Martin Luther King Jr

PROFILES IN POWER

General Editor: Keith Robbins

Martin Luther King Jr

John A. Kirk

Harlow, England • London • New York • Boston • San Francisco • Toronto
Sydney • Tokyo • Singapore • Hong Kong • Seoul • Taipei • New Delhi
Cape Town • Madrid • Mexico City • Amsterdam • Munich • Paris • Milan

PEARSON EDUCATION LIMITED

Edinburgh Gate
Harlow CM20 2JE
United Kingdom
Tel: +44 (0)1279 623623
Fax: +44 (0)1279 431059
Website: www.pearsoned.co.uk

_____

First edition published in Great Britain in 2005

© Pearson Education Limited 2005

ISBN 0 582 41431 8

British Library Cataloguing in Publication Data
A CIP catalogue record for this book can be obtained from the British Library

Library of Congress Cataloging in Publication Data
A CIP catalog record for this book can be obtained from the Library of Congress

10 9 8 7 6 5 4 3 2 1
08 07 06 05 04

Set by 35 in 9.5/12pt Celeste
Printed in Malaysia

The Publisher's policy is to use paper manufactured from sustainable forests.

For Charlene

Contents

Acknowledgements

My thanks go to a number of people for their help in the writing of this book. Series editor Keith Robbins suggested that I write a study of Martin Luther King Jr and provided patient yet constant encouragement to finish it. Likewise, Heather McCallum at Pearson Education has been very supportive. The staff at the British Library, Humanities 1, kept me efficiently supplied with a constant stream of books over several long hot summers of research. Colleagues in the History Department at Royal Holloway, University of London, provided a friendly and convivial academic environment within which this book was written. One of those colleagues, Rudolf Muhs, another ever-present at the British Library, was there to share pleasant coffee and lunch-break conversations. Dan Stone, hired at the same time as me in the History Department at Royal Holloway, has shared many similar life and career trials, tribulations and celebrations, throughout our friendship. The Institute of Historical Research (IHR) American History seminar has provided an important meeting point and a forum for sharing ideas with fellow London-based Americanists, centred upon a number of papers delivered by visiting speakers. Regulars at the seminar include Melvyn Stokes, Adam Smith, Vivien Miller, John Howard, Mara Keire, Elizabeth Clapp and Arlene Hui. Students who take my final year 'Martin Luther King Jr and the Civil Rights Movement' course challenge me to rethink various aspects of the subject each year and provide an invaluable link between teaching and research. Although I cannot list all of my academic debts here, a number are particularly notable for their longevity of help, support and friendship: Brian Ward, Tony Badger, Richard King, David Chappell, Adam Fairclough, George Lewis, Sylvia Ellis, Jenny Ward, Clive Webb and Philip Clark. I am grateful to Richard King for agreeing to read parts of this manuscript and for his helpful and instructive comments. Underpinning everything I do are my parents and my family. I should not forget to mention my Arkansas family-in-law. Finally, this book is dedicated to my wife, Charlene, with love.

Abbreviations

ABC	American Broadcasting Company
ACHR	Alabama Council on Human Relations
ACMHR	Alabama Christian Movement for Human Rights
AFSCME	American Federation of State, County and Municipal Employees
BSCP	Brotherhood of Sleeping Car Porters
CBS	Columbia Broadcasting System
CCCO	Coordinating Council of Community Organizations
CFM	Chicago Freedom Movement
COFO	Council of Federated Organizations
COME	Community on the Move for Equality
CORE	Congress of Racial Equality
CREB	Chicago Real Estate Board
CRS	Community Relations Service
CUCRL	Council for United Civil Rights Leadership
DCPA	Danville Christian Progressive Association
EOA	Economic Opportunity Act
FBI	Federal Bureau of Investigation
FEPC	Fair Employment Practices Committee
FOR	Fellowship of Reconciliation
FRCC	Freedom Rides Coordinating Committee
ICC	Interstate Commerce Commission
IRS	Internal Revenue Service
LDF	NAACP Legal Defense and Educational Fund, Inc.
MCL	Montgomery City Lines
MFDP	Mississippi Freedom Democratic Party
MIA	Montgomery Improvement Association
NAACP	National Association for the Advancement of Colored People
NCLC	Nashville Christian Leadership Council
NOI	Nation of Islam
NUL	National Urban League
OEO	Office of Economic Opportunity
PPC	Poor People's Campaign

SCLC	Southern Christian Leadership Conference
SCOPE	Summer Community Organization and Political Education
SNCC	Student Nonviolent Coordinating Committee
SRC	Southern Regional Council
UNIA	Universal Negro Improvement Association
VEP	Voter Education Project
WPC	Women's Political Council

Introduction: King in Context

Early histories of the civil rights movement that appeared prior to the 1980s were purely biographies of Revd Dr Martin Luther King Jr. Collectively, these works helped to create the familiar 'Montgomery to Memphis' narrative framework for understanding the history of the civil rights movement in the United States. This narrative begins with King's rise to leadership during the 1955–6 Montgomery bus boycott in Alabama, and ends with his 1968 assassination in Memphis, Tennessee. Since the 1980s, a number of studies examining the civil rights movement at local and state levels have questioned the usefulness and accuracy of the King-centric Montgomery to Memphis narrative as the sole way of understanding the movement. These studies have made it clear that civil rights struggles already existed in many of the communities where King and the organization of which he was president, the Southern Christian Leadership Conference (SCLC), ran civil rights campaigns in the 1960s. Moreover, those struggles continued long after King and the SCLC had left those communities. Civil rights activism also thrived in many places that King and the SCLC never even visited.

The historiography of Martin Luther King Jr and the civil rights movement, as that term itself implies, has consequently developed in two distinct strands. On the one hand, the literature comprises biographies of King in the 'Montgomery to Memphis' mould, while on the other hand it also comprises histories of the civil rights movement that have increasingly tended to frame that movement within the context of a much larger, ongoing struggle for black freedom and equality unfolding in the twentieth century at local, state, national, and even international levels. Partisan movement activists have played their own role in reinforcing the idea that there is a division between the 'man and the movement'. Notably, there is the overused quote from Ella Baker (a former SCLC staff member who, disillusioned with the organisation and King, went on to become instrumental in the formation of the Student Nonviolent Coordinating Committee (SNCC)) that 'The movement made Martin rather than Martin making the movement.'[1] Contrast this with the claim by the Revd C.T. Vivian (a stalwart SCLC staff member, and like King a black Baptist minister) that 'Man, Dr King was the movement.'[2]

My contention in this book is that King did not create or control the civil rights movement and that neither did the civil rights movement create or control him. Rather, I maintain that movement leaders and the movements that they lead continually shape each other, and it is precisely that dialectical process that needs to be explored further. King is best understood as an integral and organic part of the civil rights movement and not, as has too often been the case, above or apart from it. The *Profiles in Power* series, which does not aim to produce biographies, but instead locates individual historical agents within the broader context of their times, provides the perfect vehicle for doing this.

As the title of the series suggests, the central focus is on the theme of power. The various competing theories on and debates about power could fill this book and several others besides. Acknowledging from the outset that there are a number of different approaches that I could take, I prefer here to keep things relatively straightforward and to use King's own definition of power as 'the ability to achieve purpose ... the strength required to bring about social, political and economic changes' as my benchmark.[3] King's definition of power informs the central questions that this book addresses: To what extent was King able to 'bring about social, political and economic changes'? How and why did King seek to bring about those changes? What strengths and abilities did King in particular contribute in the context of the wider civil rights movement?

In utilising the 'Montgomery to Memphis' narrative I do not seek to simply repeat earlier versions of it, but to rethink and to recast it within the light of recent scholarship. The first way in which this study differs from other, particularly shorter, studies of King is that, unconstrained by the demands of a biography, it seeks to locate King firmly within the context of other leaders and organisations, voices and opinions, and tactics and ideologies, that made up the movement as a whole. Reassessing the conventions of the Montgomery to Memphis narrative also means moving beyond the laudatory and even reverential tone that popular histories of the movement take. Instead, I seek to point out not only what specific contributions King made to the civil rights movement, but equally what he failed to do. Likewise, I seek to highlight King's weaknesses as well as his strengths, his defeats as well as his victories, and the roles played by others in making King's reputation, as well as the role played by King himself. This approach arises from the conviction that King is far too important a historical figure to be drawn over-simplistically as a mythic heroic, even saintly figure, as has too often been the case. King's life and public leadership demand careful and critical analysis and there is much to be learned (and unlearned) in that process. As historian Charles

Payne has noted of certain populist elements of the Montgomery to Memphis narrative, they make 'a good story but useless history'.[4]

The second way in which this study is different from previous studies of King is in its more conceptual approach to the development of his leadership. The typical approach to King has been a methodical chapter-by-chapter account of his life and career that steadfastly runs campaign by campaign, year by year, and even sometimes, seemingly, day by day. This tendency is driven by the fact that King's career unfolded in a relatively short space of time – just over twelve years elapsed between Montgomery and Memphis – but that it was packed with incident. Even the Montgomery to Memphis time frame is deceptive. Most of the achievements and victories identified with King came within the space of just two years between 1963 and 1965: the Birmingham campaign in which Public Safety Commissioner Bull Connor used police dogs and water from fire hoses to break up demonstrations; the March on Washington and the 'I Have a Dream' speech; the 1964 Civil Rights Act and King's 1964 Nobel Peace Prize; and the Selma campaign that led to the introduction of a voting rights bill to Congress, which eventually became the 1965 Voting Rights Act. In this book, I seek to identify what I see as the different phases and major periods of development within King's career as a civil rights leader by using a different sort of structure that places individual events and episodes within a much broader conceptual framework.

There were, I argue, four distinct stages to King's development as a civil rights leader. The first stage (covered in Chapter 1) was King's rise to leadership during the 1955–6 Montgomery bus boycott. During the bus boycott, King used his status as a black southern Baptist minister to help mobilise the black community, and he harnessed the black church both as a spiritual base for legitimising and shaping the nature of the protest movement and as a physical base for mass meetings and information dissemination. King would later claim that 'Christ furnished the spirit and motivation, while Gandhi furnished the method' for the bus boycott.[5] But it was not until a couple of months into the bus boycott that King began seriously to consider, prompted by representatives from northern-based pacifist groups, how the Christian spirit in which the boycott began might be more formally channelled through nonviolent, direct-action techniques.

The second stage of King's career, stretching from the 1955–6 Montgomery bus boycott to the 1963 Birmingham campaign (covered in Chapters 2 and 3) saw King struggling to translate the mass black community activism of the Montgomery bus boycott, and the idea of nonviolence, into a coherent strategy for social and political change. To that end, King, along with other movement activists, helped to found the SCLC. However, early efforts to expand mass black activism through bus boycotts and through voter registration campaigns met with little success. Events elsewhere, unfolding largely independently of King and the SCLC, fared much better. The 1960 student sit-in movement led to the formation of a new student-oriented organisation, SNCC, and forced concessions for the desegregation of public and private facilities in a number of communities. The 1961 Freedom Rides were instigated by the Chicago-based civil rights organisation the Congress of Racial Equality (CORE), and forced federal intervention to uphold civil rights in inter-state transportation facilities. The sit-ins and the Freedom Rides led the way in demonstrating how nonviolent direct action might effectively be applied to bring about social change.

King tried to capitalise on these developments in 1961–3 in two community-based campaigns in Albany, Georgia, and Birmingham, Alabama. Although King and the SCLC's campaign in Albany at the end of 1961 and the beginning of 1962 encountered a number of difficulties, it proved a vital learning experience in running a far more successful campaign in Birmingham in 1963. In Birmingham, King and the SCLC developed a strategy of short-term black community mobilisation in nonviolent, direct-action demonstrations that successfully forced concessions from whites for civil rights at a local level, and engaged support and action from federal government for civil rights at a national level. Historian David J. Garrow notes that the Birmingham strategy marked a significant break from King's earlier attempts to use 'nonviolent persuasion', relying on the moral aspects of nonviolence to persuade whites to instigate racial change, to a use of 'nonviolent coercion' to force change through nonviolent, direct-action demonstrations.[6]

The third stage of King's career, and his most successful, unfolded between the 1963 Birmingham campaign and the 1965–6 Chicago, Illinois, campaign (covered in Chapters 4, 5 and 6). During this time, King and the SCLC attempted to repeat the strategy of the 1963 Birmingham campaign in other communities. The main campaigns in the Birmingham mould were held in St. Augustine, Florida, in 1964, in Selma, Alabama, in 1965, and in Chicago, Illinois, in 1966. Of these, King and the SCLC's Selma campaign was by far the most successful, engaging the highest level of public attention, of northern white support, and of federal intervention and action. Following on from the 1964 Civil Rights Act, which had legislated an end to segregation in public facilities and accommodations, President Lyndon B. Johnson introduced and oversaw the passage of the 1965 Voting Rights Act, which removed obstacles to black voting rights and provided active federal assistance to black voters. The campaigns in St. Augustine and Chicago produced far more ambiguous results for a variety of reasons, indicating that the Birmingham strategy did not guarantee successful outcomes in all places, on all issues, and at all times.

The fourth stage of King's career is the most complex and the least familiar. It began with the 1965–6 Chicago campaign and ended with King's assassination in Memphis in 1968 (covered in Chapters 5 and 6). During this period, King was forced to re-evaluate the Birmingham strategy in the face of a rapidly changing struggle for black freedom and equality. With the goal of legislation to compel desegregation and to enforce the black franchise achieved, King and the civil rights movement looked to consolidate these victories while expanding their remit to other areas. A number of urban riots in black ghettos of the west and north of the United States between 1965 and 1968 highlighted the problems faced by blacks outside the South, where King and the civil rights movement had been predominantly based. The popularisation of the 'Black Power' slogan emerged from the experiences of SNCC workers in the rural counties of Alabama and Mississippi, areas where King and the SCLC's influence was also slight, since the Birmingham strategy was focused more on towns and cities.

Amid these changes, the Vietnam War increasingly overtook civil rights as the most important domestic issue in the United States, and the anti-war movement began to sap civil rights movement activists and volunteers. The urban riots, the rise of black power, and the anti-war demonstrations all played their part in prompting a white conservative political backlash to the perceived excesses of liberalism, which conservatives believed was the cause of these developments. King, the SCLC, and the civil rights movement as a whole, were challenged to move beyond their initial goals of desegregation and black enfranchisement, to tackle the fundamental economic problems that underpinned black powerlessness and to engage with unfolding larger social and political developments.

King responded in a number of ways. He tried to tackle the problems faced by urban blacks in Chicago by implementing the Birmingham strategy of nonviolent, direct-action demonstrations there. He sought to temper black power's anti-white rhetoric and advocacy of black nationalism, black separatism and black armed self-defence, by insisting that integration and nonviolence were still relevant and important to the struggle for civil rights. He joined the anti-war movement to oppose the actions of the United States in Vietnam and attempted to fuse the energies of the anti-war movement and the civil rights movement in a coalition against incipient white political conservatism. King further looked to broaden the base of the civil rights movement by forming a coalition of blacks, ethnic minority groups, and poor whites, in a Poor People's Campaign (PPC) to take the Birmingham strategy to a new level of mass civil disobedience by staging demonstrations for economic justice in Washington, DC. Before he could lead the PPC, however, King was assassinated while supporting a strike by sanitation workers in Memphis in April 1968.

Thus, at the time of his death, King was beginning the next stage of his career, moving from a regional civil rights base to a vision of national, and indeed even international, human rights. He was also engaged in developing a fundamentally new strategy of nonviolence and civil disobedience in the pursuit of social, political and economic power – an agenda cut tragically short by his assassination and one that he would never get the chance to implement.

Chapter 1

Becoming a Leader, 1929–56

The Montgomery bus boycott thrust King into a leadership position that he did not expect and for which he was largely unprepared. His early life was dedicated to study in pursuit of a career as a Baptist church minister. Growing up in a family with a ministerial tradition, King attended a northern, predominantly white theological seminary for his divinity degree, before gaining a PhD in theology at the also predominantly white Boston University. He had been in his first job at Dexter Avenue Baptist Church in Montgomery, Alabama, for only fifteen months before the bus boycott began. As the protest developed, King found himself called upon by others rather than volunteering himself to perform a leadership role. Once King had agreed to assume that responsibility, however, it changed the entire trajectory of his life. As the bus boycott grew beyond its initially projected, short-term life, King was drawn into an ever more demanding position of responsibility. By the end of the bus boycott, at the age of 27, King would be one of the most well-known black leaders in the United States and a national symbol of an emergent civil rights movement.

Civil Rights in the Mid 1950s

King's civil rights leadership emerged at a critical point in the continuing struggle for black freedom and equality. The onset of the Cold War between the United States and the Soviet Union after the Second World War had a profound and often contradictory impact on civil rights activism. On the one hand, the Cold War led to a more politically conservative and socially repressive climate in the United States, which found its apotheosis in the anti-communist witch-hunts of Republican senator Joseph T. McCarthy in the late 1940s and early 1950s. Any perceived left-of-centre cause risked the accusation of harbouring communist sympathies, and opponents of civil rights used McCarthyite sentiments and anti-communist rhetoric to curtail the activities of many existing civil rights leaders and organisations. On the other hand, the Cold War made the United States acutely aware of the contradiction between existing racial discrimination and claims to represent global democracy for all. The Soviet Union responded to criticism about its denial of human rights in Eastern Europe by pointing to the United States's own track record in race relations. Anti-colonial struggles by non-whites in Africa, Asia and the Far East created newly emerging nations where the stance of the two superpowers on the question of race would be influential in winning support.

One of the civil rights organisations that did continue to flourish in Cold War America, largely because of its staunch anti-communist stance, was the National Association for the Advancement of Colored People (NAACP), the oldest civil rights organisation in the United States. Founded by black activists and northern white liberals in 1909, with its head-quarters in New York, the NAACP's early campaigns centred on lobbying Congress to pass anti-lynching legislation and defending black civil rights in the courts. It was not until the 1940s, however, that the NAACP became a truly effective and potent force as a mass-membership organisation. As blacks strived during the Second World War to win their share of wartime prosperity in the rapidly expanding economy, and fought in segregated US armed services for what the black press termed the 'Double V' – victory against a racist foe abroad as well as racism at home – NAACP membership swelled tenfold from 50,000 in 1940 to 500,000 in 1946. The bulk of new members flocked to southern local NAACP branches, which they used as a base to pursue better employment opportunities, voter registration campaigns and fairer treatment from whites.

While the NAACP's mass southern membership base grew, the national organisation underwent significant changes. Under pressure from the Internal Revenue Service (IRS), which denied the NAACP tax-exempt status because of its lobbying activities, in 1939 the NAACP created the NAACP Legal Defense and Educational Fund, Inc., known later as the LDF or 'Inc. Fund'. The LDF dealt with legal and educational matters only, thus ensuring its tax-exempt status. The LDF provided black attorney Thurgood Marshall, who became director–counsel of the LDF and special counsel to the NAACP, with a platform to pursue civil rights in the courts. In the late 1930s and early 1940s, Marshall won a number of favourable rulings to equalise the salaries of black and white teachers. Throughout the late 1930s, and the 1940s and 1950s, Marshall success-fully argued a number of landmark cases before the US Supreme Court. *Smith* v. *Allwright* (1944) outlawed the use of all-white Democratic Party primaries that blocked black access to politics in a number of southern states. *Morgan* v. *Virginia* (1946) made segregated seating on interstate bus routes illegal. In a series of court cases in higher education, *Missouri ex rel. Gaines* v. *Canada* (1938), *Sipuel* v. *Oklahoma State Regents* (1948), *McLaurin* v. *Oklahoma State Regents* (1950), and *Sweatt* v. *Painter* (1950), Marshall successively rolled back the parameters of segregation in higher education.

The critical legal breakthrough came with *Brown* v. *Board of Education* (1954), when the US Supreme Court ruled that segregation in schools was unconstitutional. Marshall introduced evidence from black psychiatrist Kenneth B. Clark, based on his experiments in southern schools, that convinced the Court that segregation 'generates a feeling of inferiority as to [black children's] status in the community that may affect their hearts and minds in a way unlikely ever to be undone'. The Court concluded that 'in the field of public education the doctrine of "separate but equal" has no place'. In attacking the legal doctrine of 'separate but equal', the Court reversed its earlier ruling in *Plessy* v. *Ferguson* (1896), when it had declared that the southern states' practice of segregation did not contravene the Fourteenth Amendment to the US Constitution, which guaranteed 'equal protection of the law'. The Court then ruled that 'separate' facilities for the races were constitutional so long as they were of an 'equal' standard. In reality, few of the facilities that the southern states provided for blacks were equal to those provided for whites, if indeed they were provided at all. By reversing the legal doctrine of 'separate but equal' in school education, the Court challenged the legal underpinnings of segregation as a whole, and paved the way for yet more challenges to segregation in other areas of southern life.

After handing down the *Brown* decision the Court delayed its implementation for a year to take advice on how next to proceed. Many white southerners opposed *Brown*. Some vowed a campaign of 'massive resistance' and Mississippi led the way in the formation of the first White Citizens' Council dedicated to preventing school desegregation. Mississippi senator James O. Eastland denounced *Brown* and advised his constituents that they were 'not required to obey any court which passes such a ruling'.[1] Not all whites took this hard line. Alabama governor James 'Big Jim' Folsom declared that 'when the Supreme Court speaks, that's the law', and even Mississippi governor James P. Coleman appealed for 'cool thinking' on the matter.[2] Many white southern newspaper editors echoed these sentiments. Yet as massive resistance grew such voices of reason were increasingly drowned out. Declaring total opposition to any change in the segregated order fast became an electoral necessity for southern politicians wishing to successfully stay in or to stand for public office. The NAACP bore the brunt of the white southern backlash to *Brown*. Many of its southern members were persecuted for their activities and local branch membership figures began to dwindle, leading to the collapse of a number of local branches altogether. In 1956, Alabama effectively barred the NAACP from operating in the state.

The reaction to *Brown* at a national level was not encouraging either. President Dwight D. Eisenhower refused to back the *Brown* decision strongly in public. In private he confided that his recent appointment of Earl Warren as US Supreme Court chief justice was the 'biggest damn fool mistake' he had ever made.[3] A US Congress containing many powerful southern politicians also refused to back the Court's decision. In March 1956, 101 southern congressmen signed the 'Southern Manifesto' in outright opposition to *Brown*. There were even rumours of dissent within the Supreme Court. Some justices who had been persuaded to sign up to a unanimous decision in *Brown* now argued for a lenient implementation order to appease opponents. Consequently, when the Court issued its implementation order in May 1955, it appeared to backtrack. The Court set no definite guidelines for when school desegregation should begin, nor did it indicate how it should be carried out. It devolved these responsibilities to local school boards and to local and state judges. Many of these were white southerners opposed to desegregation. School desegregation, the Court informed them, should proceed 'with all deliberate speed'. Many interpreted this as a mandate for indefinite delay.

By the mid 1950s, the legal struggle for black freedom and equality appeared to have stalled. The leading civil rights organisation, the NAACP, had won its greatest victory in the courts after decades of litigation. Yet having won the legal argument against segregation in schools through the courts, white southerners now insisted that they would even go so far as to oppose the law of the land if it meant having to grant black equality. It was at this delicately poised impasse in race relations that the Montgomery bus boycott began in December 1955.

The Origins of the Montgomery Bus Boycott

On the late afternoon of 1 December 1955, 42-year-old Rosa L. Parks, a seamstress in a downtown Montgomery, Alabama, department store boarded her bus home from work. As the bus moved along its route it began to fill with people. White bus driver J. Fred Blake told Parks and other black passengers sitting next to and across the row from her to 'let me have those front seats'. In the system of racial segregation that existed in Montgomery at the time, the ten seats at the front of the bus were reserved for white passengers and the ten seats at the back of the bus were reserved for black passengers. In the middle section, whites filled the seats from the front, and blacks filled the seats from the back, on a first-come, first-served basis. On that particular evening, blacks occupied all of the seats in the middle section. Parks was sitting in the row next to the white section. The white section was crowded with standing passengers but there was space for blacks to stand at the back. 'You all make it light on yourselves and let me have those seats,' Blake warned. Those sitting next to and across from Parks moved. Still, that was not enough. The city bus segregation ordinance decreed that black passengers could not sit parallel to white passengers. Every black person in the row had to move before a white person could sit down. Parks, however, refused to budge. 'Well, if you don't stand up, I'm going to call the police and have you arrested,' Blake told her. 'You may do that,' Parks replied. Blake then went to inform the police. A few minutes later, a squad car arrived, and two policemen boarded the bus. 'Why don't you stand up?' asked one of the officers. 'Why do you push us around?' Parks demanded. 'I do not know, but the law is the law and you are under arrest,' the officer replied.[4] The policemen then hauled Parks off to the police station where she was charged with breaking Montgomery's city bus segregation ordinance.

News of Parks's arrest quickly reached one of Montgomery's leading black activists, Edgar Daniel (E.D.) Nixon. A railroad porter, Nixon was head of the black Brotherhood of Sleeping Car Porters (BSCP) union in Alabama, and president of the Progressive Democratic Association, the political voice of black Democratic Party supporters in Alabama. A former president of the Montgomery NAACP, Nixon had known Parks for a number of years as she had served as his branch secretary. When Nixon called the Montgomery police station to find out exactly what had happened, he was curtly told by a police officer that it was 'None of your so-and-so business.'[5] Nixon then attempted to contact black attorney Fred D. Gray. The young, recently qualified attorney was, alongside Charles D. Langford, one of only two black attorneys practising in Montgomery at the time, and the only one willing to accept civil rights cases. When Nixon discovered that Gray was out of town on business, he contacted white attorney Clifford Durr. Clifford and his wife Virginia belonged to a small section of the Montgomery white community, a section found in white communities in many other southern cities, that sympathised with the plight of southern blacks. Such a stance came at a cost. According to Fred Gray, the Durrs 'endured public scorn and social ostracism' as a result.[6] The Durrs knew Parks personally since they had hired her on a regular basis as a seamstress to alter their daughter's dresses. The Durrs accompanied Nixon to the police station, where Nixon signed the bail bond for Parks's release. Enthusiastic about using the incident as a legal test case, Nixon told Parks, 'with your permission we can break down segregation on the bus[es]'. Despite her husband's objections – 'Rosa, the white folks will kill you,' he warned her – Parks agreed.[7]

In a separate development, attorney Fred Gray, upon his return to Montgomery, contacted Jo Ann Robinson of the Women's Political Council (WPC) about the Parks incident, and told her, 'if you ever planned to do anything with the council, now is your time'.[8] The WPC, formed by Mary Fair Banks in 1949, was made up of a small number of black women educators, all of whom were affiliated with Montgomery's black Alabama State College. In its relatively short life the WPC had established itself as one of the most active political groups in the city. Banks's friend and colleague, Jo Ann Robinson, was president of the group and had spearheaded previously unsuccessful attempts to petition the city to alter segregation practices on buses in the light of previous incidents. Gray and Robinson had held 'many discussions . . . with reference to what should be done in the event another incident occurred'.[9] Robinson contacted Nixon, and both agreed that the Parks case offered the possibility of mobilising the black community in a united protest at her treatment. They agreed that a mass meeting should be organised to engage the support of the black community, and that a one-day bus boycott should be organised for the following Monday. Nixon took the job of making the necessary arrangements for the mass meeting and Robinson, along with other members of the WPC, made leaflets reading 'Don't ride the bus to work, to town, or any place Monday December 5' and began to distribute them in the black community.[10]

Members of Montgomery's black community knew that Park's refusal to surrender her seat was not the first time a black person had challenged their treatment by whites on a city bus. Ten years previously, Geneva Jordan had been arrested for 'talking back' to a white driver who had complained about her lack of correct change. In the ensuing years, Viola White, Katie Wingfield, and two children visiting from the state of New Jersey, had all been arrested for sitting in the section of the bus reserved for whites. In 1952, a city policeman shot dead a black man who argued with a bus driver over the correct fare. The following year, Epsie Worthy was fined after a fracas with a bus driver in another fare dispute. In 1955, in the months leading up to Parks's arrest, both Claudette Colvin and Mary Louise Smith had been arrested for refusing to move to the back of the bus. Of these incidents, the Claudette Colvin case had come closest to sparking a challenge to segregation on the buses, since she was the only person to be charged under the city segregation ordinance and, on the advice of attorney Fred Gray, to plead 'not guilty' in court. For various legal and personal reasons, however, the attempt to use the Colvin incident as a legal test case had collapsed.

Montgomery's black population was not alone in its discontent with bus segregation. As a site of frequent close contact between blacks and whites, public transportation was often a place of racial friction in southern cities. When segregation statutes had first been introduced on streetcars at the turn of the century, the black community in Montgomery had organised a boycott in protest, as had a number of other black communities in cities across the South. During and after the Second World War, instances of interracial pushing, shoving and jostling on buses increased in correspondence with increasing black discontent with and action against the segregated order. In 1953, the Revd Theodore J. Jemison organised a bus boycott in Baton Rouge, Louisiana, to protest against segregated seating arrangements there. Utilising taxis and then a car pool as alternative transportation systems for black passengers, the boycott lasted for ten days until whites finally acquiesced in black demands to modify segregation practices. Under the new arrangements, reserved sections for the races were abolished and whites sat from the front of the bus to the back, and blacks sat from the back of the bus to the front, on a first-come, first-served basis. Crucially, blacks were no longer forced to surrender their seats to whites and they would not have to stand if white seats were empty.

Many incidents over many years, not just in Montgomery but right across the South, formed the background to Parks's refusal to move from her seat. Yet Parks's arrest and the subsequent bus boycott produced a unique outcome leading to the eventual desegregation of buses in the city. The Parks case was different for a number of reasons. Rosa Parks was a well-respected community figure. As she put it, 'The white people couldn't point to me and say that there was anything I had done to deserve such treatment except to be born black.'[11] As someone involved in civil rights organisations over many years, Parks was fully aware of the consequences of her actions. Although not premeditated, her decision not to surrender her seat was, historian Adam Fairclough notes, a 'purposeful act of a politically aware person' and support could be rallied for her cause.[12] Montgomery's black community, which at around 42,750 people comprised over a third of the city's total population, and accounted for over 70 per cent of bus passengers, was large enough to make an impact with a bus boycott. At the same time, the black community was relatively small and compact enough to effectively coordinate such a protest. Montgomery also possessed more than its fair share of able black leaders and existing black organisations that were able to mobilise the black population. The 1954 *Brown* decision swung the legal initiative over desegregation towards the black community and added further leverage to its demands. Just as importantly, the way in which the city's white power structure handled the bus boycott did much to contribute to its success. Making a series of tactical blunders, Montgomery's white leaders escalated rather than dissipated the boycott at critical points in its development. One further ingredient in the boycott's success was the leadership of Martin Luther King Jr.

King's Early Years

Born in Atlanta, Georgia, on 15 January 1929, King's life was steeped in the traditions of the black southern Baptist Church. 'Religion for me is life,' King wrote in one college essay.[13] His mother, Alberta Williams King, was the only daughter of successful Atlanta minister Adam Daniel (A.D.) Williams, who was the son of a black slave preacher. King's father, Martin Luther King Sr, known affectionately to family and friends as 'Daddy' King, was raised in rural Georgia and was the son of a farmer. An ambitious man, at the age of 18 Daddy King set off for Atlanta determined to better himself through education. After graduating from Morehouse College he married into the influential Williams family and later inherited his father-in-law's pulpit at Ebenezer Baptist Church on downtown Auburn Avenue.

King spent his early years living with his parents, his older sister Christine, his younger brother Adam Daniel (A.D.), and his maternal grandmother, at 501 Auburn Avenue, located just a short distance from Ebenezer. King's familial involvement with the church placed him at the heart of black community life. As one of the few institutions wholly funded by blacks, the church provided a hub of black religious as well as of black social and cultural life, and offered a degree of shelter and independence from whites. Reflecting the historically prominent status of the church in the black community, the job of a black minister conferred considerable social standing and authority. In the South at the time, most black men were employed in menial and low-paid jobs, while many black women worked in white homes as domestics to supplement family income. The ministry was one of the few occupations for blacks that enjoyed economic independence from whites since the church congregation funded the position. Black ministers were, behind black teachers who taught in segregated public schools, the largest representatives in a tiny black middle class. Other members of the black middle class included professionals such as doctors and lawyers who administered to black clients, and black businessmen who owned businesses that served the needs of the black community. Daddy King's standing in the black community, together with his financial frugality, ensured a relatively comfortable existence for the King family. 'It is quite easy for me to think of the universe as basically friendly mainly because of my uplifting hereditary and environmental circumstances,' Martin Luther King Jr later reflected.[14]

Yet although King's upbringing ensured that he was relatively isolated from the harsher aspects of southern racism, it was impossible to hide completely from that wider social reality. Indeed, some of King's most vivid recollections of childhood involved instances of racial discrimination. As a child, like many other black southerners, King counted white children among his playmates. However, when it was time to start school, the veil of segregation began to fall on those friendships. When they enrolled at their respective segregated schools in Atlanta at 6 years old, King's best white friend informed him that 'his father had demanded that he would play with me no more'.[15] This ended their friendship. At the age of 14, King travelled to Dublin, Georgia, where he participated in a school oratorical contest, speaking on the subject of 'The Negro and the Constitution'. On the way back, he and his teacher were forced to surrender their coach seats to white passengers and to stand for 90 miles until they reached Atlanta. 'It was', King recalled, 'the angriest I have ever been in my life.'[16] Such episodes made King wonder 'how could I love a race of people [who] hated me' and how he could reconcile that feeling with the demands of Christianity to love all people.[17]

After graduation from high school in 1944 at the age of 15, King followed in his father's and his maternal grandfather's footsteps by enrolling at Atlanta's Morehouse College. King entered Morehouse at such a young age because, in the words of college president Benjamin E. Mays, a respected scholar of black religion, 'The Second World War was playing havoc with the College, for our students were being drafted in large numbers. In this crisis, we decided to take into the freshman class students who had only finished the eleventh grade.'[18] Given the family's church tradition there was great expectation that King would enter the ministry. Yet King initially contemplated becoming a doctor or a lawyer while opting to major in sociology at Morehouse. Immersed in the black church from birth, King felt that he had simply wandered into religion rather than actively accepting it into his life. He had joined the Ebenezer congregation at the age of 5, 'not out of any dynamic conviction, but out of a childhood desire to keep up with my sister'.[19] Even when he was baptised, King simply went through the motions of the ceremony without comprehending its full significance. Thus, by 13 years old, King was already beginning to question fundamental Christian orthodoxy, shocking 'my Sunday school class by denying the bodily resurrection of Jesus. Doubts began to spring forth unrelentingly.'[20]

King's reservations about the southern black Baptist Church continued to grow. He disapproved of the way that many black preachers used raw emotionalism by employing the whooping and hollering of the black folk pulpit to engage their congregations. King preferred a more cerebral approach by using intellectual arguments to get his message from pulpit to pew. He was also concerned at the way many black preachers sermonised about the promise of a better life in the next world instead of tackling the more immediate problems that blacks faced under segregation. Nevertheless, King's continuing studies of the Bible at Morehouse convinced him that, despite his continuing vocational doubts, scripture contained 'many profound truths which one could not escape'.[21] Moreover, academic clerics at Morehouse demonstrated to King that a ministerial career could be successfully combined with intellectual rigour. To Daddy King's delight, his son finally decided to enter the ministry, serving as assistant pastor at Ebenezer while continuing his studies at Morehouse. In February 1948, Daddy King presided at his son's ordination as a Baptist minister.

As a young entrant into college, King struggled to make good grades at Morehouse. Yet the experience influenced more than just his academic development. While at Morehouse he became a member of the NAACP. He also participated in an interracial Intercollegiate Council with other Atlanta schools and colleges. This experience softened King's attitudes towards whites somewhat and convinced him that a new generation of white southerners might offer hope for more enlightened race relations in the future. While in college, King got his first taste of life outside the South on summer trips to earn money by picking tobacco in Connecticut. Although the young King idealised just how free life for blacks in the north was – racial discrimination did exist there, albeit not in the same legally mandated form as in the South – the escape from southern segregation was a revelation to him. King found that he could enjoy more personal freedom in the north than he ever could in Atlanta. Changing trains in Washington, DC, for a segregated journey back home to the South, King felt the curtain 'dropped on my selfhood' yet again.[22]

The desire to escape the South was one factor in King's decision to study at Crozer Theological Seminary in Chester, Pennsylvania, after graduating from Morehouse. The move also fulfilled King's desire to gain greater independence from his father. Moreover, the small, liberal, and predominantly white Crozer came highly recommended by King's professors at Morehouse because of its good national reputation. This time, a longer stay in the north opened King's eyes to racial attitudes there. One day, he and a friend went into nearby Philadelphia for food. They sat ignored for 30 minutes before finally demanding service. When the food came there was sand deliberately scattered in the vegetables. On another occasion, while on a double date in New Jersey, a restaurant proprietor chased King and his friends out of the establishment with a gun after refusing them service. While at Crozer, King became romantically involved with a white woman and even considered a proposal of marriage. Friends intervened, warning of how difficult life would be for an interracial couple and how it would make a return to the South impossible. Painful though it was, the two agreed to end their six-month relationship. King learned from these episodes how profoundly race shaped social attitudes and conduct in the north as well as in the South.

King's academic performance at Crozer was much better than at Morehouse, with a more serious and mature attitude to study earning him the status of class valedictorian when he graduated in 1951. Studies at Crozer exposed King to a number of ideas that he eagerly explored, from Karl Marx's critique of capitalism, to theologian Walter Rauschenbush's writings about the Social Gospel, to lectures on pacifism and Gandhian nonviolence. Throughout his studies, King took a stance of healthy scepticism in all his encounters with new theories and philosophies. Notably, he developed a fondness for philosopher G.W.F. Hegel's dialectic method of analysis. This involved taking two opposite sides of an argument, weighing both positive and negative points in each, and finding an answer by using a synthesis of elements in both. This dialectical method of reasoning, which sought compromise and reconciliation between different points of view, would remain central to King's approach to problem-solving throughout his life.

After graduating from Crozer, King applied to several schools to study for a PhD before finally deciding to enrol in the philosophy faculty at Boston University. King chose Boston at the recommendation of his Crozer professors, and because he was keen to study under Dr Edgar S. Brightman, whose ideas on 'personalism' had aroused King's interest. Personalism insisted that human personality intrinsic in all individuals was the ultimate value in the world. This reaffirmed King's belief in the essential worth of all human beings. Applied to his developing ideas about religion and race, this meant that segregation, which denied the equal humanity of black and white citizens, was fundamentally evil and at odds with God's will. After Brightman's death at the end of King's first year of study, King transferred his registration to Brightman's protégé L. Harold DeWolf in the theology faculty. Further broadening his knowledge of philosophy at Boston, King took classes at nearby Harvard University.

While studying at Boston, through a mutual friend King met his future wife Coretta Scott. Scott, from rural Alabama, was studying on a scholarship at Boston's New England Conservatory of Music with aspirations to become a classical singer. Initially, Daddy King opposed his son's plans to marry Coretta since he preferred a match that would see Martin Jr marry into a family in Atlanta's black elite. At his first meeting with Coretta, Daddy King 'went a little too far, mentioning names, women to whom M.L. had proposed marriage' in his eagerness to dissuade her. King took his father to one side and told him, 'I must marry Coretta. She's the most important thing to come into my life . . . I know you don't really approve, but this is what I have to do.'[23] King's father eventually relented. On 18 June 1953, Daddy King married the couple at the Scott family home in rural Alabama and soon after baptised his new daughter-in-law at Ebenezer.

As King's residential studies at Boston came to a close he began the search for a pastorate where he could work while writing up his PhD dissertation. Daddy King was keen for his son to return to Atlanta as co-pastor of Ebenezer and persuaded Benjamin Mays to offer his son a faculty position at Morehouse to combine with his church duties. Although King did want to preach in a southern city, he still yearned for independence from his father. He therefore rejected the idea of returning to Atlanta and arranged to deliver a trial sermon for a position at First Baptist Church in Chattanooga, Tennessee. At the same time, through a family friend, King learned of a vacant position at Dexter Avenue Baptist Church in Montgomery. Dexter had recently fired its controversial and outspoken pastor Vernon Johns, a reflection of the notoriously tough treatment that the church handed out to its ministers. Unperturbed, King arranged a trial sermon there, which was well received. In April 1954, King accepted Dexter's offer of the post and took up his new job the following September.

King quickly set about putting his stamp on his new role. He made it quite clear that he would oversee major decisions affecting the church. King informed the Dexter church board members that 'leadership never ascends from the pew to the pulpit, but invariably descends from the pulpit to the pew'.[24] Although such an assertion might at first glance seem arrogant, King understood and fully accepted that taking on such authority also meant accepting a burden of responsibility. In return for being given the reins of leadership, King offered total commitment and devotion to duty. In his leadership of the church, as with his later leadership of the civil rights movement, King was both conscientious and dutiful. For King, leadership constituted both a blessing and a curse. As he revealingly told his congregation on one occasion, 'The honors and privileges that often come as a result of leadership contribute only one side of the picture. The greater the privileges, the greater the responsibilities and sacrifices.'[25]

King proceeded to set up a host of new church committees, including a social and political action committee. He linked church-based activities to the wider community by joining the local Montgomery branch of the NAACP. King also attended meetings of the Montgomery branch of the Alabama Council on Human Relations (ACHR), a state affiliate of the white liberal organisation the Southern Regional Council (SRC), which had its headquarters in Atlanta. The ACHR was the only interracial organisation prepared to address the question of racial change in Montgomery at the time. King went about proving himself worthy of his new church position by investing a great deal of time preparing polished sermons that pleased his new congregation with their performance from the pulpit on Sunday mornings. On top of this, King completed his PhD thesis and was awarded his doctorate in June 1955. On 17 November 1955, the Kings' first child, Yolanda Denise King, was born.

The Montgomery Improvement Association (MIA)

King first became involved in the developing protest movement in Montgomery when E.D. Nixon telephoned him to ask if Dexter could be used as the venue for a mass meeting to discuss Rosa Parks's arrest and to make plans for a bus boycott. 'We have taken this type of thing too long already,' Nixon told King. 'I feel the time has come to boycott the buses.'[26] At first, King hesitated, saying 'Brother Nixon, let me call you back.' King had no objection to the meeting being held at his church but, as a new pastor in the city and having just become a father for the first time, he did not want to get too deeply involved in what was bound to be a controversial protest. After hearing of King's hesitancy, fellow Montgomery pastor and King's good friend, the Revd Ralph D. Abernathy, the young minister of First Baptist Church, called to urge his help.

King assured Abernathy that he was glad to lend his support to the boycott and his church for the meeting, but insisted that he could not take a leading role. When Nixon called back, King told him, 'Brother Nixon, I'll go along with it.' Nixon replied, 'I'm glad to hear you say so because I've talked to eighteen other people and I told them to meet in *your* church tonight. It would have been kind of bad to be getting there without you.'[27]

The mass meeting at Dexter took place on the evening of 2 December 1955. It revealed both the strengths and weaknesses of a potential bus boycott in Montgomery. In its favour, Montgomery had a black community that was close-knit and well organised, with a large number of influential leaders and groups. This provided pre-existing networks and structures of support that could act as the foundations upon which a successful protest movement could be built. Militating against a successful boycott, however, was the fact that in the past the relationship between black leaders and organisations in Montgomery had been one of competition rather than cooperation. True to form, when the meeting began, the Revd L. Roy Bennett, president of Montgomery's Interdenominational Ministerial Alliance, commandeered the proceedings. Bennett declared that he knew best about how to organise a bus boycott and extolled his own leadership abilities. After half an hour had passed, people began to leave. At that point, Ralph Abernathy intervened and suggested that everyone at the meeting should have the chance to speak. WPC president Jo Ann Robinson seconded the proposal. Robinson suggested that everyone should endorse the proposed Monday bus boycott. After Monday, they could reconvene to reassess the situation. Though some were still uncertain about even a one-day boycott, there was general agreement to go along with Robinson's plan. Over the weekend, the WPC circulated more leaflets and black leaders canvassed support for the Monday boycott. Black drivers of taxicabs were persuaded to charge black passengers a standard ten-cent fare for journeys to provide an alternative means of transportation.

The first signs on Monday morning were encouraging. King watched nearly empty buses pass by his window, counting only eight black passengers over the course of an hour. Others in the black community witnessed a similar scene. The same day, it took an all-white jury just five minutes to find Rosa Parks guilty. The one significant development in the trial was a switch in the charge from breaking a city law to breaking a state law. Under the city segregation ordinance, a black bus passenger could only be asked to move if other seats were available in the black section of the bus. In Parks's case there had been no vacant seats, which meant that she had not in fact broken that particular ordinance. However, a state law gave more sweeping powers to bus drivers to enforce segregation. It was therefore under the state law that Parks was tried and convicted. Several hundred blacks turned up at the courthouse that morning, providing an unprecedented and highly visible degree of community support for Parks's action.

Later that afternoon, black leaders met at the Revd Bennett's Mount Zion AME (African Methodist Episcopal) Church to discuss what to do next. At first, it seemed that the meeting would follow the previous pattern with Bennett moving to stamp his authority on proceedings. When it was suggested that a smaller group retreat in private for more detailed discussions, plans for an extended bus boycott developed at a much quicker pace. The first order of business at the small group meeting was to ratify a proposal outlined by Nixon, Abernathy and another black minister, the Revd Edgar N. French. They proposed to issue three demands to city officials that must be met before blacks returned to the buses. The most important of these demands was for the implementation of seating arrangements on buses as previously suggested by Jo Ann Robinson and the WPC. Modelled on a system used in Mobile, Alabama, this allowed blacks to sit from the back of the bus to the front, and whites to sit from the front of the bus to the back, on a first-come, first-served basis, and abolished reserved seats for the races altogether. There was no demand for total bus desegregation, which blacks knew the city would reject outright. Rather, they demanded suggested a more acceptable modification to existing segregated arrangements. The other two demands were that white bus drivers should treat black passengers with courtesy, and that blacks should be allowed to apply for the job of bus driver.

Next, the meeting ratified Abernathy's proposal to create a new organisation called the Montgomery Improvement Association (MIA) to take charge of the bus boycott. It was hoped that the creation of the MIA would help the black community to move beyond the petty factionalism that had hampered past collective efforts. The idea was that the new organisation would co-opt black leaders and their respective organisations under its own umbrella, and thereby channel community resources into the common goal of sustaining the bus boycott. The structure of the MIA was designed to prevent one group or individual leader from dominating the protest, while also making sure that no one was excluded.

There remained the delicate question of who should lead the MIA. Two of the prime candidates were long-time rivals E.D. Nixon and black businessman Rufus Lewis, a former Alabama State College football coach and president of the civic group the Citizens Steering Committee.

It would be disastrous for the fledgling MIA to become embroiled in old rivalries that might destroy the organisation, and the bus boycott, before either had been given a chance to get off the ground. When nominations for president were invited, Lewis immediately put forward King's name, and Lewis's friend P.E. Conley seconded the proposal. It was a shrewd move on Lewis's part. He certainly did not want to see Nixon, or for that matter any other of his rivals, in charge of the MIA. As a relative newcomer to, and junior member of the black community, as well as the pastor of his church, King offered little threat to Lewis or to any existing leaders, and was therefore an ideal neutral candidate to head the new organisation.

There were other reasons behind the choice of King for president. The fact that he was a minister was crucial. Since the church congregation funded his job, King was able to head the MIA with more impunity than someone like Jo Ann Robinson, who as a black teacher was reliant on white state funding for her salary. For blacks in public employment, antagonising whites almost automatically meant being fired. A minister was also a good choice for leader because he had access to a church, one of the few places where the black community could hold mass meetings to rally support for the boycott. Moreover, a minister's link to a black congregation placed him at the head of an important information network within the black community. As head of the church, a minister could help to sway his members to support the boycott and lend sanction and authority to it.

King fulfilled these and two other important criteria. Firstly, he was one of the few ministers actually willing to accept the role. Many black ministers initially preferred to stay out of the controversy because they were doubtful of its potential success and because they did not want to become a target for white anger. Secondly, King's congregation contained many influential members of Montgomery's black middle class. Their inclusion would give added weight to the boycott, uniting both the 'classes' and the 'masses' in the black community. They were also in a position to provide practical material help. When the boycott needed to develop a car pool at a later date, they were the ones who supplied the automobiles that made it possible. Although King had been reluctant to become involved in the first place, after a slight pause he agreed to accept the MIA presidency. Although King would not have thought of putting his own name forward for the job, the fact that he had been chosen by his peers for that position meant that he felt a responsibility to accept it. 'I'm not sure I'm the best person for this position,' King told them, 'but if no one else is going to serve, I'd be glad to try.'[28]

After unanimously agreeing to install King as president of the MIA, the meeting moved on to the pressing issue of whether or not the bus boycott should be extended. MIA committee members decided to leave that question aside until they had had a further opportunity to gauge community sentiment at a mass meeting arranged that evening at Holt Street Baptist Church. King had barely twenty minutes to prepare for what in effect would be his inaugural speech as president of the MIA. When he spoke to the crowd, MIA leaders caught a first glimpse of King's true leadership potential.

The speech King delivered that night to a thousand blacks packed inside Holt Street Baptist Church, and to four thousand more who stood outside listening over loudspeakers, set the tone for his leadership in the bus boycott and for his later leadership in the civil rights movement. King began by summarising the many injustices that Montgomery blacks had endured on city buses in the past that had now brought them to this point. Then he explained the justification for the bus boycott and how it would be conducted. Firstly, King asserted the right to protest against the treatment of blacks on city buses, citing the US Supreme Court, the US Constitution and 'God Almighty' as supporters of their cause. Secondly, King told the audience that they should stick together, that they should not be afraid, and that at all times they must keep 'God in the forefront. Let us be Christian in all our actions.' Love and justice, not hatred of whites, should be their guiding principle, King insisted. Finally, King framed the bus boycott in epic terms, telling the audience that 'when the history books are written in the future, somebody will have to say "There lived a race of people, a black people . . . who had the moral courage to stand up for their rights. And thereby they injected a new meaning into the veins and history of civilization."'[29] When the question of whether to continue the bus boycott was subsequently put to the crowd it unequivocally roared back its approval.

White Montgomery and the Failure of Compromise

Montgomery's white authorities were taken aback by the show of support for the bus boycott and the decision to continue the protest. They had fully expected the venture to fizzle out in due course, just as past efforts had. When the ACHR approached officials of the bus company, Montgomery City Lines (MCL), with an offer to mediate, it met with the response that the company was following established city segregation laws and that there was nothing to discuss. Montgomery mayor

William A. Gayle was a little more accommodating, although largely because the most prominent white member of the ACHR in Montgomery, the Revd Thomas Thrasher, was the rector of his church. Gayle offered to meet with MIA and MCL representatives in an effort to resolve their differences.

When the two parties assembled on Thursday, 8 December, for their meeting with the mayor, King spoke first, outlining the MIA's three demands. MCL attorney Jack Crenshaw insisted that the seating arrangements proposed by the MIA did not comply with state segregation laws. He did concede that black passengers were entitled to courteous treatment and gave his assurance that any bus driver found mistreating black passengers would be reprimanded. On the question of hiring black drivers, Crenshaw said that he did not think that the time was right for such a change in policy. King and MIA attorney Fred Gray pointed out that the city of Mobile, which was in the same state, operated the same type of seating arrangements that they were asking for. Crenshaw simply refused to accept their argument and further discussion failed to bring any progress.

The first meeting between Gayle, the MIA and the MCL marked a critical point in the development of the bus boycott. The MIA had fully expected that their relatively modest demands would be accepted and that the boycott would last no more than a week. After all, they were only asking for a modification of segregation, not its complete abolition. The total inflexibility of the MCL took the MIA by surprise, but at the same time it strengthened its resolve to press home its demands. If the MCL had accepted the MIA's initial demands for a modification of seating arrangements, the bus boycott would most probably have been called off. King might never have progressed beyond being anything more than a notable local black leader. The refusal of whites to compromise, however, further escalated the dispute.

The deadlock over negotiations was very much a product of post-*Brown* southern race relations. Increasingly after the Second World War, many white southern communities had proved willing to reform some of their segregation practices when petitioned to do so by the black community. Such limited reform was often undertaken to appease the black community in the hope of staving off potential lawsuits from the NAACP. *Brown* signalled a change in that arrangement. Blacks saw the *Brown* decision as both a mandate and a lever for further changes to the segregated order. Whites, in contrast, correctly viewed *Brown* as a potential threat to the whole structure of segregation. Since *Brown* struck down the legal doctrine of 'separate but equal' that underpinned segregation, whites who had previously been certain that segregation would never end, and had been willing to implement limited reforms based on that under-standing, now became far more resistant to any changes in segregation practices at all. Thus, at the same time that blacks were seeking more concessions after *Brown*, whites were much less receptive to their demands. These two very different responses to *Brown* were in many ways at the heart of the dispute over segregated seating arrangements on Montgomery buses.

The MIA next wrote to the MCL's national headquarters at National City Lines in Chicago, asking them to send a representative to Montgomery to arbitrate. Reflecting the rising concern about developments among whites in the city, leading white newspaper the *Montgomery Advertiser* looked to exert pressure on the MIA to halt its protest by noting an obscure section of state law that forbade boycotts in Alabama. Montgomery police commissioner Clyde C. Sellers pointed to a city ordinance that required all taxicabs to charge a minimum fare. This would potentially strip the boycott of its alternative transportation arrangements for the city's black population.

These moves backfired by further strengthening the resolve of the MIA and the black community. In response to the minimum cab fare ordinance highlighted by Sellers, King contacted the Revd Theodore Jemison who had organised the successful ten-day bus boycott in Baton Rouge in 1953. Blacks in Baton Rouge had run a car pool system of alternative transportation to help sustain the bus boycott, and King took Jemison's advice on implementing a similar system in Montgomery. When the plan was put into operation, over two hundred volunteers signed up their vehicles to participate in the car pool. Unwittingly, the MCL also helped to bolster the bus boycott by cancelling some services on routes that had become unprofitable because of a lack of black passengers. The move virtually forced the remaining black passengers on those routes to use the car pool and to participate in the boycott. When National City Lines sent Kenneth E. Totten to Montgomery, his meeting with MIA and white community representatives proved a disappointment. Totten simply backed the position of the local MCL officials.

Events at the beginning of 1956 further distanced the black and white communities. On 6 January, Police Commissioner Clyde Sellers appeared at a White Citizens' Council meeting, an organisation sworn to opposing desegregation, and announced that he was becoming a member. This in effect placed law enforcement in the city squarely behind the militant segregationist cause. Dismayed by this development, the MIA requested a meeting with the City Commission and presented new, watered-down demands. The new demands included provisions for black and white passengers seated in the middle section of the bus to voluntarily move to the back and to the front of the bus as seats became available in those sections. The City Commission dismissed the plan. Feeling more frustrated than ever over the failure of compromise, the MIA began to discuss the possibility of filing a court suit to seek the complete desegregation of city buses. Since the dispute looked like continuing for some considerable time, the decision to seek desegregation would bring outside help and support from the NAACP. MIA attorney Fred Gray had been in touch with NAACP attorneys from an early stage in the bus boycott, but because of the MIA's request for the modification rather than the total abolition of segregation on buses, the NAACP had refused to become actively involved. The NAACP would only support cases that raised a constitutional question about the legal validity of segregation.

In a new development, on Saturday, 21 January, Mayor Gayle met with three little-known black ministers who were not members of the MIA. Disgruntled at what they perceived as being left out of the MIA loop, the ministers looked to make their own names by gaining independent concessions. Gayle subsequently announced to the press that 'prominent Negro leaders' had agreed to a settlement that would end the bus boycott. The proposal was to retain the ten front seats for whites, the ten back seats for blacks, and to fill the middle seats from the front and back on a first-come, first-served basis. Since it remained ambiguous as to whether blacks would have to give up seats to whites upon request in the middle section, this merely represented a restatement of existing practice. The City Commission still refused to press MCL on hiring black drivers. The *Montgomery Advertiser* ran the story, and rumours about the end of the bus boycott soon began to spread to national newsrooms. When black reporter Carl T. Rowan heard the news in Minneapolis, he contacted King for confirmation that the boycott had ended. King told Rowan, 'this can't be true because I was in a strategy meeting this morning and all of the "prominent ministers" were there'.[30] He then asked Rowan to call Mayor Gayle to find out more. Rowan was unsuccessful in getting full details of what had transpired from the mayor, but he did at least elicit the denominations of the ministers. From that limited information the MIA was able to work out who the ministers were. When the ministers were contacted, they denied making any deal with the city. Moving quickly, the MIA issued a press release declaring that 'The bus protest is still on and it will last until our proposals are given sympathetic consideration by our appointed leaders.'[31] The MIA contacted members of the black community through Saturday night gatherings and Sunday morning congregations to let them know that the bus boycott had not ended. On Monday, blacks still refused to ride the buses and the boycott remained in place.

The failure to end the bus boycott left Mayor Gayle fuming. He had wrongly assumed that the meeting with the three black ministers indicated that the MIA was not representative of wider black community sentiment. Having revealed himself as someone willing to compromise over segregation, Gayle was left in a vulnerable political position among white voters, particularly since his police commissioner had so publicly declared his support for the White Citizens' Council. Evidently feeling the need to assert his own segregationist credentials, Gayle denounced the boycott leaders as 'a group of Negro radicals' determined to 'stir up racial strife' and to destroy 'our social fabric'.[32] The response to Gayle's stance from the white community was overwhelmingly positive. Recognising this, Gayle, along with the third city commissioner Frank Parks, announced that they too had joined the White Citizens' Council. The dispute over bus segregation had escalated to yet another level.

As part of the city's new 'get tough' stance, city police began to disperse blacks when they gathered at car pool meeting points and to harass black car pool drivers with tickets for the slightest, sometimes even non-existent infringements. Just as this new pressure looked as though it might break the boycott – 'I began to have doubts about the ability of the Negro community to continue the struggle,' King admitted – the city made another tactical blunder.[33] On Thursday, 26 January, city policemen arrested King for travelling at 30 miles per hour in a 25-mile-per-hour speed zone. Hauled off to jail, he was fingerprinted and locked up in a squalid communal cell, and shortly after Ralph Abernathy arrived to bail him out. The jailer informed Abernathy that he needed a certificate to show that he owned sufficient property to cover the bond money. Since it was too late in the evening to obtain such a certificate, Abernathy went to get the hard cash that the jailer would accept. Meanwhile, hearing of King's arrest, a crowd of concerned blacks began to gather at the jailhouse. King's arrest was helping to galvanise sentiment in the black community to persevere with the bus boycott in the face of further attempts by whites to intimidate them. The growing crowd unsettled the jailers, who released King before Abernathy's return.

Although King spent only a short time in jail before being released, the arrest shook him. He had never experienced such treatment before and the episode brought home not only the full weight of the task that he had taken on in agreeing to become MIA president, but also the implications of that decision for himself and his family. The longer the bus boycott continued, the more likely it was that King would become the focus for white hostility. 'Almost every day,' King recalled, 'someone warned me that he had overheard white men making plans to get rid of me.'[34] When he arrived home, King received another of the anonymous threatening telephone calls from whites that he and other MIA members had been subjected to since the boycott began. 'Nigger, we are tired of you and your mess now,' said the caller. 'And if you are not out of town in three days, we're going to blow your brains out and blow up your house.'[35]

Later that night, unable to sleep, King sat in his kitchen over a cup of coffee and pondered his future. He wondered if he could find a discreet way to back out of his leadership role without appearing to be a coward. At his lowest ebb since the boycott began, and wracked with doubt, King prayed for guidance: 'I am here taking a stand for what I believe is right. But now I am afraid. The people are looking to me for leadership, and if I stand before them without strength and courage, they too will falter. I am at the end of my powers. I have nothing left. I've come to the point where I can't face it alone.' In prayer, King heard an inner voice telling him not to give up. 'Stand up for righteousness,' the voice said. 'Stand up for truth; and God will be at your side forever.'[36] King always believed that the episode provided him with the personal religious revelation and calling that he had never truly experienced before. So strong was its impact that it immediately assuaged his doubts and fears and left him more determined than ever to continue on as MIA president.

King's new-found strength of conviction was tested to the limit just a few nights later when segregationists carried out their threat and bombed his home with Coretta, the Kings' two-month-old daughter Yolanda, and a visitor, Roscoe Williams, inside. King was preaching at Dexter at the time of the attack. When word came through of the bombing he immediately rushed home. Upon arrival, King found several hundred black onlookers as well as the city police at his home. Mayor Gayle, Police Commissioner Sellers and Fire Chief R.L. Lampley were there to inspect the damage. To King's relief, no one had been injured by the blast, but the front-room windows were shattered and there was a sizeable hole blown in the concrete porch outside. Sellers assured King that despite their differences he would do everything in his power to find those responsible for the atrocity. As they spoke, the arrival of more blacks swelled the increasingly belligerent crowd. Attempts by the police to disperse the crowd failed and the threat of violence loomed. Sellers turned to King for help. True to the principles that he had set out at the beginning of the boycott, King told the crowd 'Don't do anything panicky at all. Don't get your weapons. He who lives by the sword shall perish by the sword.' He urged the crowd to leave peacefully and not to seek revenge. 'I want you to love your enemies. Be good to them . . . What we are doing is just. And God is with us.'[37] Most observers later agreed that only King's words had prevented a riot from taking place. 'If it hadn't been for that nigger preacher,' one white policeman was overheard to say, 'we'd all be dead.'[38]

Taking a Stand: The Road to Desegregation

The day after the bombing, MIA attorney Fred Gray filed a suit in the federal court under the title of *Browder* v. *Gayle*. The suit demanded an end to the harassment of car pool drivers and challenged the constitutional basis of segregation on Montgomery buses. After discussing the possibility of such a suit since early January, the bombing of King's home acted as the final catalyst for the launch of legal action. With all prospect of a negotiated settlement having vanished, the MIA leadership decided that only the courts could now settle the issue. The decision to launch a new lawsuit, independent of Rosa Parks's case, which was already on appeal in the courts, sprang from a desire to untangle the specifics of the Parks case from the general principle of challenging segregation. Therefore, it was not Parks's name, but those of other volunteer plaintiffs that were attached to the case.

As well as the legal counter-attack to the bombing, attempts were made to try to ensure King's personal safety. Armed men from Dexter's congregation began to stand guard in front of King's home every night. King and Abernathy decided that it would be prudent to carry firearms themselves to defend against possible future attacks. They went to the sheriff's office to request permits to carry pistols but their application was denied. That night, justifying their fears of further attacks, a bomb was thrown at E.D. Nixon's house from a passing car, although it failed to explode. Nixon was working out of town at the time and did not learn of the attack on his home until the following morning.

The breakdown in negotiations between the City Commission and the MIA, together with the bombings and the MIA lawsuit, moved a group of white city businessmen, the 'Men of Montgomery', to intervene. The businessmen were worried about the escalating racial conflict in the city because of the unfavourable publicity that it was generating for Montgomery. Such negative press made it difficult to lure new investment from northern industries and damaged the city's business interests. As the civil rights movement unfolded in the 1950s and 1960s, white businessmen in southern cities played an important role in mediating racial conflict. They were increasingly forced to confront the question of whether the preservation of segregation and the racial conflict that it generated was worth the economic losses that such conflict often entailed. The Men of Montgomery spent the first three weeks in February trying to mediate between the City Commission and the MIA to reach a negotiated settlement. Their efforts, however, were too little, too late. With the MIA lawsuit attacking the principle of segregation on city buses, the time for negotiation and compromise had passed. It was now all or nothing.

The Montgomery City Commission certainly recognised that there was no going back. It responded to the MIA lawsuit with mass indictments of MIA members. On 18 February, Fred Gray was indicted for allegedly using the name of a woman as a plaintiff in the MIA lawsuit without her permission. On 20 February, a further 89 MIA members, including King, were indicted under the state's anti-boycott laws. King was in Atlanta visiting his father at the time. Upon hearing the news, Daddy King pleaded with his son not to return to Montgomery, telling him it was 'better to be a live dog than a dead lion'.[39] He assembled some of Atlanta's leading black community figures at his home to help persuade his son to stay. King told his father and the black Atlantans that 'I must go back to Montgomery. My friends and associates are being arrested. It would be the height of cowardice for me to stay away. I would rather be in jail for years than to desert my people now. I have begun the struggle and I can't turn back. I have reached the point of no return.'[40] A tearful Daddy King, along with the others present, reluctantly agreed.

Back in Montgomery, MIA members gathered at the city courthouse to be booked together in a show of unity and resolve. 'You looking for me?' asked E.D. Nixon, marching up to the counter. 'Well, here I am.'[41] The following day, when King returned, he too presented himself at the courthouse to be booked. Later that evening, he addressed a mass meeting of over five thousand people. The developments in Montgomery brought increased national attention, with even the New York daily papers carrying front-page news of the boycott. National television networks also began to cover the story.

The national attention brought two people to Montgomery who would play an important role in the development of King's leadership, and in particular his understanding of nonviolence. The first was Bayard Rustin. Born in Chester, Pennsylvania, in 1910, Rustin had a long and varied career as a social and political activist. In his twenties, Rustin belonged to the Young Communist League before switching his allegiance to the US Socialist party. He also became an employee of the international pacifist organisation the Fellowship of Reconciliation (FOR), with its headquarters in New York. In 1942, Rustin assisted James Farmer in setting up the Chicago-based Congress of Racial Equality (CORE), an offshoot of FOR, which pioneered the use of Gandhian passive resistance techniques against racial discrimination in the United States. Rustin also became a close associate of one of America's foremost black leaders, A. Philip Randolph, national president of the black BSCP union. In 1942, Rustin assisted Randolph's March on Washington Movement for fair employment. The threat of the march led to President Franklin D. Roosevelt issuing Executive Order 8802, which banned racial discrimination in wartime industry hiring practices, and set up of the Fair Employment Practices Committee (FEPC) to enforce the ban. During the Second World War, Rustin served time in jail as a conscientious objector. In 1947, he participated in CORE's 'Journey of Reconciliation', an interracial ride through the South that tested southern compliance with a court order to desegregate interstate buses. At the time of the bus boycott, Rustin was actively involved in the War Resisters League.

A southern white writer and FOR board member, Lillian Smith, first alerted Rustin to King's role in events in Montgomery. In a telegram she suggested to Rustin that 'since [Rustin] had worked with the Gandhi movement in India, that it would be a good idea for [him] to go to see Dr. King because [King] was a young man and he had not had great experience in handling nonviolent tactics'.[42] Rustin was enthusiastic about using the Montgomery bus boycott as a launch pad for mass nonviolent, direct-action campaigns across the South. He consulted with a group of prominent New York-based leaders, including US Socialist Party president Norman Thomas, CORE national director James Farmer, FOR director A.J. Muste and A. Philip Randolph about his possible involvement. There were mixed feelings about Rustin's participation. His former involvement with communists, his past arrest for conscientious objection, a past arrest related to his homosexuality, and his status as an 'outside agitator' in the eyes of local whites (and, indeed, some blacks), would make his presence in Montgomery, should it become widely known, controversial and potentially damaging. Nevertheless, with Muste and Randolph's backing, Rustin travelled to Montgomery with black journalist and friend William Worthy, arriving on 21 February, the same day the City Commission was issuing the mass indictments.

Rustin wasted no time in immersing himself in the boycott. Carrying letters of introduction to vouch for his credentials he spoke with Abernathy, Nixon and ACHR executive director Robert Hughes, and attended MIA mass meetings. It was at Rustin's suggestion that the mass turnout of MIA members for indictment at the courthouse occurred. Though King had been out of town on his arrival, Rustin finally caught up with him on Sunday evening having attended King's sermon at Dexter that morning. Rustin spoke with King and found him 'very simpatico to discussing the whole question of nonviolence'.[43]

Yet Rustin's stay in Montgomery lasted only a week. MIA members were wary about his presence. White journalists soon uncovered his true identity and were ready to expose his undercover mission. With these ominous signs of trouble, Randolph phoned to tell Rustin to move on. Though Rustin left, it was not a total retreat. From nearby Birmingham, Alabama, Rustin remained in contact with King and continued to play an important role in the boycott. Rustin, according to one biographer, 'wrote correspondence and publicity material; composed songs for the regular mass meetings [and] organized car pools and other alternatives to bus transportation'.[44] Rustin also continued to have an important influence in shaping King's developing understanding of nonviolence.

As Rustin was on his way out of Montgomery, a second arrival, the Revd Glen E. Smiley, a white FOR field secretary, moved in on 27 February as a replacement. Born in Texas, the Methodist minister had worked with FOR since 1942 and, like Rustin, had been imprisoned as a conscientious objector during the Second World War. Smiley's arrival represented the desire of the New York-based groups for a much lighter touch in terms of outside help for the bus boycott. In contrast to Rustin's wholehearted enthusiasm to develop the boycott as a launch pad for wider mass activism, Smiley's more specific brief was to lend assistance and support to local leaders in their use of nonviolence. In conversation, Smiley discovered that King knew 'very little' about Gandhi and his teachings, but reported that he was willing to learn. Smiley was delighted at his receptivity but was concerned about his ability to adhere to nonviolence. 'I believe that God has called Martin Luther King to lead a great movement here in the South,' Smiley reported. 'But why does God lay a burden on one so young, so inexperienced, so good? King can be a Negro Gandhi, or he can be made into an unfortunate demagogue destined to swing from a lynch mob's tree.'[45]

Despite the talk of mass activism and nonviolence, it was in the courts that the victory over bus segregation in Montgomery was finally won. Events came to a head with a series of legal rulings during 1956. On 20 March, in agreement with the prosecuting and defence attorneys, King was the first member of the MIA to be tried under the state's anti-boycott law. As expected, three days later King was found guilty. He was fined $500 and ordered to pay $500 court costs. MIA attorneys announced that they would appeal against the decision. With the appeal process expected to take the best part of a year, the trials of the other 88 MIA members were held in abeyance until the higher courts reviewed King's case.

On 23 April, the US Supreme Court affirmed the decision of a lower court in upholding *Flemming* v. *South Carolina Electric and Gas Company*, an NAACP-sponsored case against segregated buses in Columbia, South Carolina. In the light of this, the MCL announced that segregation on city buses in Montgomery would end immediately. However, Mayor Gayle declared that any driver who failed to uphold segregation laws would be prosecuted. The MCL responded that it would stand behind any drivers the city tried to prosecute. For its part, the MIA was determined to continue the boycott until *Browder* v. *Gayle* had been heard in the courts and the specific situation in Montgomery had been clarified. That hearing took place on 11 May in front of a special three-judge federal court panel in Montgomery. On 5 June, the court struck down Montgomery's use of segregation on the buses. When the city announced that it intended to take the case to the US Supreme Court on appeal, the federal court suspended its injunction against segregation until the appeal was heard. Again, the MIA decided to continue the bus boycott until the US Supreme Court provided a definitive ruling.

In the meantime, the City Commission used another legal device to try to end the bus boycott. On 30 October, it filed a request in a state court for an injunction against the MIA's car pool on the basis that it infringed MCL's operating franchise. The idea for this came from the way white city officials had handled a bus boycott initiated by blacks in Tallahassee, Florida, in May 1956, under the leadership of former Montgomery minister C. Kenzie Steele. By targeting the operation of the car pool, whites in Tallahassee had effectively hampered the bus boycott. The MIA petitioned the federal court to prevent the state court from handing down the injunction requested by the City Commission. Federal district court judge Frank M. Johnson Jr set a hearing for the MIA petition on 14 November. State circuit court judge Eugene Carter then set a date of 13 November to hear the city's case for an injunction. On 13 November, Judge Carter granted the city an injunction against the car pool, dealing a major blow to the boycott. Yet even as the state court hearing was in session, news that the US Supreme Court had affirmed the federal court decision to strike down bus segregation in Montgomery filtered through. 'God Almighty has spoken from Washington D.C.,' a courtroom bystander exclaimed.[46] Still, that order would not come into effect until it was formally served upon Montgomery officials. Moreover, the city was given leave for one final rehearing of the case in the US Supreme Court. The following day, Judge Johnson declined to lift the state court's injunction against the MIA car pool. The MIA hastily acted to implement a share-a-ride transportation system to ensure that the boycott would last until a decisive court victory was won. On 19 November, the MIA petitioned Supreme Court justice Hugo Black to make the court's order banning segregation effective immediately, but its request was turned down.

As the black community in Montgomery awaited a final, decisive court order, the MIA organised an 'Institute on Nonviolence and Social Change' from 3 to 9 December in preparation for bus desegregation. At King's opening address on 3 December at Holt Street Baptist Church, where a year earlier he had made his first speech as president of the MIA, he echoed his call for adherence to Christian values. 'The end is reconciliation; the end is redemption; the end is the creation of the beloved community,' King told the gathering.[47] The week-long institute looked to reaffirm this principle, and guidelines were drawn up to help ease the process of integration and to ensure that the conduct of blacks followed the same nonviolent principles that the boycott had adhered to throughout.

Finally, on 17 December, the US Supreme Court rejected the city's final appeal. On 20 December, the order to desegregate buses was served on city officials. The next morning, at 5.45 a.m., King, along with Glenn Smiley, Ralph Abernathy and E.D. Nixon, boarded a bus in a black neighbourhood. 'I believe you are Reverend King, aren't you?' asked the white bus driver. 'Yes, I am,' replied King. 'We are very glad to have you this morning,' said the driver. King took his seat towards the front of the bus next to Glenn Smiley. Downtown, the group transferred to a bus travelling through a white neighbourhood. King observed a generally peaceful compliance with the court order. However, there was evidence of some resistance to change. One elderly white man remained standing rather than move to the back of the bus, declaring that he 'would rather go to hell than sit behind a nigger'. A white woman who unwittingly sat next to a black passenger jumped up at the discovery and exclaimed, 'What are these niggers going to do next?' Elsewhere, a white passenger slapped a black woman as she alighted but, heeding King's words about nonviolence, the black woman refused to strike back. Overall, the *Montgomery Advertiser* reported a 'calm but cautious acceptance of this significant change in Montgomery's way of life ... without any major disturbance'.[48]

However, the initial peaceful compliance quickly turned into a 'reign of terror'.[49] The integration of Montgomery's buses met with a violent backlash from whites. In the early morning of 23 December, someone fired a shotgun blast through King's front door. On 28 December, white snipers firing at a city bus wounded black passenger Rosa Jordan who was eight months pregnant. Police Commissioner Clyde Sellers immediately halted the city's bus service and the following day the City Commission decided to suspend all evening and night services. Extra police officers were hired to protect the reinstituted daytime service, but white snipers continued to shoot at buses. In another development, on 10 January 1957, four black churches, Ralph Abernathy's home and white minister and boycott sympathiser Robert Graetz's home were all bombed in a coordinated attack. Only a vigilant nightwatchman prevented the bombing of King's church. On 27 January, a bomb destroyed the home of black hospital worker Allen Robertson, who lived just a few hundred yards from King's parsonage. A second disarmed bomb was found at the parsonage. Though arrests were made and charges were brought against the suspected bombers – all with links to the local white terror group the Ku Klux Klan – no convictions were ever secured.

Yet if the bus boycott had led to a violent white response, it had equally helped to strengthen the resolve of the black community not to be cowed by it. NAACP attorney Thurgood Marshall too quickly dismissed the bus boycott when he declared, 'All that walking for nothing. They could just as well have waited while the bus case went through the courts, without all this work and money of the boycott.'[50] Marshall was right that ultimately the conflict had been settled in the courts, but wrong that the bus boycott had made no other impact. Crucially, the boycott had demonstrated the ability of a united black community to defy segregation nonviolently and to thereby overcome it. In doing so, blacks found a new self-confidence and self-respect in the face of white efforts to intimidate them. When 40 Ku Klux Klan cars drove through black Montgomery on the night of the decision to desegregate the buses, the Klansmen expected the usual black response of silence, fear and retreat. Instead, King reported, 'the Negroes behaved as though they were watching a circus parade. Concealing the effort it took them, they walked about as usual; some simply watched from their steps; a few waved at the passing cars. After a few blocks, the Klan, nonplussed, turned off into a sidestreet and disappeared into the night.'[51] As a black janitor in Montgomery told a white northern reporter, 'We got our heads up now, and we won't ever bow down again – no, sir – except before God!'[52] Moreover, it appeared that the impact of the bus boycott did not stop at Montgomery, but that it had a regional, even national resonance among blacks. As James Forman, later executive secretary of SNCC testifies, the 'Montgomery bus boycott had a very significant effect on the consciousness of black people throughout the United States'.[53] Many others who joined later demonstrations were, like Forman, affected and inspired by the Montgomery bus boycott.

Despite the stir created by the Montgomery bus boycott its immediate impact on the continuing struggle for black freedom and equality remained unclear. Did the bus boycott represent a unique, one-off development in one particular locality? Or could the Montgomery model of protest be successfully repeated elsewhere? What of the boycott leader Martin Luther King Jr? Was he simply a talented local leader or could he build upon his new-found notoriety to establish himself as a regional, even national, black leader? During the years after the Montgomery bus boycott, King and other civil rights activists sought to address and to find answers to these questions.

Chapter 2

Catching Up, 1956–61

Indian independence leader Mohandas K. Gandhi is purported to have said on one march, after being stopped for an interview by a reporter, 'There go my people, I must catch up with them, for I am their leader.'[1] Gandhi's meditation on the relationship between a social movement and its leader is particularly perceptive in the way that it emphasises that social movements often lead their leaders as much as leaders lead those movements. Martin Luther King Jr understood those movement dynamics, echoing Gandhi's sentiment by declaring that 'It was the people who moved their leaders, not the leaders who moved their people.'[2] In the years after the Montgomery bus boycott, King's meteoric rise to leadership and the inexperience that accompanied it were telling. King was clearly intimidated by his new-found responsibilities. He told one old family friend, J. Pious Barbour, that he was 'worried to death. A man who hits the peak at twenty-seven has a tough job ahead. People will be expecting me to pull rabbits out of the hat for the rest of my life.'[3] As King strove to capitalise on the Montgomery bus boycott by founding, with the help of others, the SCLC, it was developments elsewhere, such as the student-led sit-ins and the CORE-inspired Freedom Rides, that forged the agenda for the civil rights movement. Throughout the period, King strove to catch up with the expectations placed upon him by the rest of the movement. By 1961, he was in danger of falling behind so far that he risked becoming merely a bystander in unfolding events.

King on the National and the International Stage

Appearances with established black leaders, black celebrities, and white politicians in the period after the Montgomery bus boycott confirmed King's status as a potent symbol of a developing new black movement in the United States. In May 1957, King spoke at a 'Prayer Pilgrimage for

Freedom' at the Lincoln Memorial in Washington, DC, sharing the platform with A. Philip Randolph and NAACP executive secretary Roy Wilkins. However, King's speech, 'Give Us the Ballot,' emphasised the importance of black voting rights rather than nonviolent direct action.[4] Like many other black leaders, King believed that 'if the Negro achieved the ballot throughout the South, many of the problems which we faced would be solved'.[5] The speech placed King centre stage in proceedings. Black reporter James Hicks, writing in the *New York Amsterdam News*, claimed that King was now 'the number one leader of sixteen million Negroes in the United States'.[6] In October 1958 and again in April 1959, Randolph invited King to speak at a 'Youth March for Integrated Schools' in the nation's capital. In June 1957, King, along with Ralph Abernathy, met privately with Vice President Richard M. Nixon. A year later, President Dwight D. Eisenhower agreed to meet with a delegation of black leaders at the White House, including King, Randolph, Wilkins and Lester B. Granger, executive director of the National Urban League (NUL). Founded in 1909 and based in New York, the NUL was dedicated to pursuing better black living conditions and employment opportunities in America's cities.

Two trips abroad confirmed that King was not just a national, but also an international symbol of black America. On 5 March 1957, King and his wife Coretta, along with other black leaders from the United States, attended the independence ceremonies marking the transfer of power from the British colony of the Gold Coast to the Republic of Ghana. The trip, King's first outside the United States, provided a global context within which to locate the unfolding struggle back home. 'I thought it [Ghanaian independence] would have worldwide implications and repercussions,' King later reflected, 'not only for Asia and Africa, but also for America . . . I thought Ghana would become a symbol of hope for hundreds and thousands of oppressed peoples all over the world as they struggled for freedom.'[7] In February and March 1959, King, Coretta and Lawrence D. Reddick, a history professor at Alabama State College and a friend of the Kings, visited India at the invitation of the Gandhi National Memorial Fund. In India, King met with many of Gandhi's compatriots, including Prime Minister Jawaharlal Nehru. India's attempts to overcome the centuries of injustice inflicted by the caste system provided King with another instructive parallel for attempts by blacks in the United States to overcome second-class citizenship there. King noted that 'India appeared to be integrating its untouchables faster than the United States was integrating the Negro community . . . I left India more convinced than ever before that nonviolent resistance was the most potent weapon available to oppressed people in their struggle for freedom.'[8]

King's notoriety brought its own problems. Competition with other black leaders was one of them. With the bus boycott over, both old and new rivalries began to surface in Montgomery's black community. King had initially been chosen to head the MIA because he was not perceived as posing a threat to existing black leaders, and because he was not involved in their squabbles. Subsequent events meant that King's star rose far higher than that of any other black leader in the city. Media accounts placed King at the centre of the boycott. Even though King's own account of the Montgomery bus boycott, published as *Stride Toward Freedom: The Montgomery Story* in 1958, was at pains to acknowledge the efforts of others, many still felt that the young preacher was unjustly emphasising his role in events while diminishing theirs.

Among the most vociferous critics of King was E.D. Nixon. At one point he offered his resignation as MIA treasurer, complaining at being 'treated like a child' by its leadership.[9] King tried to smooth matters over and refused to accept the resignation. After further complaints about MIA finances and more threatened resignations, Nixon finally left to pursue his own voter-registration campaign. This placed him directly at odds with his old rival Rufus Lewis, who was running MIA voter-registration efforts. Nixon intended to hire Rosa Parks, who was disgruntled about being left out of MIA activities altogether, but by that time she had already accepted another job in Virginia. Tensions between MIA lawyer Fred Gray and others in the organisation continued. The Revd Uriah J. Fields, the MIA's recording secretary, resigned to form the Restoration and Amelioration Association as a rival to the MIA.

With all the infighting, the MIA failed to make progress in addressing the needs of the black community. Its first post-boycott project of forming a credit union for Montgomery blacks met with little success. When the MIA launched a lawsuit to desegregate city parks it did manage to win a favourable court ruling. However, the city responded by closing all of the public parks for blacks and whites alike. This hurt blacks more, since many well-to-do whites had access to private park facilities. Plans to launch a legal challenge to continuing segregation in Montgomery's public schools brought the threat from incoming Alabama governor John Patterson to close all of the city's public schools rather than desegregate them. As with the parks, this would disadvantage the black population more, since whites would have better access to private schools. Moreover, there were worries among the city's black teachers that the closure of black public schools would lead to them losing their jobs. In the light of this, the MIA put its plans to challenge school desegregation on hold.

King's difficulties with local black leaders were echoed at the national level. In particular, King found himself in conflict with NAACP leader Roy Wilkins. Wilkins was wary of King, who appeared far better at reaching out to and communicating with the black masses than he did. Moreover, King and Wilkins placed a different emphasis on the future of the black struggle for civil rights. Although both agreed that litigation and legislation would form an important basis for gaining equal rights, Wilkins did not accept that the use of nonviolent direct action had any significant role to play. King's experience with the Montgomery bus boycott convinced him that nonviolent direct action, working alongside litigation and legislation, would be imperative in the fight against segregation. Wilkins feared that King and the SCLC were trying to usurp not only the NAACP's influence over the future direction of the movement but also, with far-reaching consequences for the very existence of the NAACP, its membership and donations. King was at pains to placate Wilkins and the NAACP and tried to convince them that the SCLC would work alongside and not in competition with them. Such assurances, however, did little to assuage Wilkins's constant doubts.

King's arrest in September 1958 demonstrated that although he could mix with national and international dignitaries, back in his home state and in much of the South the white population considered him public enemy number one. King was back in Montgomery to attend the trial of Edward Davis, who had attacked Ralph Abernathy in his church office after accusing him of having an affair with his wife. When King and Coretta tried to enter the courtroom, the police refused to admit them. King told them he was waiting to see his lawyer, Fred Gray, who was there to assist Abernathy. When King peered into the courtroom to try to attract Gray's attention a nearby police sergeant took offence, telling him, 'Boy, you done done it now.'[10] King was placed under arrest for loitering. The next morning, King was summarily tried and convicted and handed a $14 fine or a 14-day prison sentence. For the first time, drawing upon his growing understanding of nonviolent methods of protest, King refused to pay the fine and accepted imprisonment to draw attention to the injustice of his arrest.

King's arrest and his decision to go to jail appeared to rekindle the spirit of the bus boycott in Montgomery. Abernathy marched the crowd waiting outside the courtroom to King's church and made plans to hold a vigil outside the jail. However, in a wholly unexpected development, King was refused entry into prison. Alert to the fact that King's incarceration could potentially reunite the black community, Police Commissioner Clyde Sellers paid King's $14 fine himself. The irony of this event was made light of at a mass meeting afterwards, but it contained a prescient warning that law enforcement officers were learning quickly about how to respond to nonviolent protest tactics. Nevertheless, the whole episode clearly demonstrated that King was, as long-time family friend the Revd J. Raymond Henderson reminded him after his arrest, a 'marked man'.[11]

Henderson's point was dramatically brought home the following month when a black woman, Izola Ware Curry, stabbed King in the chest with a Japanese letter opener as he signed copies of his book *Stride Toward Freedom* in New York. Curry casually came up to King and asked 'Are you Martin Luther King?' King replied 'Yes.' Curry then plunged the letter opener into King's chest.[12] The blade lodged perilously close to King's heart and required delicate surgery to remove it. Even a slight movement between the store and the hospital might have killed him. 'If you had sneezed,' King's doctor later told him, 'your aorta would have been punctured and you would have drowned in your own blood.'[13] Curry's incoherence at the trial led to her diagnosis as a paranoid schizophrenic and she was admitted indefinitely to a state hospital for the criminally insane. King's period of recovery after the stabbing did at least offer some respite from his relentless schedule. Between marches, meetings and overseas visits, King toured incessantly with speaking engagements. Even the birth of the Kings' second child, Martin Luther King III, on 23 October 1957, did little to slow him down. Surviving a life-threatening injury only served to convince King even more of his call to leadership. 'I was intensely impatient to get back to continue the work we all knew had to be done regardless of the cost,' he reported. 'I did not have the slightest intention of turning back.'[14] Family commitments and his duties as a pastor increasingly came second to his new responsibilities as a leader in the civil rights struggle.

Despite his expenditure of time and energy, King failed to maintain the momentum of the bus boycott in Montgomery and to expand black activism across the South and the nation. Progress on civil rights still lagged. Although President Eisenhower sent federal troops to enforce the integration of Central High School in Little Rock, Arkansas, in September 1957, such federal intervention proved the exception rather than the rule. School desegregation met with widespread non-compliance in the South. The Civil Rights Act passed by the US Congress in September 1957 was a move in the right direction – it had been 82 years since the last one – but it ultimately provided only token legislation. Ferocious opposition from southern congressmen such as South Carolina senator Strom Thurmond, who held the senate floor by speaking continuously for over 24 hours to stall action on the bill, meant that many of its original provisions, such as empowering the Justice Department to sue for the enforcement of school desegregation, were struck down. White resistance looked as though it might put a stop to the embryonic black protest movement before it had even had a chance to get off the ground. King therefore sought to strengthen the movement and to give it greater coherence by helping to form a new civil rights organisation.

The Southern Christian Leadership Conference (SCLC)

Even before the bus boycott ended King, with the help of others, had explored ways to capitalise on events in Montgomery. Two distinct possibilities emerged. First, Glenn Smiley and FOR national chair Charles Lawrence promoted the idea of a southern-based nonviolent organisation that would be an affiliate of the Fellowship of Reconciliation, or an independent organisation in its own right with FOR backing, along lines similar to CORE. FOR sponsored meetings in May and July 1956 and invited 150 southern black leaders to a regional conference in Atlanta held on 8–10 January 1957 to discuss these plans.

However, these discussions were overtaken by a second set of proposals developed by Bayard Rustin, Ella Baker and Stanley Levison. These three seasoned activists had previously worked together to organise In Friendship, chaired by A. Philip Randolph, in 1956. In Friendship helped to raise funds for black activists who had lost homes or jobs because of taking a stand for civil rights. Initially, funds were directed towards black activists taking part in the struggle to desegregate schools. In Friendship subsequently played an important role in raising funds for the MIA during the bus boycott. Baker and Levison, like Rustin, had a long history of social and political activism. Baker, from North Carolina, worked with the Young Negro Cooperative League and the New Deal agency the Works Progress Administration in the 1930s before joining the national office of the NAACP as national field secretary. She later became the NAACP's director of branches. In the course of her work, Baker met with many black activists across the South, as well as US Communist Party members and other left-wing activists. One of those contacts was Stanley Levison, a white, Jewish New Yorker, who was a trained lawyer and had been involved with groups such as the American Jewish Congress and the NAACP. It was through the NAACP that Levison met Baker. Like Baker and Rustin, and like many other social and political activists of the time, Levison moved in left-wing circles and was a former communist sympathiser.

Rustin, Baker and Levison, like FOR's Smiley and Lawrence, urged King to think about how to expand the Montgomery example of black activism. In contrast to FOR's proposals, however, they successfully persuaded King that such an organisation should be completely independent of other organisational ties. On New Year's Day 1957, King, along with C. Kenzie Steele, head of the Inter-Civic Council in Tallahassee, Florida, and Fred Shuttlesworth, founder of the Alabama Christian Movement for Human Rights (ACMHR) in Birmingham, Alabama, sent 100 invitations to a meeting in Atlanta on 10 and 11 January to discuss the matter. The 60 or so respondents who attended that meeting agreed, based upon working papers provided by Rustin and Baker, to establish a temporary 'Southern Leadership Conference on Transportation and Nonviolent Integration'. At a further meeting organised by Rustin in New Orleans on 14 February, it was agreed to establish a permanent organisation. Finally, in August, at its first annual convention, the group changed its name to the Southern Christian Leadership Conference (SCLC), with the conference theme providing the motto of the organisation: 'To Redeem the Soul of America'.[15]

The idea for the SCLC formulated by Rustin, Baker and Levison held important differences from the organisation envisioned by FOR's Smiley and Lawrence. Firstly, the SCLC was predominantly composed of and led by southern blacks. This meant that it had a strong indigenous base in the South. This, in turn, addressed Rustin's concern that the new organisation should be different from existing civil rights organisations in distancing itself more from white, middle-class, northern intellectuals and liberals. An organisation led by and for southern blacks, and especially led by black ministers (although Rustin had opposed the addition of Christian to SCLC's title, fearing that it could alienate non-religious members) increased the likelihood of black support for it. Secondly, the involvement of Rustin, Baker and Levison helped to bring on board the support of A. Philip Randolph, which they considered essential. As one of black America's most respected leaders, Randolph lent credibility and respectability to the SCLC and provided an important source of political and financial support from the labour movement. Moreover, as a known staunch anti-communist, Randolph's support signalled to others that the SCLC was a mainstream organisation free from subversive or radical intent, an important criterion in the context of Cold War America.

The way that the SCLC was structured was also significant, especially in its self-conscious differentiation from the NAACP. Rustin, Baker and Levison conceived of the SCLC as being what black sociologist

Aldon Morris later termed an 'organization of organizations', that is, an organisation made up of loosely bound affiliate groups.[16] Each affiliate group paid a $25 subscription that entitled it to a certificate of affiliation, the right to send five delegates to the SCLC annual convention, and to advice and assistance from SCLC staff members. Importantly, unlike the NAACP, the SCLC did not solicit individual membership.[17] Indeed, the way that the SCLC was set up allowed its members to remain in the NAACP – in fact, many SCLC members were NAACP local and state presidents – and sought to placate the older civil rights organisation by demonstrating that both organisations could work side by side in the South.

SCLC affiliates came in two general types. The first were church-led organisations, most of them recently founded and modelled on the MIA, such as the ACMHR in Alabama, the Baton Rouge Christian Movement in Louisiana, and the Nashville Christian Leadership Council in Tennessee. The second were voter-registration organisations and civic groups. Again, ministers dominated most of these organisations, though laymen did front some of them, such as the United Christian Movement led by black dentist Dr C.O. Simpkins in Shreveport, Louisiana. There was just one non-southern affiliate, the Western Christian Leadership Conference based in Los Angeles, though this was exclusively a fund-raising outpost. The SCLC had a governing board of 33 people. All board members were black, two-thirds of them were ministers (with a preponderance of Baptists), all were from the urban South, and most were relatively well-off members of the black upper middle class. There was just one female member on the board.

Although Rustin, Baker and Levison were important facilitators in the formation of the SCLC, and sought to influence and guide its activities, the main thrust of its direction and focus came from black southern ministers and especially from King, who was elected SCLC president. From the outset, King was synonymous with the SCLC, which in effect became his own personal vehicle for civil rights leadership. Board members more often than not rubber-stamped all King's nominees, suggestions, statements and actions. Throughout his leadership of the organisation, King retained independence of thought and action. He was always willing to listen to and to contemplate the views of others, but he ultimately came to his own conclusions and made up his own mind about the direction and activities of the organisation.

Thus, it was their organisational skills and experience, rather than their political ideas, that Rustin, Baker and Levison primarily lent to the SCLC. Baker took on the task of running the SCLC headquarters in Atlanta and coordinating the activities of its affiliates. Rustin and Levison meanwhile assisted on a number of fronts, including briefing King for meetings, arranging speaking engagements, advising on handling journalists and publishers, drafting speeches and press releases, ghostwriting articles for publication, helping King to write *Stride Toward Freedom*, and telling him how best to approach individuals and groups for funding and support.

Despite this help, the SCLC was painfully slow in moving into action. It took almost all of 1957 to establish its structure and organisational procedures. The SCLC's first campaign was an attempt to expand the Montgomery bus boycott model of protest to other cities. For a variety of reasons this failed. In New Orleans, Atlanta and Mobile, white city authorities complied with court-ordered desegregation to forestall the development of a mass movement. In Miami, blacks represented too small a proportion of the population to make a bus boycott effective. In Birmingham, 'police intimidation, poor planning, black disunity, and the problem of devising alternative transportation' were all obstacles. Only in two places did a sustained bus boycott emerge. In Tallahassee the boycott failed to achieve a clear victory. In Rock Hill, South Carolina, a six-month boycott put the bus company out of business completely. These disparate developments demonstrated that the Montgomery bus boycott, as Glenn Smiley concluded, 'was not exportable'.[18]

Faced with this setback, the SCLC shifted its focus to what it thought would be the more promising endeavour of voter registration. Such a campaign coincided with the civil rights bill being debated by Congress in 1957 that included a proposal to tackle voting discrimination. The SCLC believed that there would be less white opposition to voter registration than to desegregation, since it did not raise the sensitive issue of racial mixing. A voter-registration drive also offered a way to unite SCLC affiliates in a coordinated regional programme. In July 1957, Rustin and Levison drew up a plan for an SCLC voter-registration campaign. This included raising $200,000 to set up a central office in Atlanta with an executive director and a staff of fieldworkers. The team of workers would then help to set up voter-registration committees that would hold voting clinics to encourage blacks to register to vote and collect evidence of illegal black disfranchisement. Ella Baker launched the 'Crusade for Citizenship' on 12 February 1958 from SCLC's Atlanta headquarters. In May, the Revd John L. Tilley from Baltimore joined her as the SCLC's first executive director.

The SCLC's second campaign, however, proved little more successful than the first. The planned extensive network of voter-registration committees failed to materialise, as did the overly ambitious funding target. In April 1959, King fired SCLC executive director Tilley, citing the lack of a 'dynamic program commensurate with the amount of money' spent.[19] Baker was given the job of acting executive director. The SCLC's Atlanta headquarters remained essentially a one-woman operation, with Baker left to coordinate the Crusade for Citizenship, to make field trips, to prepare the SCLC's newsletter, to arrange conventions and board meetings, to make reports to King and the SCLC's administrative committee, and to compile complaints about voting discrimination. Finally, exasperated at being left to do all the work and at the continuing lack of a strategy and direction within the organisation, in October 1959 Baker challenged King and the board of directors to re-examine the way the SCLC operated.

The review produced a number of important changes. The SCLC streamlined the number of board meetings from three to two a year, and the number of conventions from two to one. It also appointed a subcommittee of five to help Baker focus on developing a new programme for 1960. King recommended diversifying SCLC activities beyond voter registration. He picked up on Baker's suggestion of setting up literacy classes in cooperation with Highlander Folk School in Tennessee, and getting James Lawson, FOR's southern field secretary, to teach techniques of nonviolent protest to selected groups. King insisted on hiring Bayard Rustin as SCLC public relations director to boost the SCLC's profile, despite the problems that had previously beset Rustin's involvement with the Montgomery bus boycott. King was also forced to address the growing concern that he personally was not devoting enough attention to the development of the SCLC. Speaking engagements, meetings with officials, trips abroad, and pastoral responsibilities at Dexter, all compromised King's time and energy. King therefore decided that he must now devote all his attention to the SCLC: 'I came to the conclusion that I had a moral obligation to give more of my time and energy to the whole South.'[20] King therefore resigned from his post at Dexter and moved to Atlanta to share the pastorate of Ebenezer Baptist Church with his father. The move freed King from the obligation to preach every Sunday, it put him in the same city as the SCLC's headquarters, and it placed him in the city that was the central airline hub for the South, making it easier and quicker for him to reach appointments around the country. On 31 January 1960, King said goodbye to the Dexter congregation, explaining that 'History has thrust something upon me from which I cannot turn away.'[21]

The 1960 Sit-ins and the Student Nonviolent Coordinating Committee (SNCC)

Before King could make any impact on the SCLC's fortunes, however, fresh impetus for the civil rights movement came from elsewhere. The day after King delivered his farewell sermon in Montgomery, Ezell Blair Jr, Franklin McCain, Joe McNeil and David Richmond, all of them black students at North Carolina Agricultural and Technical College in Greensboro, North Carolina, went into a downtown Woolworths store. 'For about a week,' recalls Richmond, 'we four fellows sat around the A&T campus talking about the integration movement. And we decided to go down to Woolworths and see what would happen.'[22] The students bought a number of items in the store and then, keeping hold of their receipts, headed for the segregated lunch counter and ordered coffee. The waitress refused to serve them. They demanded to know why they could buy goods in other parts of the store, but were refused service at the lunch counter. They refused to leave until they were given a satisfactory answer. The students stayed until the store closed. The next day, the four students returned with others from campus to resume the sit-in. Over the following days, more students joined in the protest and initiated other sit-ins in other local stores. By the weekend, local stores decided to close their lunch counters. The sit-ins forced the local white business community to address the question of whether segregation was worth the cost of racial unrest and economic damage that it entailed. Through sustaining the pressure on them to act, the black students forced white businessmen to relent and to desegregate downtown facilities.

Like the Montgomery bus boycott, the sit-ins were not without precedent. The tactic had been used decades before by labour unions. Between 1957 and 1960, at least 16 other cities had experienced sit-in demonstrations. However, what had been a fragmented, tentative and experimental series of demonstrations in the late 1950s finally cohered in a region-wide movement in 1960. In direct contrast to the Montgomery bus boycott, the 1960s sit-ins proved immediately exportable. The sit-ins expanded via the interrelated network of southern black colleges that could mobilise student-led action in other communities. Unlike the Montgomery bus boycott, the sit-ins did not require the mobilisation of an entire community from the outset, and were therefore much easier to organise and much simpler to instigate. The week after the Greensboro sit-ins, similar demonstrations occurred in other parts of North Carolina. Then they began to occur in neighbouring states. Finally, they spread right across the South. From 1 February to 1 April, over 70 communities experienced sit-ins. By the end of 1960, over 70,000 students had participated in sit-ins or other forms of direct action, and there had been 3,600 arrests.

King first became involved with the sit-ins on 16 February when he addressed a meeting of students in Durham, North Carolina. The meeting was the idea of the Revd Doug Moore, a local black minister and SCLC board member. Moore, who had been involved in helping to organise earlier sit-in demonstrations in Durham, wanted students who had participated in sit-ins in North Carolina to establish formal and ongoing links between them. King encouraged the formation of such an organisation in his address and passed on advice about how to conduct and how to develop the sit-ins. As in the Montgomery bus boycott, King stressed the need for student protests to take place in a spirit of nonviolence and to seek reconciliation with whites. He also encouraged students to supplement sit-ins with economic boycotts of stores and to pursue a 'jail not bail' policy of choosing imprisonment over paying fines if convicted. At a later rally at White Rock Baptist Church, King assured black demonstrators that 'you have the full weight of the SCLC behind you in your struggle'.[23]

It was SCLC's acting executive director Ella Baker who most enthusiastically took on the task of supporting the sit-in movement. Baker wanted to extend Moore's idea of coordinating protests in North Carolina throughout the southern states. With $800 of SCLC money, Baker, along with Moore and Glenn Smiley, organised a conference at Baker's alma mater, Shaw University, in Raleigh, North Carolina, on 15–17 April 1960. In the letter of invitation, the stated purpose of the conference was 'TO SHARE experience gained in recent protest demonstrations and TO HELP chart future goals for effective action' in order to build 'a more unified sense of direction for *training and action in Nonviolent Resistance*'.[24] From the outset, Baker was determined to safeguard the independence of the student movement from the influence of other organisations, particularly the SCLC. Already disillusioned with what she perceived to be King's faltering leadership, and on her way out of the SCLC, Baker wanted the students to form a new organisation that would be more democratic and lean toward 'group-centered leadership' rather than the 'leader-centered group pattern of organization' that she felt hindered the SCLC with its 'prophetic leader [with] heavy feet of clay'.[25]

Baker's efforts to steer the students in a new direction was reflected in her choice of James Lawson as keynote speaker, a minister closely linked to the influential group of students from Nashville who were in attendance at the conference. Like Baker, Lawson wanted students to retain their independence and dynamism rather than to be beholden to existing organisations. He told them that nonviolence stripped 'segregation's power structure of its major weapon: the manipulation of law or law-enforcement to keep the Negro in his place'.[26] Lawson also stridently criticised the NAACP for its reluctance to support nonviolent action. King proved willing to take a back seat at the conference, even though he was the most well-known and influential black leader at the meeting. In his address, King limited his remarks to essentially the same message he had delivered at the earlier North Carolina meeting. He pointed to the need for an ongoing student organisation, advocated a nationwide selective buying campaign, and encouraged students to employ 'jail not bail' tactics.

Yet some of those close to King, such as Wyatt Tee Walker, who was already lined up as Baker's replacement to become full-time SCLC executive director, and Bernard Lee, a student leader in Montgomery, urged that any new student organisation should be formally allied to the SCLC. Had King chosen to force the issue, some observers believe that he might well have persuaded the students to become an adjunct of SCLC. Instead, King sought to avoid infighting with Baker and Lawson and allowed an independent student organisation to emerge from the conference. A 'Temporary Student Nonviolent Coordinating Committee' was set up with Marion Barry, a Nashville student, elected as chair. At further meetings held that year, students decided to drop the 'temporary' label and to make the Student Nonviolent Coordinating Committee (SNCC – pronounced 'snick') a permanent organisation. Nevertheless, SNCC remained closely bound to the SCLC. For the early part of its life, SNCC's headquarters was 'squeezed in one corner of the SCLC office' in Atlanta.[27]

As the sit-in movement unfolded, King was involved in several uncomfortable brushes with the law. On 17 February 1960, two local deputy officers arrived at Ebenezer Baptist Church with warrants for King's arrest and his extradition to Alabama. King faced two counts of perjury for allegedly falsely swearing to the accuracy of his 1956 and 1958 state tax returns. King went to Montgomery for arraignment and was released on a $2,000 bond. The arrest came as a complete shock. Alabama auditor Lloyd Hale had previously claimed that King's income was greater than King had reported. However, King thought the matter was resolved when he reluctantly agreed to pay $1,600 to dispel those accusations. The state of Alabama refused to let the matter rest there, even though the case was the first time in the history of the state that it had prosecuted anyone for perjury on a tax return. It was clearly a direct attempt to harass King and to besmirch his name.

King was particularly troubled by the allegations since they were directed at his personal integrity as a leader and insinuated that his main reason for involvement with the civil rights movement was for financial gain. In fact, quite the opposite was true. Throughout his career as a civil rights leader, King deliberately lived within modest means to avoid such allegations of corruption. Nevertheless, the charges perturbed King and successfully diverted his energy and movement funds away from civil rights activities. In New York, Bayard Rustin and Stanley Levison set up a Committee to Defend Martin Luther King, chaired by A. Philip Randolph, and with Rustin as executive director. The committee began to raise money and to assemble a team of attorneys for King's defence.

When the trial began in Montgomery on 25 May 1960, the flimsy allegations of the state were quickly laid bare. On the witness stand, Lloyd Hale came close to admitting that the tax discrepancies highlighted by the state were easily explained, and that the outstanding sums were simply back payments to King for associated travel expenses. Various witnesses testified on matters ranging from King's good character to the intricacies of tax law. To universal surprise, after hearing three days of testimony, an all-white southern jury rendered a fair verdict and took less than four hours to find King not guilty. Once again, Alabama's attempts to harass King backfired. The allegations were proved false and the amount of money channelled into the Committee to Defend Martin Luther King demonstrated the extent of white liberal support for King and the civil rights movement in the north. The successful fund-raising exercise opened up new channels of financial support and provided a springboard to more effective money-raising efforts in the future.

King and the Kennedys

Between his arrest and trial over alleged tax evasion, King was charged a second time over traffic violations. On the evening of 4 May, he and Coretta were driving their dinner guest, white writer Lillian Smith, back to her hospital room at Emory University where she was undergoing treatment. Police patrolmen, suspicious of the car's interracial occupancy, pulled King over. The officers discovered that King was driving a borrowed car with expired licence plates. Moreover, he had still not transferred his driving licence from Alabama to Georgia as state law required after 90 days' residence. After one of the police officers issued a citation, King was permitted to continue his journey. On 23 September, King appeared before Judge J. Oscar Mitchell in DeKalb County. Mitchell dismissed the charge over expired licence plates but fined King $25 and imposed a twelve-month probation period for King's failure to obtain a valid Georgia driving licence. King paid the $25 immediately and put the seemingly innocuous incident out of mind.

The full ramifications of the traffic charge only became apparent later that October when King joined the sit-in movement in Atlanta. The sit-ins had reached Atlanta as early as March 1960, but conservative black leaders in the city, including Daddy King, urged caution and restraint. Without the wholehearted support of the adult black community the sit-in movement proceeded hesitantly and failed to achieve any breakthrough over the desegregation of downtown facilities. By October, students were ready to take a more determined stand for desegregation. Three local student leaders, Lonnie King, Herschelle Sullivan and Julian Bond, asked King to join them on a sit-in. King was initially reluctant to comply with their request, since he did not want to defy the influential Atlanta black elite and not least his own father. Yet, as the students pressed King hard, he realised that he had to 'practice what I preached' and he agreed to join them.[28]

The following morning, 19 October, King and 35 others were arrested at Rich's department store downtown for refusing to leave its segregated restaurant after being denied service. King and the others were taken to Fulton County Jail where they refused bail. The following days saw more demonstrations and further arrests, prompting the city's black and white leaders to enter into negotiations to end the protests. Atlanta mayor William B. Hartsfield convened a meeting with 60 black representatives on Saturday morning, 22 October.

Meanwhile, Harris Wofford, a white friend of King's and also a campaign official for Democratic Party presidential candidate, Massachusetts senator John F. Kennedy, called white Atlanta attorney Morris Abram with an idea. Wofford suggested that Abram help King to get out of jail and let the Kennedy campaign claim a successful intervention. Such a move would be good press and curry favour with key black voters in the north. Abram, a Kennedy supporter, agreed to call Mayor Hartsfield, also a Kennedy man, about Wofford's plan. Hartsfield agreed to the plan. By the time Abram arrived at the meeting with black leaders, a settlement had already been reached. Demonstrations would be suspended for 30 days and all of the jailed protestors would be released. The city would drop its charges and ask white merchants to do likewise. Hartsfield volunteered to act as an intermediary in further discussions between merchants and students. The mayor told reporters that 'in response to Senator Kennedy's personal intervention [I have] reached an agreement with Negro leaders for the release of King and other sit-in prisoners'.[29]

After persuading the initially recalcitrant owner of Rich's department store to drop charges against the jailed protestors, they were all released. Except for King. Judge Mitchell in DeKalb County wanted to assess King's case to determine whether his recent arrest violated the probation imposed after his earlier driving licence conviction. The following morning, King was taken from Fulton County Jail to appear before Mitchell. King's attorney, Donald L. Hollowell, had already filed an appeal against King's licence conviction and argued that his client could not be imprisoned until that hearing. Mitchell ignored Hollowell's argument, ignored King's plea that he did not realise that probationary terms were attached to the $25 fine, and ignored defence witnesses' pleas from Atlanta's black elite testifying to King's good character. Mitchell decided that King had broken the terms of his probation and handed him a four-month prison sentence. Coretta and King's sister, Christine, both broke down in tears in the courtroom. Coretta was alarmed at the prospect of Martin going to jail while she was six months pregnant with their third child, Dexter Scott King.

Coretta told Harris Wofford, 'They are going to kill him, I know they are going to kill him.'[30] Wofford tried to comfort her. He told her that he was trying to persuade Senator Kennedy to issue a statement on the matter, but that the idea was being blocked by Georgia governor S. Ernest Vandiver's office, which insisted that it would handle the matter. After Wofford unsuccessfully tried to reach Kennedy, Chester Bowles, a leading Democratic Party politician, called instead. At 3.30 a.m. the following morning, without a word of explanation, two prison guards placed King in handcuffs and leg irons and took him on a long car ride into rural Georgia. 'That kind of mental anguish is worse than dying,' King later wrote, 'riding for mile after mile, hungry and thirsty, bound and helpless, waiting and not knowing what you are waiting for.'[31] Only when King realised that he was being taken to the state prison at Reidsville and not to his death could he breathe a sigh of relief.

Coretta was even more frantic than before when she called Wofford to tell him about her husband's transfer, news of which was by that time filtering through to the black community. Wofford called Kennedy's brother-in-law Sargent Shriver in Chicago to ask him to persuade Kennedy to make a reassuring phone call to Coretta. Shriver had to lurk until several staffers left before putting the idea to Kennedy. There were those in the Kennedy campaign, not least John's influential younger brother Robert Kennedy, who remained sceptical about becoming too closely involved with King. Whereas Wooford believed support for King might help win vital black votes in the north, Robert Kennedy worried that it might more damagingly alienate white southern voters and politicians.

Nevertheless, John Kennedy agreed to call Coretta. He told her, 'I'm thinking about you and your husband, and I know this must be very difficult for you. If there is anything I can do to be of help, I want you to please feel free to call on me.' Coretta replied, 'Well, I really appreciate this and if there is anything you can do, I would deeply appreciate it.'[32]

According to Harris Wofford's most often cited account of events, Robert Kennedy was furious when he heard his brother had been railroaded into making the call to Coretta. 'You've just lost the election,' he told Wofford and other staff members. 'We had three southern governors tell us that if you support Khrushchev, Castro, or Martin Luther King, we are going to throw our votes to Nixon.'[33] He then stormed off to catch a plane to New York. Somewhat surprisingly, given his attitude on departure, when he got to New York Robert Kennedy called Judge Mitchell at the DeKalb County courthouse. Wofford reports that Kennedy 'said that if he [Mitchell] was a decent American he would let King out of jail by sundown. I called him because it made me so damned angry to think of that bastard [Mitchell] sentencing a citizen for four months of hard labor for a minor traffic offense and screwing up my brother's campaign and making us look ridiculous before the world.'[34] The following morning, Mitchell granted King's release on payment of a $2,000 bond.

Historian Clifford M. Khun later discovered an overlooked interview with Georgia governor S. Ernest Vandiver that led him to reinterview the governor about events. From that interview, a very different story emerged. According to Vandiver, John Kennedy had secretly called him seeking his assistance in the release of King. Vandiver was not normally disposed to such a suggestion. After all, when King moved back to Atlanta, Vandiver had declared that 'Wherever M.L. King, Jr. has been there has followed in his wake a wave of crimes including stabbing, bombings, and inciting of riots, barratry, destruction of property and many others. For these reasons, he is not welcome in Georgia.'[35] However, Vandiver stated that for promising to help with King's release and Kennedy's presidential bid, Kennedy had promised that he would in return never federalise troops in Georgia. John Kennedy then recommended that Vandiver discuss the situation with his brother Robert Kennedy. Vandiver first discussed the matter with his brother-in-law and political confidant Bob Russell. Russell suggested making an approach to Judge Mitchell through George B. Stewart, secretary of the Georgia Democratic Party. Stewart talked with Mitchell and may, Vandiver hints, have dangled the prospect of a federal judgeship to win him round. Mitchell agreed to King's release if it was confirmed that the orders came direct from the Kennedy campaign. Vandiver then called Robert Kennedy and told him that Mitchell was amenable to King's release and that he should call the judge directly. When Robert Kennedy called Mitchell, the judge was already expecting the call, and said, 'Bob, it's nice to hear from you. And I don't have any objections to [releasing King on bail].'[36] In view of all the political shenanigans surrounding King's release, NAACP attorney Thurgood Marshall later mercilessly teased King's attorney Donald Hollowell, 'Say, Hollowell, they tell me that everybody got King out of jail but the lawyers'?[37]

Whichever version of events is true, King was released from jail, and his father Daddy King was delighted at the intercession of the Kennedys, whatever form it might have taken. He told news reporters that he was switching his lifelong Republican Party allegiance to back Kennedy and the Democrats in the November presidential election. 'As a Baptist I was going to vote against John Kennedy because he was a Catholic,' Daddy King declared, 'but if he has the courage to wipe the tears from my daughter-in-law's eyes then I have the courage to vote for him, Catholic or not. And I've got a whole suitcase of votes that I'm taking up and putting in the lap of John Kennedy.'[38] Kennedy privately remarked that it was 'a hell of a bigoted statement' but he was pleased at the metaphorical suitcase full of votes. Martin Luther King Jr was more circumspect, shrewdly noting that 'There are moments when the politically expedient can be morally wise.'[39] He had already met Kennedy twice that year and was still unconvinced about the sincerity of the presidential candidate's support for civil rights. 'He knew that segregation was morally wrong and he certainly intellectually committed himself to integration, but I could see that he didn't have the emotional involvement,' King later stated.[40] King therefore expressed his gratitude to Kennedy for helping with his release but declined to offer an electoral endorsement. That fact notwithstanding, the Kennedy campaign sought to fully capitalise on these events. Neither current Republican President Dwight Eisenhower, nor his vice president and Republican presidential candidate for 1960 Richard Nixon, publicly commented on the King arrest, although both were well aware of the unfolding events. The Kennedy campaign team put together a flyer with the banner headline '"No Comment" Nixon versus a Candidate with a Heart, Senator Kennedy: The Case of Martin Luther King' for distribution in black neighbourhoods. In November, one of the most closely fought presidential elections in US history came down to just over 100,000 votes separating the two candidates. Black votes were one of the significant factors in ensuring a Kennedy victory. Irrespective of the political machinations involved, the whole episode further identified King as one the most influential black leaders in the United States.

In the midst of the sit-ins and the drama surrounding King's arrest and jailing, there were important developments taking place within the SCLC. Trusted adviser Bayard Rustin resigned his position in the organisation under duress. The resignation stemmed from plans by King and A. Philip Randolph to announce a 'March on the Conventions Movement for Freedom Now', which would recruit and organise nonviolent pickets at the Democratic Party and Republican Party conventions in Los Angeles and Chicago respectively in July 1960. New York black congressman Adam Clayton Powell took exception to the news and launched a scurrilous public attack on King and Randolph, claiming that they were captives of socialist interests and beholden to figures such as Bayard Rustin and Stanley Levison. King, destined for South America on vacation, sent a telegram to Powell expressing his dismay at his comments and asking for a public correction. Instead, Powell exerted further pressure on King. Through an intermediary, he let King know that he intended to make public the false but potentially very damaging story that Rustin and King were involved in a homosexual affair, if King did not cut his links with Rustin and cancel the threat to picket the party conventions.

Flustered, King called Rustin to suggest calling off the convention protests, though he did not reveal the nature of Powell's threat. Rustin then called Randolph and insisted that they should not be intimidated by Powell's threats, whatever they were. Randolph agreed and told King that he was still committed to the convention protests. King reluctantly went along with Randolph's decision. When he returned from vacation, King spoke candidly to Randolph and Rustin about Powell's threat. Randolph suggested that they simply ignore Powell. King remained uncertain and had intermediaries approach Powell to see how serious his threats were, but the news kept coming back that Powell wanted Rustin to go. When King subsequently failed to leap to Rustin's defence, Rustin did the honourable thing and offered his resignation, fully expecting it to be refused. To his dismay, King accepted it. Many felt that the episode demonstrated a lack of moral courage on King's part, with FOR's A.J. Muste declaring that he was 'personally ashamed of Martin'.[41] Rustin recalled that it was 'the only time Martin really pissed me off. He didn't have the courage to come to me [in person].'[42] For all of the controversy the plans caused, the July picketing of the party conventions that finally went ahead produced little significant impact.

A second personnel change was the arrival of Wyatt Tee Walker in August 1960 as new executive director of the SCLC. A native of Merchantville, New Jersey, Walker earned degrees in science and divinity at Virginia Union University in Richmond. He went on to become pastor at Gillfield Baptist Church in Petersburg, Virginia, one of the oldest black churches in the country. Walker had a long and varied history of activism as chair of the local NAACP branch, the Virginia director of CORE, and a founder member of the Petersburg Improvement Association (PIA) and the Virginia Christian Leadership Conference, and an SCLC board member. Dynamic and ambitious, Walker set about the task of revitalising the SCLC in dedicated fashion. He brought with him two colleagues from the PIA, James Wood and Dorothy Cotton, and appointed the SCLC's first dedicated voter-registration worker. Walker's business-like, no-nonsense approach to the job contributed to an increase in SCLC funds. Moreover, Walker's more professional and strategic handling of King's various speaking engagements, which sought to capitalise on the SCLC president's ever-increasing public profile, also helped boost the organisation's coffers.

Walker also helped to develop two new SCLC-related initiatives during 1960 and 1961. The first was the establishment of the Citizen Education Program that the SCLC took over from Highlander Folk School, which the Tennessee authorities had closed down in 1960 because of alleged communist connections. Highlander director Myles Horton arranged for classes, which concentrated mainly on voter registration, community organising and literacy, to be transferred to the SCLC. With funds from the Marshall Field Foundation, the SCLC relocated classes to a disused college building in McIntosh, Georgia, and hired young black preacher Revd Andrew Young to supervise the programme. Septima P. Clark continued in her role at Highlander as the main teacher. The second initiative was the development of a Voter Education Project (VEP), with help from the Taconic Foundation, to channel funds for black voter registration in the South. Run under the tax-exempt wing of the Southern Regional Council, the VEP, supported by all the major civil rights organisations including the SCLC, hired its own director, Wiley A. Branton from Arkansas, and officially launched in 1962. Walker saw the VEP as a potential platform to extend the SCLC's own base of support in the South.

The Congress of Racial Equality (CORE) and the 1961 Freedom Rides

Despite new stirrings within the SCLC, it was again developments outside that organisation that stole the initiative in pushing forward the civil rights agenda in 1961. The Chicago-based civil rights organisation CORE and its national director James Farmer initiated the Freedom Rides that year. In 1947, members of CORE had successfully travelled on an interracial 'Journey of Reconciliation' through a number of upper South states after the *Morgan* v. *Virginia* (1946) US Supreme Court ruling outlawed segregation on interstate bus routes. In *Boynton* v. *Virginia* (1960) the Supreme Court extended the *Morgan* ruling to include the desegregation of interstate bus terminal facilities. Farmer, in the wake of the sit-in movement and of increased civil rights activity across the South, proposed to renew the Freedom Rides to test facilities at bus terminals throughout the region. As with the sit-ins, creating a symbolic confrontation would, Farmer hoped, illustrate to the nation the ugly face of white southern bigotry that might even bring with it a federal response to the continued denial of civil rights. As Farmer put it, 'Our philosophy was simple. We put on pressure and create a crisis so that they [federal government] react.'[43]

On 4 May 1961, 13 freedom riders – 3 white women, 3 white men, and 7 black men – divided into two groups and boarded Greyhound and Trailways buses in Washington, DC. The first leg of their journey through Virginia, North Carolina, South Carolina and Georgia passed largely without incident. When they reached Atlanta, King and Wyatt Walker met the riders and warned them that the next leg of their journey across Alabama would be the most difficult so far. Walker gave the riders the names of various SCLC contacts along the route and arranged for Fred Shuttlesworth to receive them when they arrived in Birmingham.

The two groups set off for Birmingham the next morning. At Anniston, Alabama, a white mob was waiting for the Greyhound bus armed with 'pistols, guns, blackjacks, clubs, chains, [and] knives'.[44] Under the circumstances, the riders decided not to test facilities there but to move on. However, when they tried to leave, the mob slashed the bus's tyres. The bus limped out of Anniston before finally grinding to a halt on the outskirts of town with the mob in its wake. When someone from the mob threw a firebomb on board, the bus burst into flames and the riders had to evacuate. One rider remembered 'yelling and screaming. They just about broke every window out of the bus . . . I really thought that that was going to be the end of me.'[45] Initially, an undercover plainclothes state investigator on board kept the white mob back with his revolver drawn, but as the riders poured out the mob began to attack them. Alabama state troopers belatedly arrived on the scene to escort the riders to Anniston Hospital.

An hour later, the Trailways bus pulled into Anniston where three whites boarded, beat up several freedom riders, and physically forced the black riders to the back seats. They remained on board for the journey to Birmingham to make sure that the bus remained segregated. Upon arrival in Birmingham, the freedom riders encountered an even more savage attack at the hands of members of the local Ku Klux Klan who, in collusion with the local police force, were allowed a fifteen-minute beating of the riders before the law enforcement authorities intervened. James Peck, a white volunteer who had been selected to test the Birmingham bus terminal lunch counter with black student Charles Person, recalled, 'This mob seized us and I was unconscious, I'd say, within a minute. I came to in an alleyway. Nobody was there. [Just] a big pool of blood.'[46] Later, Birmingham's somewhat ironically titled Public Safety Commissioner who was in charge of the police department, T. Eugene 'Bull' Connor, passed off the delayed arrival of his men by claiming that because it was Mother's Day there were fewer police on duty, since he had allowed many of his officers time off to spend at home with their families.

The riders on the Greyhound bus meanwhile found themselves still pursued by the white mob that lurked outside Anniston Hospital. Inside, the hospital authorities insisted that the freedom riders must leave, since the mob posed a threat to other patients. In Birmingham, Fred Shuttlesworth arranged a convoy to travel the 60 miles to Anniston to collect the freedom riders and to take them back to Birmingham. Although Shuttlesworth insisted that those from his congregation who chose to participate in the errand of mercy should be nonviolent, one noted that 'every one of those cars had a shotgun in it'.[47] The convoy made a successful recovery mission.

Despite all the difficulties that they had encountered, the freedom riders were determined to continue their journey out of Alabama and across Mississippi the next morning. However, bus drivers in Birmingham refused to transport them. Resignedly, the freedom riders decided to abandon their overland journey and to proceed to New Orleans by plane. Even at the airport they were delayed by bomb threats. Only when US Attorney General Robert Kennedy sent John Seigenthaler, the only white southerner on his immediate staff, along to Birmingham to assist the freedom riders did they finally escape their ordeal.

Determined that the demonstration should not end in defeat, a group of students from Nashville, one of the leading centres of the sit-in movement, declared that they would continue the Freedom Ride. 'I strongly felt that the future of the movement was going to be cut short if the Freedom Ride had been stopped as a result of violence,' said Diane Nash, one of the Nashville students. 'The impression would have been that whenever a movement starts, all you have to do is to attack it with massive violence and the blacks will stop . . . So, under those circumstances, it was really important that the ride continue.'[48] The students approached the SCLC affiliate, the Nashville Christian Leadership Council (NCLC), to release money for their bus fares. With great reluctance, since they feared for the students' safety, the NCLC finally agreed. On 17 May, ten Nashville students arrived in Birmingham. When they tried to board a bus bound for Montgomery they were taken into 'protective custody' by local police.[49] Held overnight and for much of the following day, eventually Public Safety Commissioner Connor personally led a convoy that drove the students back to the state line, where they were unceremoniously dumped by the side of the road in the dead of night. 'This is the Tennessee state line,' Connor told them. 'Cross it and save the state and yourself a lot of trouble.'[50] The students told Connor that they would see him back in Birmingham by noon the next day. Connor laughed. The students were back in Birmingham the following day to keep their appointment, but white bus drivers again refused to carry them on the next leg of their journey to Montgomery.

Robert Kennedy finally intervened to put an end to the stand-off. He persuaded the bus company to take the students to Montgomery, telling local bus officials to contact 'Mr Greyhound' if they had to, but that 'somebody better get in that damn bus and get it going and get those people on their way'.[51] Robert Kennedy also secured a grudging assurance from Alabama governor John Patterson that the riders would be afforded state protection. On 20 May, a Greyhound bus left Birmingham for Montgomery carrying the SNCC freedom riders with an escort of sixteen Alabama highway patrol cars. Fred Shuttlesworth was arrested to prevent him from participating. As he watched the buses pull away he lamented, 'Man, what this state's coming to! An armed escort to take a bunch of niggers to a bus station so they can break these silly old laws.'[52] When the buses approached Montgomery, the police escort disappeared. Downtown, a similar scene to the one previously played out in Birmingham occurred. John Doar, an assistant attorney general, witnessed events from a nearby payphone and relayed them direct to Robert Kennedy: 'The passengers are getting off . . . There are no cops. It's terrible . . . People are yelling "Get 'em, get 'em." It's awful.'[53] Right at the centre of events, Nashville student John Lewis remembered that 'People came out of nowhere – men, women, children, with baseball bats, clubs, chains – and there was no police official around. They just started beating people.'[54] Local whites, as in Birmingham, were given fifteen minutes to beat the freedom riders until the police arrived. Even John Siegenthaler, Robert Kennedy's administrative assistant, who was there simply as an observer, was beaten by the mob as he attempted to intervene. Infuriated that Governor Patterson had reneged on his promise to safeguard the riders,

Robert Kennedy sent US federal marshals to Montgomery to protect them.

Ralph Abernathy arranged a meeting at his First Baptist Church the following evening to discuss events. King cancelled an engagement in Chicago to fly to Montgomery, joined there by Wyatt Walker from Atlanta and by James Farmer from Washington, DC. As the meeting at First Baptist began, a white mob gathered outside the church, trapping all of those inside. US federal marshals used tear gas in an attempt to disperse the mob. When the mob still refused to move, King called Robert Kennedy personally. Kennedy told King that the Alabama National Guard was on its way to provide US federal marshals with back-up. Given Alabama's record of defending civil rights activists, the assurance did little to calm King. Even when the Alabama National Guard arrived, the white mob still defiantly refused to leave. Not until 4.30 a.m. the following morning, after an all-night siege, were the first of those inside First Baptist escorted home.

The Nashville SNCC students still insisted that they would continue the Freedom Ride, even though King and Farmer were reluctant to support them and the federal government openly opposed the plan. The students leant heavily on King to accompany them on their journey, insisting that he had a moral responsibility to do so. To the great disappointment of the students, King refused, saying that his participation might violate his probation. King insisted that he would choose 'the where and when of [my] own Golgotha'.[55] The students were still dissatisfied, pointing out to King that many of them were violating their own probation terms from the sit-ins by taking part in the Freedom Ride. King still refused to listen. An infuriated Robert F. Williams, a North Carolina NAACP leader and a staunch advocate of black armed self-defence, sent King a telegram telling him forthrightly that 'No sincere leader asks his followers to make sacrifices that he himself will not endure. You are a phony. Gandhi was always in the forefront, suffering with his people. If you are the leader of this nonviolent movement, lead the way by example.'[56]

On Wednesday, the first group of SNCC riders set off for Jackson, Mississippi, with a sizable Alabama National Guard escort. This did little to placate James Farmer, who decided to join the students at the last minute not knowing 'which way the National Guardsmen would point their guns in the event of a showdown'.[57] King remained behind, waving the bus goodbye as it went. A second bus set off later. Both made an uneventful journey to Jackson where the students, as Robert Kennedy had arranged in advance with Mississippi governor James O. Eastland, were arrested when they attempted to use segregated facilities at the bus terminal. Upon arrival in Jackson under intense national media scrutiny, Frank Holloway, one of the freedom riders, remembers feeling 'like the President of the U.S. . . . At the door of the waiting room a policeman stood there like a doorman at the Waldorf Astoria and opened the door for us.'[58]

Out of sight of the media in Hinds County Jail the scene was very different. 'When we went in we were met by some of the meanest looking, tobacco-chewing lawmen I had ever seen,' Holloway remembers. 'They ordered us around like a bunch of dogs and I really began to feel like I was in a Mississippi jail.'[59] Nevertheless, more civil rights activists from different parts of the country began to flood into Montgomery to take the ride to Jackson to join the Nashville students in jail. By the end of the summer, 328 of them were in Mississippi jails. In the county jail the 'cells were filthy; the food was wretched; and the crowding was so bad that one four-bunk cell held up to 23 prisoners at one time'.[60] As the jail filled to overflowing the less lucky ones were taken either to the county penal farm or to the notorious state penitentiary at Parchman. At Parchman, several freedom riders were beaten and the squalid conditions tested their endurance to the limit. The freedom riders were placed two to three each in a cell measuring only nine by six feet, and were given badly fitting prison wear. There was no 'exercise, games or cigarettes and the food was inedible'.[61] There was no reading material and inmates were allowed to send and receive only two letters a week. When they sang freedom songs to relieve the boredom, the guards removed their mattresses, meaning that they had to sleep on wire bedsteads or on a concrete floor.

Before more recruits had started rolling into Montgomery, Robert Kennedy had called King to demand a 'cooling-off' period and offered federal help to get the Nashville students out of jail in return for a temporary cessation of the Freedom Rides. King replied that the students intended to take a stand by refusing bail and by choosing to go to jail instead. Farmer responded to the news of Kennedy's call by noting that 'We've been cooling off for three hundred years. If we cool off anymore we'll be in the deep freeze.'[62] Reflecting back, Farmer believed that the Freedom Rides turned out to be a 'different and far grander thing than we had intended . . . Instead of seeking token arrests to spur legal and administrative action, we began to fill the jails of Mississippi.'[63] CORE, along with the SCLC and SNCC, agreed to form a Freedom Rides Coordinating Committee (FRCC) to orchestrate and to fund further Freedom Rides. President Kennedy warned King that 'this is not going to have the slightest effect on what the government is going to do'.[64] However, on 29 May, Robert Kennedy took up King's suggestion to petition the Interstate Commerce Commission (ICC), an independent body that had direct responsibility for interstate travel facilities, to issue regulations to ban segregation. After holding hearings on the matter, the ICC issued a comprehensive ban on all forms of segregation in interstate transit and in interstate terminal facilities, effective from 1 November 1961. Although this took time to enforce, historian Catherine Barnes notes that 'By mid-1963, legacies of a Jim Crow transit structure lingered on, but . . . systematic discrimination in interstate transport had ended.'[65]

As the freedom riders trickled out of jail over the summer of 1961, discussion over the future direction of SNCC produced heated debate. Some, such as SNCC chair Charles McDew, advocated switching the organisation's attention to voter-registration campaigns and building upon the work already started by activists like Robert Moses in Mississippi. Others, especially the Nashville students who had played such a prominent role in the Freedom Rides, staunchly advocated continuing mass direct action through dramatically expanding the number of Freedom Ride participants. Many of these students were suspicious of the eagerness of the Kennedy administration to support voter registration as a less controversial form of protest. To calm dissent, Ella Baker suggested that SNCC resolve its internal differences by operating for a short while as two wings, one involved in direct action and the other in voter registration. This suggestion largely resolved the matter, although as events unfolded the presumed dichotomy between direct action and voter registration turned out to be a false one. Attempting to register black voters in Mississippi would prove every bit as dangerous and contentious as the sit-ins and the Freedom Rides.

In the wake of the sit-ins and the Freedom Rides, Martin Luther King Jr's credibility as a civil rights leader was on the line. His refusal to join the Freedom Rides dismayed SNCC students. Soon, they would be calling him 'de Lawd', part teasing and part mocking King for what they perceived as his pomposity at likening himself to Christ.[66] As King and the SCLC floundered and failed in their search for new direction, SNCC's brand of fearless, nonviolent direct action was dominating the movement. King understood the need to regain the initiative if he was to fulfil his role as a civil rights leader. An invitation from the local movement to join demonstrations in Albany, Georgia, in 1961, held out the prospect of doing this. Instead, it led to not one, but two embarrassing defeats.

Chapter 3

Forming a Strategy, 1961–3

Two community-based campaigns within the space of eighteen months between December 1961 and June 1963 proved to be a turning point in King's civil rights leadership. In Albany, King was drawn into a developing local movement without any advance planning, and he and the SCLC consequently ran into a number of problems. Conflicts of interest and bickering between the SCLC, SNCC, the NAACP and local leaders undermined black unity. Albany's white City Commission remained unmoved by black demands for change and steadfastly refused to negotiate. Albany chief of police Laurie Pritchett made mass arrests instead of meeting demonstrations with force, denying the movement the dramatic confrontation that had inspired federal intervention during the Freedom Rides. A divided black movement, a unified white community, and a largely unconcerned federal government, meant that King and the SCLC were forced to retreat from Albany twice without gaining any concessions.

Although the Albany Movement ended in defeat for King and the SCLC, it provided a valuable learning experience. King and the SCLC used their experiences in Albany to reflect on the mistakes that they had made there and to devise a better-planned strategy for their next campaign in Birmingham, Alabama. In choosing Birmingham, King and the SCLC went to a place that symbolised violent white southern racism, personified in Public Safety Commissioner Bull Connor, who had allowed freedom riders to be beaten by a white mob in the city in 1961. At the same time, Birmingham's white business community was wary of the damage that its racist reputation was having on the city's image in the nation. Birmingham businessmen had therefore already indicated a tentative willingness to introduce limited changes in racial practices. The Alabama Christian Movement for Human Rights (ACMHR), under the leadership of the Revd Fred Shuttlesworth, was one of the SCLC's most active affiliates and the leading civil rights organisation in the city, which King and the SCLC hoped would ensure greater unity in demonstrations.

Despite their best-laid plans, however, King and the SCLC encountered a number of difficulties in Birmingham. Political developments in the city delayed the start of the campaign. Complaints from local black leaders and white sympathisers about the use of nonviolent, direct-action tactics threatened movement unity. Too few blacks were willing to join demonstrations. King and other SCLC staff members fast discovered that, although they could target the places most conducive to successful demonstrations, no movement that involved so many different factors for victory could ever totally be under their control. To be successful, movement leadership required tactical innovation in the field, continual improvisation, and dynamic responses to unpredictable developments. Learning as they went along, King and the SCLC overcame a number of obstacles to form a strategy for change in Birmingham that would provide the basic blueprint for future demonstrations.

The Albany Movement

In August 1961, SNCC field secretary Charles Sherrod sought to establish a voter-registration campaign in south-west Georgia. Initially, he targeted 'terrible' Terrell County, one of the most notoriously hostile counties to black voting rights in the country. The depth of white opposition in Terrell soon convinced Sherrod that the larger city of Albany, where 26,000 blacks represented around 40 per cent of the city's 56,000 population, would be a far safer and more inviting base. Joined by SNCC volunteer Cordell Reagon, Sherrod moved into Albany in October. The two SNCC workers expanded their vision for the movement in Albany to incorporate nonviolent, direct-action demonstrations as well as voter registration. They canvassed student support for such demonstrations at local black high schools and among the 650 black students at Albany State College. They hoped that by winning student support for their plans they would, in turn, engage the support of Albany's black adult population, which was more wary about launching a campaign of direct action. In anticipation of the ICC order to desegregate interstate bus terminal facilities on 1 November, Sherrod and Reagon encouraged students to test those facilities in Albany on that date.

However, when Sherrod and Reagon left the city to stand trial for previous arrests in McComb, Mississippi, the local Albany NAACP branch stepped in to dissuade students from participating in the planned demonstration. When Sherrod and Reagon, accompanied by white SNCC worker Salynn McCollum, rode into Albany from Atlanta on 1 November, they found that the local police had been forewarned of their arrival and were ready to meet them. The SNCC workers decided to rally local students before testing the bus terminal facilities. They returned later that day with Albany State College students and were moved on by the city police under threat of arrest.

The low-key policing of demonstrations at the bus terminal was down to Albany chief of police Laurie Pritchett. Pritchett had followed the development of the civil rights movement with keen interest and had, he claimed, 'researched Dr. King [and] read about his early days in Montgomery, his methods there'.[1] Pritchett had also witnessed the handling of the Freedom Rides in Alabama the previous year. He observed that much of the success of nonviolent direct action was down to the hostile and often violent reaction of whites to demonstrations. He also noted that many local law enforcement officers, such as Birmingham's Bull Connor, did little to dissipate this violence and sometimes even encouraged it. This convinced Pritchett that it would be best for him to handle demonstrations in Albany differently. Pritchett prepared his officers for demonstrations in advance and told them that there would be 'no violence, no dogs, no show of force . . . We're going to out-nonviolent them.'[2] King later noted that 'Pritchett felt that by directing his police to be nonviolent, he had discovered a new way to beat [nonviolent] demonstrations.'[3] By foregoing explicitly brutal policing, and by instead arresting demonstrators on charges that did not directly raise the issue of segregation, such as obstruction and public order offences, Pritchett hoped to contain the movement and to deny it any publicity. Also, anticipating the use of 'jail not bail' tactics, Pritchett made contingency plans to use jails in surrounding counties if Albany's jails became overcrowded. In doing so, Pritchett correctly bargained on the movement running out of demonstrators before he ran out of jails.

Sherrod and Reagon, joined by fellow SNCC worker Charles Jones, continued their organising efforts at Albany State College in preparation for further demonstrations. This placed SNCC further at odds with local NAACP branch members who felt SNCC was poaching its own NAACP Youth Council recruits. 'I wouldn't say we didn't want the students here,' said one NAACP spokesperson, but 'I would say that they found us not too receptive to them.'[4] The friction between SNCC and the NAACP led to the intervention of Albany's Criterion Club, a community organisation of black professionals and businessmen. Three younger members of the Criterion Club, osteopath Dr William G. Anderson, attorney Chevene B. King and his brother, estate agent Slater King, discussed developments in community meetings. They concluded that it would be best to work with SNCC representatives so that at the very least they could exert some control over them. To that end, on 17 November, they formed the Albany Movement. Like the MIA in Montgomery, the Albany Movement joined together a number of local black groups and leaders for the purpose of coordinating community protest efforts. Ambitiously, it decided to tackle racial discrimination on a number of fronts simultaneously, including demands for fair employment, an end to police brutality, and the desegregation of bus and train terminals and other city facilities. Anderson was elected president, with Slater King and postal worker Marion S. Page making up a three-man coordinating committee.

The local NAACP president, dentist E.D. Hamilton, refused to sign up to the Albany Movement without first getting the consent of state and regional NAACP representatives. When Hamilton consulted with NAACP state field secretary Vernon Jordan and NAACP regional director Ruby Hurley, they both insisted that the local NAACP branch should take charge of any new demonstrations. Accordingly, plans were made for three NAACP Youth Council members, acting independently of the Albany Movement, to test bus terminal facilities on 22 November. When the three youths asked for service at the lunch counter in the white waiting room at the bus terminal they were arrested. News of the arrests quickly spread, and SNCC supporters from Albany State College descended on the bus terminal. Many of the students left when college dean Charles Minor arrived and made a personal appeal for them to halt the demonstration. However, two students with close links to SNCC, Bertha Gober and Blanton Hall, refused to leave and were arrested. Minor later expelled them from college for defying him. The arrested NAACP Youth Council members were all released on bail, but Gober and Hall chose to go to jail instead. 'From that moment on,' SNCC's Charles Sherrod maintained, 'segregation [in Albany] was dead.'[5] Black students had taken the first crucial step in defying both white supremacy and the black adults in the community who had urged restraint. The movement's first mass meeting took place at Mount Zion Baptist Church three days later. All five students arrested at the bus terminal were handed fifteen days probation and $100 fines.

Continuing efforts to heal the rift between the local NAACP branch and the Albany Movement proved unsuccessful. In an attempt to usurp control of the demonstrations, the NAACP even approached Dr Anderson with an assurance that he would be installed as local NAACP branch president if the Albany Movement disbanded and agreed to work under the NAACP's banner. Anderson refused the offer. SNCC tried to recapture the initiative on 10 December by organising a Freedom Ride from Atlanta to Albany to test the city's train terminal facilities. When eight SNCC freedom riders entered the white waiting room at the train terminal, Pritchett ordered them out. As they moved outside, several hundred local supporters were on hand to greet them. Annoyed by the show of solidarity, Pritchett announced, 'I told you to get off the street. You are all under arrest.' Later, Pritchett admitted that this loss of composure had been 'a mistake'.[6] The SNCC freedom riders, together with Charles Jones and Bertha Gober, were arrested for blocking the sidewalk and for obstructing traffic.

The new arrests sparked further activity in the black community. As the trial of the freedom riders arrested on 10 December began, over 250 black students marched on City Hall to demonstrate their support for them. Pritchett arrested them all, asserting that 'We can't tolerate the NAACP or SNCC or any other nigger organization to take over this town with mass demonstrations.'[7] The following day, further marches brought more arrests. Despite Pritchett's best efforts to avoid publicity, the movement in Albany began to make national headlines as the scene of the 'first large-scale Negro uprising since the Montgomery bus boycott'.[8] The reaction of the Albany Movement to the burgeoning protests was twofold. Firstly, it began to exert economic pressure on Albany's white business community by organising a boycott of city stores and city buses. Secondly, it invited outside help from the SCLC and asked Martin Luther King Jr to come to Albany.

SNCC workers were unhappy with the decision to enlist outside help and saw 'no necessity for King to come'.[9] They believed that local protest efforts were working sufficiently well already and that the self-confidence of local blacks was beginning to build. They were afraid that inviting King might introduce a 'Messiah complex' into the movement and that 'people would feel that only a particular individual could save them and would not move on their own to fight racism and exploitation'.[10] However, Anderson was adamant about the need for King's help. He pointed out that the local movement had already run out of cash to bail local students out of jail. According to Anderson, SNCC 'provided what was needed – a stimulus – but once the movement got going they did not have the resources to manage the massive movement'.[11] For his part, King was not especially interested in going to Albany and getting sidetracked from his primary goal of building the SCLC into a regional force. Yet, according to his wife Coretta, 'his [King's] conscience and his sense of the obligation of leadership made him go at once to try to help'.[12] King finally agreed to put in a token appearance.

Concerned at the escalation of the protests in Albany and urged on by President Kennedy's civil rights assistant Burke Marshall, the city authorities attempted to put a stop to the demonstrations. On 15 December, Albany mayor Asa D. Kelley announced that he was 'ready to . . . discuss all problems with responsible Negro leaders'.[13] Meanwhile, Georgia governor S. Ernest Vandiver sent 150 Georgia National Guardsmen to the city should reinforcements be needed. That afternoon, an informal biracial negotiating committee of three blacks not belonging to the Albany Movement (the city's definition of 'responsible leaders') and three whites met to discuss developments. The committee members agreed that if the city's train and bus terminal facilities desegregated and an ongoing biracial negotiating committee was formed to discuss further desegregation in Albany, the demonstrations would be halted. The only hitch was what would happen to those demonstrators already arrested. Black negotiators insisted that they should all be released immediately, while white negotiators did not believe that the City Commission would agree to such a move. With the situation delicately poised, King arrived in Albany.

King's Defeat in Albany, 1961

On the evening of 15 December, King, Ralph Abernathy and Wyatt Walker attended a mass meeting at Albany's Shiloh Baptist Church. King told the audience, 'Don't stop now. Keep moving. Don't get weary. We will wear them down with our capacity to suffer.'[14] Also present at the meeting were the Freedom Singers, a group formed in Charles Sherrod's local SNCC workshops. The powerful use of freedom songs, many of which were adapted from black slave spirituals with lyrics amended to reflect movement concerns, became a hallmark of the Albany Movement. The songs, which surfaced not only at church meetings but also on marches, demonstrations and even in the jails, forged a bond between movement participants and bolstered their collective confidence and strength. King called the songs 'the soul of the movement . . . They are adaptations of the songs slaves sang – the sorrow songs, the shouts for joy, the battle hymns and the anthems of our movement . . . It is not just a song, it is a resolve.'[15] From 'the singing movement' in Albany, the exportation of such songs by the Freedom Singers to other localities soon made them a hallmark of the entire civil rights movement.

At the meeting, Anderson invited King to march with him in Albany the following day. King had not bargained on such a development, but agreed to put aside existing commitments to participate. Anderson told the crowd to reassemble at the church the next morning. Afterwards, Anderson sent a telegram to Mayor Kelley demanding a more constructive approach from the city to the current situation. He demanded a response by 10 a.m. the following morning. Kelley and other city commissioners did not take kindly to the ultimatum. Moreover, they knew from Pritchett's police intelligence reports that plans were already afoot to launch more demonstrations in concert with King. The City Commission accused the movement of 'not acting in good faith and until you can do so we can give no response to your demand'.[16] King's arrival thus polarised opinion in Albany. Whites refused to make concessions while pressured by his presence in the city, whereas the local black community was even more emboldened because of it.

On 16 December, King and Anderson led over 250 people in a march to City Hall. As they reached Ogelthorpe Avenue, the dividing line between the black and white downtown areas of Albany, Pritchett and his men blocked their way. When the marchers refused to disperse, Pritchett arrested them for parading without a permit and for obstruction. Anderson, King and Abernathy were separated from the rest of the marchers as they were taken into custody. Abernathy subsequently made bail to rally outside support. King told reporters 'If convicted I will refuse to pay the fine. I expect to spend Christmas in jail. I hope thousands will join me.'[17] Privately, King still held reservations about becoming embroiled with the local movement. He told confidants in the SCLC 'that we could not stay there more than three months. But if the sentences were less than three months we would serve the time.'[18]

Events beyond the jail proved more influential than King's plans. Persisting divisions between the various civil rights organisations involved in the Albany demonstrations hampered efforts to capitalise on the new wave of arrests. With King in jail and Abernathy back in Atlanta, SCLC executive director Wyatt Walker took over operations in Albany. Forceful and abrasive, Walker's actions antagonised other organisations and leaders. One newspaper reported that Walker was now in charge of the movement in Albany. In Atlanta, Abernathy appeared on television urging civil rights activists to go to Albany and to support the struggle there. Yet back in Albany, local leader Marion Page insisted that he was the one in charge of the movement. SNCC, meanwhile, smarted over the fact that the SCLC had taken over a movement that they had begun. SNCC's Charles Jones held his own press conference, telling reporters that he personally intended to renew negotiations with the city's white leaders. Further compounding these problems was the fact that Albany Movement president Dr Anderson was beginning to crack under the strain of imprisonment and appeared to be suffering some sort of mental breakdown. Fearing that Anderson could not last out much longer, and mindful of the rapidly deteriorating interorganisational relations, King told Walker to get them out of jail as quickly as possible.

When Anderson and King were taken for trial on 19 December their hearings were postponed while new negotiations continued. SCLC attorney Donald Hollowell joined the Albany Movement's Marion Page and C.B. King in negotiations with Mayor Kelley and Chief of Police Pritchett. Existing movement divisions, which Kelley and Pritchett were both well aware of, gave them the upper hand in the negotiations. Knowing that many in the Albany Movement wanted King and the SCLC out of Albany as much as they did, they forged a settlement that offered essentially the same deal on the table before King's arrival. In exchange for a cessation of demonstrations and the departure of King from Albany, the city's bus and train terminals would be desegregated, the city would establish an eight-member biracial committee, and all local citizens would be released from jail. Kelley and Pritchett gave their word on the settlement but refused to sign up to anything on paper. Despite reservations about this, the Albany Movement agreed to the deal.

The Albany Movement subsequently claimed a significant victory. It told reporters that all demonstrators would be released, that the city's bus and train terminals would be desegregated, and that there would be further biracial discussions with the City Commission when it met in January 1963. The city, which briefed journalists at a slap-up steak dinner in a segregated restaurant '[i]n appreciation for the accurate coverage of Albany's difficulties', denied all of these claims.[19] Kelley and Pritchett told reporters that blacks were being released from jail only because they had agreed to provide bail money. They insisted that both bus and train terminals in Albany already obeyed the ICC desegregation ruling, although they refused to say whether that meant blacks would actually be free to use them without arrest. It was true that the city had agreed to listen to black complaints further at its January meeting, they said, just as it would listen to any group of concerned citizens that approached them. Moreover, there was no formal agreement on any of these points. In fact, they maintained, all they had really done was to clarify the existing status quo. Kelley noted that Attorney General Robert Kennedy had already called him to congratulate the city on its handling of the crisis.

Almost universally to onlookers it appeared that King had been comprehensively outmanoeuvred and outwitted by Kelley and Pritchett. The *New York Herald Tribune* described Albany as a 'devastating loss of face' and a 'stunning defeat' for King. 'Segregation 1, King 0', read other headlines.[20] Many reports focused upon and congratulated Pritchett's policing methods and his strategy of neutralising nonviolence by making mass arrests instead of using force.

Despite the criticism, King was relieved to have been extricated from Albany. Refusing to dwell on the negative press, he returned to what he viewed as his central task of strengthening the SCLC. It turned out to be an important period 'of laying permanent foundations, re-structuring the organization, building a team and charting the course we should travel', as Wyatt Walker later put it.[21] King undertook several 'People-to-People' tours to Mississippi, Virginia and South Carolina, in an effort to recruit volunteers for the SCLC's proposed 'Freedom Corps'. Under the tutelage of James Lawson, it was planned that the 'corps' of 'troops' trained in nonviolence would work on the SCLC's voter-registration drives and nonviolent, direct-action campaigns. New funds from the Field Foundation ensured the continuation of the SCLC's citizenship training programme. The SCLC staff increased further, with the appointment of field secretaries for Mississippi and Virginia, the appointment of assistants for voter registration in Georgia, and the promotion of Jack O'Dell, who had previously run the SCLC's New York office, to SCLC director of voter registration. At the suggestion of white New York attorney Harry H. Wachtel, the SCLC established a charitable foundation to which tax-free donations could be made, calling it the Gandhi Society for Human Rights.

Annoyed at the absence of support from the Kennedy administration over the situation in Albany, King became increasingly vociferous in his criticism at the lack of executive action on civil rights. The Kennedy administration had its own concerns about the workings of the SCLC, and in particular about the role being played by Stanley Levison. The FBI provided the president with information about Levison's alleged communist connections, inferring that he provided a direct link from King to Moscow. The FBI began electronic surveillance of Levison through wiretaps and planted bugging devices in the SCLC's headquarters. Several Kennedy aides informally warned King about Levison, and also Jack O'Dell, another SCLC member who had been involved with the US Communist Party in the 1950s. King listened to but ultimately rejected these warnings, preferring to trust Levison rather than the Kennedy administration and the FBI. King was quite right to do so. Although Levison still remained in contact with the US Communist Party, he had severed official links with it in 1955. The FBI's alarmist accusations appeared to have little substance to them, a fact that it attempted to conceal by remaining vague about specific details. Much of the information the FBI claimed to have was outdated and, even more damning, the FBI itself had attempted to recruit Levison twice in the past, which hardly pointed to him being a highly suspect communist agent. Nevertheless, the FBI persisted in its campaign to smear King and others in the civil rights movement as communists or, at the very least, as unwitting communist dupes.

King's Defeat in Albany, 1962

Amid continuing efforts to strengthen SCLC operations, King briefly returned to Albany for trial on 27 February 1962 and was convicted on charges of disorderly conduct and for parading without a permit. Judge A.N. Durden Sr delayed sentencing and did not recall King for over five months. The fervent segregationist candidate for Georgia governor, Marvin Griffin, running against the more moderate Carl Sanders, declared that if elected he would 'put Martin Luther King so far back in jail that you will have to pump air to him'.[22] In King's absence, Albany Movement leaders tried to keep the faltering local movement going. They discovered that the previous promises of the city counted for little. On 23 January, when Anderson and Page requested that the City Commission put in writing its 18 December agreement, the commissioners undertook to give the matter 'serious consideration' and adjourned the meeting without any further discussion. 'I was a naive little boy from a country town,' Marion Page ruefully admitted. 'The [City Commission] put things over on me.'[23] In fact, the short shrift given to the Albany Movement in part reflected the internal divisions that existed within the City Commission. Mayor Kelley was actually willing to accept the full terms of the December agreement, but there were hard-line segregationists on the City Commission who were adamantly opposed to any concessions. Chief of Police Pritchett strongly advised against any public airing of the City Commission's divisions. The most important thing for the white community to do was to keep up a united front, Pritchett insisted. If it did so, he predicted that segregation would remain intact.

Yet pressure was mounting in Albany's white business community for the City Commission to be more receptive to black demands. A boycott of white businesses remained in effect and was hurting many downtown merchants. Even more pressing was a renewed bus boycott organised by SNCC after the arrest of 18-year-old black student Ola Mae Quarterman on 12 January. When the bus driver had asked Quarterman to move to the back of the bus she had replied, 'I paid my damn 20 cents and I can sit where I want.'[24] She was jailed for using obscene language. Since it relied heavily upon black patronage, by the end of January the bus company faced collapse. The Albany Movement agreed to call off the bus boycott and to save the bus company on condition that buses desegregated, that the bus company accepted black job applications, and if, this time learning from previous mistakes, the city gave a written assurance not to interfere. The bus company contacted the City Commission to indicate that it would be willing to accept these terms. Mayor Kelley and local businessmen supported the bus company's request but other city commissioners still refused to give in to any black demands. The bus company therefore went out of business. With the help of local white businessmen, the service was revived again for a short while before collapsing for a final time on 6 March. With no city buses left to boycott, the Albany Movement stepped up its downtown economic boycott to a larger number of stores. In April, several sit-ins led to the first arrests since the previous December demonstrations. This prompted a brief but unfruitful resumption of negotiations with the City Commission.

On 10 July, King and Abernathy returned to Albany and were sentenced to 45 days in jail or a $178 fine. In an attempt to revive protests and to pressure the City Commission back to the negotiating table, they chose jail. King's jailing appeared to have the intended reinvigorating effect on the Albany Movement. The following day, 32 people took part in a downtown march. Pritchett arrested them all. A new round of demonstrations looked set to ignite. However, on the morning of 12 July, King and Abernathy were called into Pritchett's office. Pritchett told them that their fines had been paid and that they were free to leave. 'Well,' King told Pritchett, 'we want to serve this time, we feel that we owe it to ourselves and the seven hundred and some-odd people of this community who still have these cases hanging over them.' Pritchett simply replied, 'I don't want you in my jail.'[25] In fact, Mayor Kelley, echoing Police Commissioner Clyde Sellers's earlier ploy after King's 1960 arrest in Montgomery, had arranged King's release from jail to prevent a re-emergence of demonstrations. Once again outmanoeuvred by the city authorities, King walked free. 'I've been thrown out of lots of places in my day,' Ralph Abernathy told a mass meeting afterwards, 'but never before have I been thrown out of jail.'[26]

SNCC workers tried to persuade King to lead further demonstrations, to invite arrest again, and to return to jail. They warned that to let the movement lose momentum for a second time would have disastrous consequences. Yet King refused their request. He told them that the SCLC needed him to help with its fund-raising efforts, that a lack of bail money meant that risking further arrests of local people would be irresponsible, since they could not afford to remain in jail indefinitely with jobs to attend and families to feed, and that therefore the movement should first seek negotiations before escalating demonstrations. As SNCC predicted, King's decision had a dire impact on local blacks who, SCLC programme director Andrew Young reported, were 'somewhat outraged because Dr. King would not lead them in mass demonstrations ... And the talk going through all the Negro community was that Martin Luther King was going "chicken".'[27] When the City Commission still refused to enter into negotiations, King scheduled a mass march for Saturday 21 July.

In response, the city obtained a temporary restraining order from federal district judge J. Robert Elliott that forbade King and other named members of the Albany Movement from marching. Movement attorneys tried but failed to secure a vacation of the order. King therefore called off the march, arguing that he could not disobey a federal court order since it would be inconsistent with the movement's demand that whites should obey federal laws that required desegregation. 'Some of us, myself included, felt that [the] movement should not be stopped by the injunction and that we had to teach the people that such an injunction wasn't valid,' remembers SNCC's James Forman. Forman believed that King 'could have used his status and moral authority' to proceed with the march.[28] That evening, local pastor the Revd Samuel B. Wells declared at a mass meeting, 'I see Dr. King's name, I see Dr. Anderson's name, and I see Charles Sherrod [on the retraining order] but I don't see Samuel Wells.'[29] Wells then led a march of 200 people not cited in the restraining order to City Hall. King watched them go, observing that 'They can stop the leaders, but they can't stop the people.'[30] Pritchett arrested all the marchers.

On Tuesday morning, 24 July, movement attorneys successfully managed to get Judge Elliott's temporary restraining order vacated. Movement leaders used the decision to try to reopen negotiations with the city before launching new demonstrations. Earlier that day a sheriff in Mitchell County had beaten the pregnant Marion King, wife of Albany Movement leader Slater King, while she was visiting an arrested friend in jail. This inflammatory news threatened to strain appeals for nonviolence. However, after the meeting broke up, a white CORE member from New York led a group of 40 marchers downtown. Pritchett arrested them all. Almost two thousand black onlookers followed the progress of the march, fully expecting a confrontation with the police. Angered by the arrests, the black onlookers began to throw rocks and bottles. Missiles struck a city police officer and a state trooper. Pritchett used the outbreak of violence to question the movement's use of marches and the wisdom of the courts in allowing them to take place. Pritchett asked reporters if they had seen 'them nonviolent rocks?'[31] King insisted that the violence had been caused by blacks who did not belong to the Albany Movement. Nevertheless, he announced a 'Day of Penance' with a 24-hour lapse in demonstrations as atonement for the violence.[32] King appealed to local blacks to maintain the movement's nonviolent stance, telling them that 'We don't need guns and ammunitions – just the power of souls.'[33] SNCC was again aghast that King could so blithely call a halt to demonstrations.

On 27 July, King led a delegation including Abernathy, Anderson and Slater King to City Hall to request face-to-face talks with the City Commission. When they refused to leave they were arrested. A second group of fifteen people led by SNCC's Charles Jones and William Hansen headed to City Hall several hours later. They too were arrested. Despite these new arrests, there were few other volunteers willing to go to jail. As SNCC had feared, many local blacks were disillusioned with King's recent vacillation over demonstrations. The movement stuttered on with smaller demonstrations, some of which Pritchett considered so insignificant that he did not even bother to make arrests. Between Pritchett's successful policing tactics, the steadfast refusal of the City Commission to negotiate, the waning support of the black community, and the absence of federal intervention, the local movement in Albany appeared to be grounding to a halt. To cap it all, Judge Elliot began hearings on the city's request for a permanent restraining order against any further demonstrations.

With the local movement in Albany getting increasingly bogged down, on 1 August President Kennedy appeared to offer at least a glimmer of hope. Throughout the Albany campaign, the position of the Kennedy administration had been to prefer a local settlement without the need for its intervention. Yet the last thing the administration wanted was a protracted campaign of demonstrations and arrests without any sign of resolution. Asked about developments in the city at a press conference, Kennedy observed that the United States was currently 'involved in sitting down at Geneva with the Soviet Union. I can't understand why the government of Albany, City Council of Albany, cannot do the same for American citizens.'[34] King congratulated Kennedy for his comments and expressed his hope that 'you will continue to use the great moral influence of your office to help this crucial situation'.[35] Mayor Kelley dismissed the president's comments as 'inappropriate [since] this is a purely local problem'. He added that the city would 'never negotiate with outside agitators'.[36] King countered this by offering 'to call off the marches and return to . . . Atlanta to give the commission a chance to "save face" and demonstrate good faith with the Albany movement'.[37] The city believed that it was King who was trying to save face by fleeing a failing local movement in Albany. One city official boasted that 'firm but fair law enforcement [has] broken the back of the Albany Movement'.[38] The following night, various representatives of civil rights organisations, including the SCLC, CORE, and the NAACP, met with Robert Kennedy and Burke Marshall in Washington, DC, to discuss developments in Albany. Kennedy and Marshall both indicated that the administration favoured a swift local settlement, but insisted that this could not be achieved while King remained on the scene.

Further federal intervention came on Wednesday, 8 August, when the Justice Department joined movement attorneys in opposing the city's attempts to win a permanent injunction against demonstrations. On Friday, 10 August, King and Abernathy were both found guilty over their 27 July arrest, but had their 60-day jail sentences and $200 fines suspended, thus paving the way for them to leave the city. After speaking at mass rallies that night, King left Albany. Over the weekend, city commissioners poured scorn on King's retreat by declaring that while they were pleased at his departure it did nothing to change their existing stance.

Angered by the city commissioners' remarks, King returned to Albany on Monday with renewed gusto, vowing to 'keep on marching until victory is finally ours'.[39] Sitting alongside Albany Movement president Dr Anderson, King announced a number of new measures designed to press home black demands. He declared that the boycott of white businesses would be stepped up. Anderson's daughter would apply to attend an all-white city high school to begin the process of school desegregation. A black candidate would run for a place on the City Commission in November. On Wednesday, Marion Page presented the black community's grievances to the City Commission. He again asked for a clarification of the previous December settlement. Demonstrating that it was utterly unmoved by the new developments, the City Commission dismissed the petition out of hand and declared that all the issues raised were now matters for the courts to decide. On Thursday, Anderson, indicating that the City Commission had been right to call the movement's bluff by refusing to negotiate, announced that there would be no more demonstrations and that the local movement would now turn its attention to voter registration and 'settling down for the long haul'.[40]

King tried several last-ditch attempts to keep the local movement in Albany alive. He returned on 27 August to offer support for two groups of white northern ministers who offered to mediate in the dispute. The city subsequently arrested 75 of the ministers for holding a prayer vigil outside City Hall. King then sent a telegram appealing to President Kennedy to assist in mediation efforts. There was no reply. Having achieved the goal of ending demonstrations, the Kennedy administration had no desire to further involve itself with the Albany Movement. The City Commission continued to hold fast against any changes to the segregated order. When advised that the federal courts would ultimately order the desegregation of public facilities, the City Commission closed down all the city's parks and swimming pools, and the public library. Furthermore, it extended its existing policy at bus and train terminals – contending that they were desegregated while still in practice enforcing segregation with the use of trespass laws – to hotels, restaurants and other facilities. The Albany Movement had left blacks 'disillusioned, frightened and bitter', reported Albany Movement leader Slater King. Writing two years after the 1961–2 movement, one news reporter concluded that Albany still represented a 'monument to white supremacy'.[41] At the end of 1963, Chief of Police Laurie Pritchett could boast that 'Albany is as segregated as ever.'[42] NAACP executive secretary Roy Wilkins, commenting on the Albany Movement, noted that 'Direct action, for all the exhilaration it had produced in Montgomery, with the sit-ins and the Freedom Rides, had suddenly come up against a hard, unmoving rock. If the entire South had been as deft and devious as Albany in avoiding integration we would have been in very serious trouble.'[43] Fortunately for the movement, not every city was as 'deft and devious' as Albany.

Learning from Albany, Preparing for Birmingham

On 10 and 11 January 1963, King and SCLC board members met to reflect on the lessons of Albany at a staff retreat at the Dorchester Center in Georgia. King felt that one of the main problems in Albany was that the movement there had been too ambitious in attacking segregation on all fronts at once. King believed that focusing limited resources on one particular issue at a time would have proved more effective. Another important lesson, King felt, was the question of exactly where movement pressure should be applied in a community. Negotiations in Albany targeted the political power structure, yet it was the economic power structure that was most vulnerable to boycotts and to demonstrations, and that was therefore more likely to respond to black demands. King concluded that, particularly in places where few black voters were registered, and where they were therefore not able to exert political pressure on whites, future campaigns should focus on the white economic power structure that could in turn apply pressure on the white political power structure for change.

King and SCLC board members were adamant about the need to conduct another campaign quickly to counter the defeat in Albany. The most promising place for such a campaign was Birmingham, Alabama. The largest centre of heavy industry in the South, Birmingham's economy was built around iron and steel production. The city held a fearsome reputation as one of the most violent and racist cities in the United States. In the post-war era, racial violence had manifested itself most visibly in the city in the dynamiting of black residents who attempted to move from cramped black neighbourhoods into white neighbourhoods. The violence earned the city the nickname of 'Bombingham'.[44] It was, the SCLC's Wyatt Walker noted, 'the biggest and baddest city of the South'.[45] King felt that Birmingham's reputation as a symbol of white violence meant that if the SCLC could 'break the back of segregation' there it could do it 'all over the nation'.[46] Birmingham's black population, like Albany's, stood at around 40 per cent of the city population. Yet with a much larger total population of 350,000, the city held out the prospect of a campaign on a much larger scale.

Another important factor in the decision to hold a campaign in Birmingham was the presence of the ACMHR, one of the SCLC's strongest and most active affiliates. The SCLC's existing relationship with the ACMHR, King hoped, would avoid the debilitating divisions that had undermined the local movement in Albany. Much of the ACMHR's success lay in the leadership of its president, the Revd Fred Shuttlesworth, who had helped to place the organisation at the forefront of black protest in the city after Alabama outlawed the NAACP in 1956. Shuttlesworth had invited the SCLC to hold its annual conference in Birmingham in September 1962. Using the threat of accompanying demonstrations, Shuttlesworth managed to elicit some concessions from white businessmen, such as painting over segregation signs in downtown stores. As a result of the concessions, the SCLC decided not to hold demonstrations in the city. However, after the SCLC conference, under pressure from Public Safety Commissioner Bull Connor, the businessmen reinstated the signs. Angered by the businessmen's backtracking, Shuttlesworth asked the SCLC to return to the city for a full-fledged campaign against segregation. In doing so, he was fully aware that 'King's image was slightly on the wane' and that 'The SCLC needed a victory.'[47] Birmingham's white businessmen, in an attempt to improve the city's image and to rein in the excesses of Bull Connor, successfully campaigned for city government reform in November 1962. In changing from a City Commission to a mayor–council form of government, the businessmen hoped to oust Connor from office.

Many historians have highlighted two further important considerations on the part of King and the SCLC in launching the Birmingham campaign. Firstly, they point to the fact that in Bull Connor the SCLC had the opportunity to take on a lawman who, in contrast to Albany's Laurie Pritchett, could be counted on to use confrontational policing tactics. Secondly, they point to the fact that by engaging in a symbolic struggle in a violent city like Birmingham, the Kennedy administration would inevitably be forced to intervene to a greater extent than it had done in Albany.

Although both these points were ultimately borne out in the SCLC's Birmingham campaign, historian of the local Birmingham movement Glenn T. Eskew casts doubt upon the extent to which these two goals were in fact important prior to the actual demonstrations taking place. Eskew points out that the Birmingham campaign was initially scheduled to begin only after Bull Connor had been ousted from office in elections for the new mayor–council city government. Elections to fill the new government positions were scheduled to take place in early March 1963. The SCLC, Eskew insists, purposely set the start date for its campaign to begin after the elections, when Connor should have been removed from office and a potentially more sympathetic city government should have been installed.

Eskew also asserts that, given the Kennedy administration's previous civil rights record, its intervention in the local movement in Birmingham was by no means a foregone conclusion. In fact, the idea that taking on Connor and engaging the Kennedy administration was part of the SCLC's Birmingham campaign master plan, Eskew argues, is largely the result of SCLC executive director Wyatt Walker's subsequent evaluation of the Birmingham campaign. Eskew claims that after the fact, Walker intentionally interpreted the eventual successful outcomes of the SCLC's Birmingham campaign as being part of the SCLC's initial goals. This was done to give the appearance that the SCLC stage-managed the Birmingham campaign to a greater extent than was actually the case, and to make the SCLC look more professional and organised than in fact it was.

It is certainly true that King and the SCLC scheduled demonstrations in Birmingham to start after Connor's expected removal from office. The extent to which it believed that demonstrations would bring federal intervention is more uncertain. Whatever the degree of advance planning in the SCLC's Birmingham campaign, however, Eskew is certainly right to point out that much of its success depended upon ad hoc decision-making and in-the-field innovation. 'No revolution is like a ballet,' reflected King later, in typically prosaic fashion. 'Its steps and gestures are not neatly designed and precisely performed.'[48] SNCC's James Forman put it in his typically more forthright manner by noting that 'In many ways [the] success [of the Birmingham campaign] was due to flukes.'[49]

The Birmingham Campaign

Developments in Birmingham stalled the SCLC campaign before it had even started. Elections for the new mayor–council government were scheduled for 5 March 1962. Bull Connor was running for mayor in a bid to retain political office against two other candidates, former state lieutenant governor Albert Boutwell and Thomas King. Both Boutwell and Thomas King declared themselves supporters of segregation, but insisted that they disagreed with Connor's brutal policing methods. The SCLC scheduled the start of its campaign for 14 March, after the elections had been held. However, on the day of the election there was no clear majority winner, with Boutwell narrowly ahead on 39 per cent to Connor's 31 per cent of votes. A run-off election between Boutwell and Connor was set for 2 April. The run-off forced the SCLC to 'remap strategy' and to delay the start of the campaign until 3 April.[50] On a personal note, the delay allowed King to be in Atlanta for the birth of the Kings' fourth child, Bernice Albertine King, on 28 March, before the Birmingham campaign began in earnest. On 2 April, Boutwell beat Connor in the run-off election by 58 per cent to 42 per cent of votes. Connor, however, refused to surrender. He sued in the courts for the right to see out his original term of office. This in effect meant that two different administrations laid claim to city government. Boutwell decided to wait until the courts ruled on the matter before taking office, which left Connor still in charge. Against this backdrop of political confusion, the SCLC launched its campaign on 3 April. Soon, Birmingham would have, as one local put it, 'two mayors, one King, and a parade every day'.[51]

As King and his SCLC advisers had previously agreed, demonstrations began with small groups targeting downtown lunch counters with sit-ins. A number of arrests were made in the first few days of demonstrations. King continued to stress the importance of putting pressure on the city's white businessmen with a boycott of selected downtown stores during the busy Easter shopping period. He believed that Birmingham's large black population possessed 'significant buying power so that its withdrawal could make the difference between profit and loss for many businesses'.[52]

No sooner had the campaign got under way than several unanticipated problems came to light. The number of local blacks willing to volunteer to participate in demonstrations was far below the SCLC's expectations. In the run-up to the Birmingham campaign, Fred Shuttlesworth had noted that 'some few Negroes are not for D.A. [direct action] at this time'.[53] To keep the SCLC interested, however, he had downplayed just how widespread that sentiment was. Likewise, Shuttlesworth glossed over his rivalries with influential black middle-class leaders in Birmingham. Those black middle-class leaders now began to voice strong reservations in private about the timing of the SCLC's demonstrations. They insisted that the Boutwell administration should be given a chance to address the city's racial problems before SCLC demonstrations began. Local black newspaper the *Birmingham World* declared that 'this direct action seems to be both wasteful and reckless'.[54] White clergymen in the city who were sympathetic to black demands, and the Kennedy administration, both insisted that the timing of the demonstrations was inappropriate.

While King strenuously defended his decision to launch the Birmingham campaign, another problem arose. Bull Connor, aware of Laurie Pritchett's successful policing tactics in Albany, was attempting to emulate them. At Connor's request, the Ku Klux Klan violence that had long plagued the city disappeared overnight. King admitted that he was 'surprised at the restraint of Connor's men'.[55] Still vying for public support to remain in office, Connor insisted that he would 'fill the jail if they violate the laws as long as I am at City Hall'.[56] However, Connor's policy of appeasement did not last long. On Sunday, 9 April, King's brother, A.D. King, who was a church minister in Birmingham, led a march downtown. Connor brought out snarling police dogs to keep the marchers in line. Watching the scene unfold, Wyatt Walker stumbled upon an important discovery. Although the actual demonstration was made up of barely twenty people, the number of black onlookers it attracted gave the impression that a much larger demonstration was taking place. Viewing this as a way to make up for a lack of movement volunteers, Walker planned further demonstrations at peak times of the day when they might receive the most residual support. As it had in Albany, this carried with it the risk of undisciplined, even violent demonstrations. Yet in Birmingham the tactic would be vindicated to a large extent by the disproportionate counter-violence used by the police. This meant that it was white, and not black violence, that would make the headlines in Birmingham. Walker and SCLC staffer Dorothy Cotton were jubilant at the discovery, exclaiming 'We got a movement! We had some police brutality. They brought out the dogs.'[57] Walker renamed the Birmingham campaign from its initial 'Project X' to 'Project C' for confrontation. SNCC's James Forman found Walker and Cotton's outburst 'a disgusting moment . . . for it seemed very cold, cruel, and calculating to be happy about police brutality coming down on innocent people'.[58]

On 8 and 9 April, King met with groups of Birmingham's black ministers and black middle-class leaders to convince them that this was the opportune time for the movement to press home its demands. Gradually winning them around, they agreed to open negotiations with white businessmen, but made little progress. In an attempt to place pressure on the white business community to hold meaningful negotiations, King declared that he and Ralph Abernathy would lead a march on Good Friday, 12 April, and that they would face arrest and if necessary go to jail. Already anticipating this move, the city won a state court injunction against further marches or demonstrations. The hope was that such legal action, as in Albany, would stop the movement in its tracks. This time, however, King was prepared for such a move and was willing to accept the previous arguments made by SNCC that the movement had a duty to break unjust laws. Nevertheless, he was careful to make the distinction between defying a state court order from courts that still upheld segregation laws, and a federal court order from federal courts that were more willing to rule segregation laws invalid. King declared that the march would go ahead despite the state court injunction.

King began Friday morning with a new problem. The SCLC's funds for bail money were already depleted and anyone now arrested in Birmingham could not be guaranteed release from jail. This point was crucial since, as in Albany, few local people could afford to commit to remaining in jail on an indefinite basis since they had jobs to go to and families to feed. Thus King faced a dilemma. Should he leave Birmingham to raise bail money for the movement or should he stay in Birmingham and go to jail? If he left it would look like another retreat. If he stayed he would be stuck in jail and unable to help those incarcerated alongside him. As he deliberated, King felt that he was 'standing . . . at the center of all that my life had brought me to be'.[59] Despite the problems that it might entail, King told his advisers that he had resolved to 'make a faith act' and to go to jail as planned.[60] The SCLC's Andrew Young later reflected that the decision marked 'the beginning of [King's] true leadership' of the movement, in that King showed himself willing to move beyond his previous cautious stance and that he began to take more risks to provide more dynamic movement leadership.[61] That afternoon, King and Abernathy, clad in blue denim overalls to show their unity with Birmingham's ordinary black citizenry, led 50 demonstrators on a march from Sixth Avenue Baptist Church to City Hall. After a few blocks, Connor told his men to 'Stop them. Don't let them go any farther.'[62] Police officers arrested all the marchers and drove them downtown to the city jail.

In jail, King was placed in solitary confinement. Movement attorney Norman Amaker's request to see King in private was rebuffed. When Wyatt Walker heard this he sent a telegram to President Kennedy asking that at least 'a modicum of human treatment' be afforded to King while in jail.[63] Kennedy conferred with his civil rights assistant Burke Marshall, who told him that there were no grounds for federal intervention in Birmingham. Walker then convinced King's wife Coretta to telephone the president. After all, Walker reasoned, in his 1960 telephone call after Martin's Atlanta arrest, Kennedy had told Coretta to call him if she ever needed help. Coretta reached presidential press secretary Pierre Salinger who promised to pass her message on to the president. Three quarters of an hour later, Robert Kennedy called back with a promise to make inquiries on Coretta's behalf. Keeping up the pressure in the streets, A.D. King led a march of 30 people downtown. Police clashed violently with black onlookers, ensuring front-page headlines for the movement the following day.

On Monday, 15 April, President Kennedy called Coretta to express his concern at her husband's imprisonment, to tell her that FBI agents had reported that Martin was safe, and to tell her that Martin would be allowed to call her from jail. Half an hour later King called and hurriedly enquired about his family and about movement developments in Birmingham. The next day, King penned his 'Letter From Birmingham City Jail' in response to the earlier criticisms of eight prominent white Alabama clergymen about his use of nonviolent, direct-action tactics.[64] The letter was one of King's most eloquent and thoughtful defences of the use of nonviolence and civil disobedience, although its publication and widespread dissemination came only after the major events of the Birmingham campaign had passed. On Thursday, Coretta and Ralph Abernathy's wife Juanita visited their husbands in jail. On Saturday, King and Abernathy left jail having been helped to raise bail money by black entertainer Harry Belafonte and other SCLC supporters. They returned to Atlanta to preach at their churches, arriving back in Birmingham on Monday morning, 22 April, for trial.

King and ten other defendants were found guilty on the charge of violating the court injunction against marching or demonstrations. Each was sentenced to five days in jail and a $50 fine, which was held in abeyance on appeal. At a mass meeting on Friday evening, King again underlined the importance of the economic boycott of white-owned down-town stores and announced an expansion of demonstrations. Yet, as King left Birmingham for speaking engagements elsewhere that weekend, Wyatt Walker and Revd James Bevel, an SCLC field secretary recruited from the student sit-in movement in Nashville, were left in charge of operations and found it increasingly difficult to recruit movement volunteers. 'We needed more troops,' Walker explained. 'We had run out of troops. We had scraped the bottom of the barrel of adults who could go [to jail].'[65]

Bevel noted that the most eager recruits were black high school students. When King arrived back in Birmingham on Monday, 30 April, Bevel urged him to tap this student support. Bevel explained that 'A boy from high school . . . can get the same effect in terms of being in jail, in terms of putting the pressure on the city, as his father – and yet there is no economic threat on the family because the father is still in his job.'[66] Using children in demonstrations would undoubtedly be a controversial move. Many black adults naturally objected to their offspring being placed in danger. Much earlier in the movement, when King had suggested encouraging the use of nonviolent direct action in high schools, NAACP attorney Thurgood Marshall had stated that he did not 'approve of using children to do men's work'.[67] Strong opposition to the tactic in Birmingham came from an array of sources. Birmingham's mayor elect Albert Boutwell condemned the movement for using 'innocent children as their tools'. Robert Kennedy warned that 'An injured, maimed or dead child is a price that none of us can afford to pay.' In Harlem, Nation of Islam minister and spokesperson Malcolm X stormed that 'real men don't put their children on the firing line'.[68]

Recognising just how damaging the tactic of using child demonstrators might be to the movement, and the criticism that it would draw, King was hesitant about giving an open endorsement to Bevel's plan, but he did agree to explore its potential further. Even contemplating such a move was a reflection of King's desperation at that point. It was evident that the movement in Birmingham was stalling. As historian Glenn T. Eskew notes, 'Nearly everything pointed to another Albany, another failure.'[69]

Birmingham and the Children's Crusade

While King hesitated, Bevel acted. Without King's explicit approval, Bevel began to mobilise black student support from Birmingham's high schools. On Thursday, 2 May, hundreds of young would-be demonstrators filled

Sixteenth Street Baptist Church. At the same time, Connor's police forces gathered at Kelly Ingram Park, a small patch of grassland that divided a predominantly black part of the city from the white downtown. With a stand-off in the making, Bevel and Walker moved to implement what turned out to be the decisive tactical decision of the Birmingham campaign, entirely without King's consent, although King would later call it 'one of the wisest moves we made'.[70] Bevel and Walker sent a first wave of several hundred high school demonstrators on a march to City Hall. Birmingham police arrested the marchers. A second, then a third wave of demonstrators followed. Again the police arrested them all. Bevel took charge of organising the youngsters while Walker coordinated the demonstrations, communicating with other SCLC staff over walkie-talkies. By the evening, over five hundred arrests had been made. For the first time ever, the SCLC was actually able to hold good on its promise to fill the jails. As Bevel had predicted, with their children involved the black adult community rallied to the aid of the movement. Over two thousand local blacks attended a mass movement that night.

The following afternoon the demonstrations continued. Fast losing patience, Connor set free the police dogs and had the fire department, also under his control, train water from high-powered hoses on demonstrators. David Vann, a white Birmingham attorney, reported that because of Connor's tactics 'in a twinkling of an eye, the whole black community was instantaneously consolidated behind King'.[71] Moreover, the scenes of violence got the attention of the president. Although there was still no mandate for federal intervention, Kennedy admitted that the news reports and images of the police dogs attacking demonstrators had made him 'sick'.[72] Burke Marshall and Joseph Dolan, an assistant deputy attorney general, were dispatched to the city to assist in a negotiated settlement. Under pressure from federal representatives and fearing a mass outbreak of violence and disorder, white businessmen in Birmingham agreed to open negotiations with black community representatives. The movement continued to keep up the pressure in the streets. A demonstration on Friday, 4 May, resulted yet again in the use of high-powered fire hoses against demonstrators. Bevel, sensing an increasingly agitated and violent mood among black demonstrators, feared that he might lose control of events. Borrowing a bullhorn from one of the policemen he told demonstrators to 'get off the streets now, we're not going to have violence. If you're not going to respect policemen, you're not in the movement.'[73]

Against the backdrop of continuing demonstrations, negotiations between white businessmen and black representatives began. The white businessmen were presented with the movement's four principal demands. Firstly, downtown store facilities must desegregate. Secondly, existing black employees must be upgraded and non-discriminatory hiring practices must be adopted in the future. Thirdly, white businessmen must put pressure on the city government to drop charges against movement demonstrators. Fourthly, white businessmen must put pressure on the city government to form a biracial negotiating committee to conduct further discussions. The reply was not promising. White businessmen refused to negotiate on points three and four since they insisted that they involved the city government and not them. They also insisted that no action on points one and two could be taken until the existing stalemate over who actually ran city government had been resolved in the courts. With little further progress made, white negotiators decided that a larger representative body was needed to encompass the scope of black demands. They therefore called upon the help of the Senior Citizens Committee, a group of senior white businessmen sponsored by the city's Chamber of Commerce, which had originally been formed to push through local government reform. Burke Marshall phoned Washington, DC, to urge the Kennedy administration to use its influence with members of the Senior Citizens Committee to reach a settlement.

On the afternoon of Tuesday, 7 May, the Senior Citizens Committee met amid further demonstrations. From past experience in Albany, King and the SCLC knew that they needed to keep pressure on the city to make concessions while negotiations took place. SNCC's James Forman and the SCLC's Dorothy Cotton helped to develop a new tactic of flooding the downtown area with black students, thereby bringing the struggle to the very doorstep of the white business community.[74] As the Senior Citizens Committee convened, another wave of demonstrators was clashing with police at Kelly Ingram Park. The calling out of state troopers or the Alabama National Guard by Governor George Corley Wallace to assist the city police was a looming possibility. Such a development would plunge the city into further chaos. Under the circumstances, the Senior Citizens Committee agreed that it had to act decisively. With only a few dissenting voices, an agreement was reached to pursue a meaningful settlement with black representatives. That afternoon, there were more clashes between demonstrators and city police. Fred Shuttlesworth was carried away on a stretcher after being hurled against a wall by a jet of water from a fire hose. Connor was overheard to say that he wished Shuttlesworth had 'been carried away in a hearse'.[75] The situation was rapidly escalating out of both the SCLC's and the city's control.

With Shuttlesworth hospitalised, King and Shuttlesworth's second in command, L.H. Pitts, discussed the situation the following morning. With negotiations already under way and with events in the streets beginning to get out of hand, King felt that a temporary halt to demonstrations was appropriate. King believed that this would demonstrate the movement's good faith in the efforts of white negotiators and would equally allow the SCLC to regroup and to restore nonviolent discipline to demonstrations. With Pitts's agreement, King announced a temporary cessation of demonstrations. When Shuttlesworth found out that King had called an end to demonstrations behind his back he was furious. For his part, Bull Connor did not take kindly to white businessmen seemingly negotiating an end to what had become his own personal crusade to maintain segregation in Birmingham, which he felt was integral to his popularity among the white population and therefore potentially his political future. In an act of defiance, Connor indiscriminately raised the bail for King and Abernathy to $2,500 and told them to pay up or go back to jail. They chose jail. With King and Abernathy out of the way, Shuttlesworth, who checked himself out of hospital while still medicated, announced that demonstrations would resume with immediate effect and set off for Sixteenth Street Baptist Church. Kennedy administration representatives had to physically restrain Shuttlesworth from his warpath. They persuaded him to contact Robert Kennedy before making any rash decisions. Soon after, Burke Marshall and local black leaders persuaded local black businessman A.G. Gaston to write cheques to bail King and Abernathy out of jail.

Negotiations between black and white representatives were meanwhile making progress. The main sticking point was the question of what would happen to the jailed demonstrators. This was resolved when Gaston agreed to put up some of the money for their bail, while the Kennedy administration persuaded sympathetic northern labour unions to help make up the rest of the necessary funds. On Friday morning, 10 May, King held a press conference to announce the settlement terms of the 'Birmingham Truce Agreement'. At the insistence of white businessmen, a number of the agreements hinged upon the expected court ruling that would allow the Boutwell administration to assume control of city government. Firstly, three days after the close of demonstrations, downtown stores would desegregate their waiting rooms. Secondly, 30 days after the court order to install the Boutwell administration, segregation signs on washrooms, restrooms and drinking fountains would be removed. Thirdly, 60 days after the court order to install the Boutwell administration, the desegregation of lunch counters would begin. Fourthly, when the court order to install the Boutwell administration was handed down a programme of black employment upgrading would begin immediately; within 60 days that programme would include at least one black sales person or cashier; and within fifteen days after demonstrations ending, a biracial Committee on Racial Problems and Employment would be established. King was at pains to emphasise that the SCLC would not repeat the mistake of Albany and simply leave after an agreement had been reached. Rather, this time, King insisted, he and the SCLC would stay to help the black community through the process of desegregation and to help launch a voter-registration drive to consolidate existing gains and to force further concessions in the long term.

On Saturday morning, King left Birmingham to return to Atlanta. That evening, the full fury of a white backlash against the truce agreement was unleashed. For six weeks the hallmark of Ku Klux Klan violence in the city, terror bombings, had been absent. With news of the truce agreement they returned with a vengeance. The targets were A.D. King's home and Martin Luther King Jr's vacated room at the Gaston Motel. Fortunately, no one was injured, but the blasts brought angry black crowds out on to the streets. Movement officials tried to calm the crowds, although they themselves were angered that the state apparently had a hand in the violence. Suspiciously, Alabama state troopers under the command of Colonel Albert J. Lingo, a figure who had close links with Bull Connor and Governor George Wallace, had disappeared after previously guarding the area around the Gaston Motel, only to reappear again after the explosion. The returning state troopers clashed with the black crowd and the situation rapidly escalated into a full-scale riot.

Robert Kennedy feared that if violence continued in Birmingham, it might spread to other cities across the country. He dispatched two more federal assistants, Ramsey Clark and John Nolan, to the city. After consulting with Burke Marshall and King, President Kennedy decided to federalise the Alabama National Guard to prevent its possible use by Governor Wallace and to move federal troops close to Birmingham for reinforcements if needed. That night, the president appeared on national television to inform the people of the United States about his decision to back the truce agreement in Birmingham. Over the following weeks, King spent time in Birmingham to help ease tensions in the city. He spoke at a number of venues to urge the black community to remain committed to nonviolence. When Birmingham school authorities insisted that eleven hundred black children would be expelled from school for skipping classes to take part in demonstrations, King persuaded local blacks to take their case to the courts rather than to the streets. They agreed, and a federal court subsequently ordered that all the students should be reinstated. Soon after, the Alabama Supreme Court ruled in favour of the Boutwell administration taking office. Bull Connor was forced to vacate his office and the timetable for many of the terms laid down in the truce agreement was triggered.

The Birmingham campaign was to King and the SCLC what the sit-ins were to SNCC and what the Freedom Rides were to CORE. After struggling to find his place in the emerging civil rights movement since the Montgomery bus boycott, Birmingham provided a strategy for King, and for the SCLC, that represented their own distinctive brand of nonviolent direct action. Moreover, the success of the Birmingham campaign inspired an upsurge in black activism in other southern communities during the summer of 1963 – a 'contagion of the will to be free', as King put it.[76] The basis of King and the SCLC's strategy was to choose a community that they felt was the most conducive and susceptible to demonstrations; they would seek negotiations with the white community for change; they would engage in the short-term mobilisation of the black population and train them in nonviolence; and if negotiations with the white community subsequently failed, they would launch nonviolent, direct-action demonstrations to highlight the injustices that existed in the community. In holding demonstrations, King and the SCLC hoped that they would force local whites to the negotiating table or encounter violent opposition to change that would bring outside help in the form of federal intervention.

In implementing this strategy, King and the SCLC encountered a number of criticisms. SNCC decried the insensitive nature of the strategy, claiming that King and the SCLC exploited communities for their own ends and failed to take into account the needs of local blacks over a desire for national headlines. Moreover, SNCC claimed, King and the SCLC failed to provide the support that black communities needed after demonstrations finished that would enable them to continue to fight for civil rights after King and the SCLC left. Though these criticisms were borne out in many cases, King and the SCLC's strategy was in many ways dictated by practical constraints. The SCLC simply did not have the committed cadre of student volunteers to conduct long-term community-organising campaigns that SNCC did, nor did it have the finances to pay staff members to engage in and to support such projects. The SCLC strategy was designed to maximise its resources: it relied upon King's national standing to bring federal action and legislation through pressure exerted in local campaigns, in the hope and expectation that federal action and national legislation would ultimately benefit blacks in the

South and the nation as a whole. Of course, ideally, the SCLC would have wanted to provide an extensive local support network to help implement this legislation. But it just could not financially afford to do so.

Whites criticised King and the SCLC's strategy by claiming that, although it pretended to be nonviolent, it in fact actually provoked violence by actively seeking out confrontation. King responded to this criticism by noting that nonviolent, direct-action demonstrations merely brought to the surface the latent violence that kept segregation and racial discrimination in place. He reasoned that if black demonstrators were allowed to exercise their constitutional civil rights, there would be no reason for whites to use violence to stop them from doing so in the first place.

King and the SCLC would return to the Birmingham strategy repeatedly over the following three years with mixed results, constantly seeking to evolve that strategy to address new issues and to respond to the variety of different local conditions and contexts in which it operated.

Chapter 4

Glory Bound, 1963–4

Much of King's reputation rests upon the two-year period between the 1963 Birmingham campaign and the 1965 Selma campaign. It produced some of King and the SCLC's most iconic moments: the deployment of police dogs and water from high-powered fire hoses against demonstrators in Birmingham; King's 'I Have A Dream' speech at the March on Washington; and confrontations with Alabama state troopers who teargassed and beat marchers on Selma's Edmund Pettus Bridge. Added to this, Congress passed the 1964 Civil Rights Act, which among other things contained a clause to end segregation in public facilities and accommodations, and the 1965 Voting Rights Act, which removed obstacles to black voting rights in many states and provided active federal assistance to black voters. King was named *Time* magazine's 'Man of the Year' in 1963 and received the Nobel Peace Prize in 1964.

Yet not everything went King's way. In the midst of triumphs were tragedies such as the bombing of Birmingham's Sixteenth Street Baptist Church that killed four black girls attending Sunday school. Amid successful campaigns at Birmingham and Selma were more ambiguous results, most notably in St. Augustine, Florida. Continuing tension between the national goals and the local needs of the civil rights movement came to a head after the 1964 Mississippi Freedom Summer, when Mississippi Freedom Democratic Party (MFDP) delegates attempted to be seated at the 1964 Democratic National Convention in Atlantic City, New Jersey. The FBI stepped up its campaign of harassment against King by placing bugging devices in his hotel rooms. The bigger King's rewards, the bigger were the responsibilities that went with them. Even as King found himself bound for glory, he often found himself equally bound by it.

The March on Washington

'History has attached the name of the Rev. King to the march,' reflects the NAACP's Roy Wilkins in his autobiography, 'but I suspect it would be more accurate to call it [A. Philip] Randolph's march – and [Bayard] Rustin's.'[1] The 1963 March on Washington had its origins in a similar demonstration planned by Randolph in 1941, which he had threatened to lead if President Franklin D. Roosevelt did not act to combat racial discrimination in wartime industries. The planned march did not take place after Roosevelt met with Randolph and agreed to take action. Roosevelt issued Executive Order 8802, which banned racial discrimination in wartime industry hiring practices and set up of the Fair Employment Practices Committee (FEPC) to enforce the ban. On a December afternoon in 1962, at the BSCP office in New York, Randolph and Rustin discussed the idea of reprising a 'March on Washington for Jobs and Freedom' to mark the hundredth anniversary of President Abraham Lincoln's signing of the Emancipation Proclamation, and to focus attention on the problems of black employment opportunities and economic injustice.

In June 1963, plans for the March on Washington evolved into an event that promised to unite all the major civil rights organisations in one single demonstration. Representatives of all the main organisations were in New York on 17 June to attend a meeting called by Taconic Foundation president Stephen R. Currier. At the meeting, Currier suggested the formation of a Council for United Civil Rights Leadership (CUCRL) that would collect and then divide large financial contributions to the movement between the leading organisations to avoid squabbles over funding. Since Currier played an important role in securing such donations, the representatives of all the organisations agreed to the plan. The following day, Currier met with King, Ralph Abernathy, Fred Shuttlesworth, Stanley Levison, Bayard Rustin and others at Randolph's office. The group agreed that a March on Washington would take place in August 1963 and they named New York black unionist Cleveland Robinson and New York pastor George Lawrence, both of whom were already involved with Randolph's plans for the march, as temporary coordinators. A meeting was set for 24 June to discuss plans further. On 21 June, Robinson and Lawrence announced the march to the press.

News of the march brought a summons for what the press called the 'Big Six' civil rights leaders – King (president of the SCLC), Roy Wilkins (executive secretary of the NAACP), Whitney Young (executive director of the National Urban League), James Farmer (national director of CORE) and John Lewis (the newly elected chair of SNCC) – to the White House. The Kennedy administration was beginning to take a more forthright stand on civil rights in the wake of the Birmingham demonstrations. On 1 June 1963, Attorney General Robert Kennedy had met with key administration strategists to advocate legislation that would empower the federal government to be more proactive in the area of civil rights. Both President Kennedy and Vice President Lyndon B. Johnson agreed, although others present protested that such legislation would be difficult to get through a Congress that included many powerful southern politicians opposed to such a measure. Yet precisely the need for such legislation was evident on 11 June when Alabama governor George Wallace stood in the doorway of the University of Alabama, Tuscaloosa, and physically barred the entrance of Deputy Attorney General Nicholas Katzenbach and two black students who were attempting to enroll there under a federal court order. President Kennedy federalised the Alabama National Guard to enforce the law and the students were eventually admitted. That night, in a separate incident, Mississippi NAACP leader Medgar Evers was shot dead in the drive of his home by white segregationist Byron De La Beckwith.[2] The same evening that Evers was killed, the president appeared on national television to deliver his strongest speech yet in support of civil rights, telling the audience that 'We are confronted primarily with a moral issue' that was 'as old as the scriptures and is as clear as the American Constitution.'[3] Kennedy announced that a civil rights bill would be introduced to Congress and that it would contain a provision requiring the desegregation of all public facilities and accommodations.

When Kennedy met with civil rights leaders on 22 June he was concerned that the proposed March on Washington might hinder rather than help the already expected difficult passage of the civil rights bill through Congress. The president told civil rights leaders that 'We want success in Congress not just a big show at the capital. Some of these people [in Congress] are looking for an excuse to be against us. I don't want to give them a chance to say "Yes, I'm for the bill, but I'm damned if I'll vote for it at the point of a gun." '[4] Both King and James Farmer resolutely defended the march and stated that it would go ahead as planned. King, undoubtedly with Kennedy's words partly in mind, later dismissed the 'prophets of doom who feared that the slightest incidence of violence would alienate Congress and destroy all hope of legislation'.[5] A. Philip Randolph also insisted that the march would take place, and told Kennedy, 'The Negroes are already in the streets. If they are bound to be in the streets in any case is it not better that they be led by organizations dedicated to civil rights and disciplined by struggle rather than to leave them to other leaders who care neither about civil rights or nonviolence?'[6]

Randolph's mention of 'other leaders' who did not care about 'civil rights or nonviolence' was clearly a reference to the growing popularity of the Black Muslim sect the Nation of Islam (NOI) and in particular its charismatic spokesperson Malcolm X. A fiery, controversial and provocative speaker (SCLC's Wyatt Walker almost got into a fistfight with him when they debated on one television show), Malcolm X was the most visible and vocal critic of King, of nonviolence and of white America. Malcolm X, born Malcolm Little in Omaha, Nebraska, in 1925, was shaped by life in the northern ghetto. His father died in a streetcar accident when Malcolm was only 6 years old and his mother was committed to a mental institution eight years later, leaving him to be raised in a juvenile home, then with foster parents, and then with his half-sister Ella in Boston. Like many black ghetto youths with few opportunities in a white-dominated society, Malcolm drifted into a life of drugs and crime. In jail after an arrest for burglary, Malcolm Little underwent a religious conversion to Islam and dropped his 'slave name' for an 'X' to signify his unknown African ancestry. Taken under the wing of NOI leader Elijah Muhammad, Malcolm fast became the organisation's most effective proponent. Malcolm's speeches espoused NOI dogma, calling whites 'snakes' and 'devils', which struck a resonant chord among many alienated black northern youths and provided a form of psychological liberation from white oppression. So too did Malcolm's stress on race pride, his encouragement of his followers to explore their African identity, and his advocacy of resistance to whites 'by any means necessary', including the use of armed self-defence and outright violence. In many ways, Malcolm X was a figure that linked earlier black nationalist and black separatist leaders and organisations, such as Marcus Garvey and the Universal Negro Improvement Association (UNIA), of which Malcolm's father had been a member, to the later development of 'Black Power'. As with Garvey, the UNIA and Black Power, however, Malcolm X often stood accused by critics of lacking a plausible programme for converting a feeling of black psychological empowerment into actual social, political and economic power for the black community. Malcolm X was (and remains) a figure who represented the very antithesis of King in the minds of many blacks and whites, although in later years, after a break with the NOI in the winter of 1963–4, he began to moderate his views and rhetoric somewhat. What direction Malcolm X might have eventually taken will never be known: in February 1965 members of the NOI assassinated him.

During Malcolm X's lifetime, King and other movement leaders often exploited his angry and incendiary rhetoric to their advantage, since they were able to point to Malcolm and the NOI's stance as the alternative that whites faced if they refused the civil rights movement's more moderate and reasonable demands.[7]

As the meeting between Kennedy and the civil rights leaders ended, Kennedy took King outside into the White House Rose Garden – 'I guess [FBI director J. Edgar] Hoover must be bugging him too,' King later speculated – and tackled him once more about the FBI's warnings about possible communist infiltration of the civil rights movement.[8] Before going to the White House, King had stopped off at the Justice Department where Burke Marshall and Robert Kennedy urged him to sever his links with Stanley Levison and Jack O'Dell. The president reiterated these comments, pointing to the Profumo scandal unfolding in the United Kingdom and warning King about the need to choose his friends and associates very carefully.[9] Under continued pressure to act, King asked for O'Dell's resignation, and Levison himself insisted that he and King sever their links for the sake of the movement. King reluctantly broke direct contact with Levison, but remained in touch through an intermediary, black New York attorney Clarence Jones.

At the 24 June meeting to discuss plans for the March on Washington, to placate anxious leaders like the NAACP's Roy Wilkins who was worried about calls for the march to employ mass civil disobedience, Randolph offered the assurance that the main focus of the demonstration would be a one-day nonviolent march held on Wednesday, 28 August. Although SNCC was not pleased at the watered-down plan, Randolph's assurance did persuade Wilkins to grudgingly give NAACP backing to the march. At the follow-up meeting on 2 July, Rustin put forward detailed plans for the march. Reflecting the original plans of Randolph and Rustin, economic issues such as demands for better jobs for blacks and a higher minimum wage were prioritised. Passage of the civil rights bill was listed only as a secondary concern. The 'Big Six' leaders would serve as co-chairs of the march, with each appointing a fellow member of their respective organisations as administrative coordinators.

When the question of appointing a director for the march arose, Wilkins moved to block the obvious candidate, Bayard Rustin, citing his already well-publicised status as a conscientious objector, his communist links, and his conviction related to homosexuality, as reasons to choose someone else. King and Farmer leaped to Rustin's defence. The NUL's Whitney Young finally resolved the matter by suggesting that Randolph should be the march director and that he should be free to choose his own deputy.

Everyone agreed. Randolph immediately chose Rustin as his deputy. As preparations got under way, plans for a more restrained demonstration pleased those who had initially worried that it would lead to a full-scale replication of the Birmingham campaign. Even President Kennedy endorsed the march at a 17 July press conference. In early August, Randolph announced four white co-chairs of the march: United Auto Workers' president Walter Reuther and three white religious leaders from the Protestant, Catholic and Jewish faiths. The new appointments emphasised the biracial and interfaith nature of the march and broadened the movement's base of support. The now ten-strong co-chair committee declared that they would seek an audience with President Kennedy after the completion of the march and the planned afternoon speeches.

King arrived late in Washington on Tuesday, 27 August, the day before the scheduled march, missing the deadline for speakers to hand in advance texts of their speeches to the press. He hurriedly sketched out his remarks for distribution the following morning. It was not the text of King's speech, however, but that of SNCC's John Lewis that was causing most concern on Wednesday morning. Lewis's controversial and incendiary tract criticised the Kennedy administration for doing 'too little and too late' in the field of civil rights. Lewis wrote of the violence being endured by civil rights workers in the South, the continual denial of black voting rights, and the economic plight of the black community, while condemning 'cheap political leaders who build their careers on immoral compromises'. Lewis also spoke of the 'revolution' taking place in America's streets and threatened to 'burn Jim Crow to the ground', metaphorically emulating the 'scorched earth' policy of Republican Civil War general William T. Sherman.[10]

Robert Kennedy and Burke Marshall were not at all happy with the text of Lewis's speech and were determined to stop it being read. One point of pressure they used was Cardinal Patrick O'Boyle, the Washington, DC, Catholic priest who was due to deliver the invocation at the march. O'Boyle threatened to withdraw from proceedings if Lewis did not change the tone of his speech. Rustin went to Lewis's hotel room to plead the case for changing the text in the interests of harmony, but Lewis was unrepentant. The controversy over Lewis's text was still raging as the march leaders gathered at the Lincoln Memorial. Eventually, Randolph persuaded a reluctant Lewis to deliver a revised version of his speech. Two Kennedy aides stood by the speakers ready to silence Lewis by literally pulling the plug if he reneged on his agreement.

In the event, it was King's 'I Have A Dream' speech that most people would remember. Some had criticised Rustin for putting King on as the last speaker. But, Rustin remembers, 'almost all the other speakers had asked me to make sure they didn't follow King. They knew that King was the key figure at that time in the civil rights history; and they realised the minute King finished speaking the program would be over, that everybody would be heading home.'[11] On a balmy August afternoon, King began with his prepared text but towards the end, responding to the emotional intensity of the occasion, he went to an improvised finale. King laid bare his vision of an integrated South with a repetition of paragraphs beginning with 'I have a dream'. Then, in a final flourish, he seized upon the peroration 'Let Freedom Ring' to bring his speech to a crescendo that brought thunderous applause from the audience.[12] Of course, King's preaching style and rhetoric was nothing new to those who knew him well, and his spontaneous break from the prepared text essentially repeated the content of earlier speeches made in Birmingham and Detroit in April and June that year. However, to those millions who watched either the live broadcast or later reruns on television, many of whom were white and who had never heard or seen a southern black Baptist preacher deliver a sermon before, King's performance was a new experience that made the speech's emotional impact even greater and framed the sense of occasion even more poignantly. This ensured that, of all the events that took place that day, King's speech remained the point of focus in the nation's collective memory.

Different people from different constituencies of the movement remember and interpret King's 'I Have A Dream' speech in different ways. To Fred Shuttlesworth, King's words were nothing short of divine intervention. 'There are good words said every day,' Shuttlesworth notes, 'But every once in a while, God intervenes in such a way that you know only God could do it. That was God preaching the Gospel to America through King. It helped to change the mind-set of America.'[13] Ralph Abernathy viewed the speech as a commanding oratorical performance, 'one of those few public utterances that inevitably becomes a part of the oral tradition of a people, never to be forgotten'.[14] The SCLC's Andrew Young saw King's speech and the March on Washington in terms of movement politics, remembering that 'The march transformed what had been a southern movement into a national movement.'[15] Others felt that King's speech revealed ongoing problems with his leadership. Mississippi activist Anne Moody was disappointed that 'we had "dreamers" instead of leaders leading us ... in Canton [Mississippi] we never had time to sleep, much less dream'.[16] Even while King enjoyed one of his finest hours on the public stage, throughout his speech a black heckler at the front of the crowd urged greater black militancy, screaming 'Fuck that dream, Martin. Now, goddamnit, NOW!'[17]

In contrast to the prominence that is often accorded to the March on Washington in the popular memory of the civil rights movement, many contemporary assessments questioned exactly what the march had achieved. The *New York Times* reported that the march 'appeared to have left much of Congress untouched – physically, emotionally, and politically'.[18] Lerone Bennett Jr, senior editor of *Ebony* magazine and a contemporary of King's at Morehouse College, noted that the march 'led nowhere and it was not intended to lead anywhere. It was not planned as an event within a coherent plan of action.'[19] Malcolm X dismissed the whole thing as a 'Farce on Washington'.[20] Even King was forced to acknowledge that 'The Negro community was firmly united in demanding a redress of grievances, but it was divided in tactics.'[21] The FBI was far more impressed. As a result of the march, the bureau labelled King the 'most dangerous and effective Negro leader in the country'.[22] Within three months it had persuaded Robert Kennedy to give the order that allowed it to start wiretapping King's home phone and SCLC offices in Atlanta and New York. Later, without even bothering to seek permission first, they extended surveillance to King's hotel rooms.

Although the direct political impact of the March on Washington on the president and Congress admittedly proved negligible, as a public relations showcase for the movement it more than fulfilled its purpose. As Ralph Abernathy perceptively later noted, 'Ceremonies of this sort have an important effect on the consciousness of a community or a people, even if they don't result in concrete actions.'[23] Around two hundred thousand people had packed the area between the Lincoln Memorial and the Washington Monument around the reflecting pool at the heart of the nation's capital, giving at least the appearance of a united and determined movement with mass support. Importantly, thanks largely to Bayard Rustin's meticulous preparations and organisational efficiency, the march passed off without any violence and emphasised the discipline and self-control of the demonstrators. This effectively underlined the movement's contention that it was white oppression and not black activism that had led to unrest in previous southern civil rights campaigns. The interracial element of the march was also significant, with whites comprising around a quarter of all those present. This demonstrated to the nation that the movement did not simply represent the special interests of one section of America, but rather that it had broad-based support. In particular, the involvement of white clergymen from different faiths emphasised the moral dimensions of the struggle. For King, the 'I Have A Dream' speech confirmed his status as the leading black spokesperson in the nation.

Bayard Rustin, the most important figure in organising the march, poignantly summed up the event by noting that, 'The march made Americans feel for the first time that we were capable of being truly a nation, that we were capable of moving beyond division and bigotry.' Being a seasoned activist, Rustin was also aware that 'The human spirit is like a flame. It flashes up and is gone. And you never know when that flame will come again.'[24]

Back to Birmingham: The Sixteenth Street Church Bombing

The triumph of the March on Washington was swiftly eclipsed by tragedy. On 15 September, Sixteenth Street Baptist Church in Birmingham was hit by a dynamite blast. Four young black girls, Addie Mae Collins, Denise McNair, Carloe Robertson and Cynthia Wesley, who had been attending a Sunday school service, were killed.[25] The city exploded with violence as angry blacks confronted the police. Two blacks were shot dead in the ensuing conflict and many others, black and white, sustained injuries. King arrived in Birmingham the same evening in an attempt to bring calm. The following morning, King demanded federal intervention to protect the black community from further white terrorism. Yet although President Kennedy roundly condemned the violence, he shied away from direct federal intervention. King later delivered a moving eulogy at the funeral of the four girls in which he referred to them as 'the martyred heroines of a holy crusade for freedom and dignity'.[26]

Outraged by one of the worst tragedies of the civil rights movement to date, the SCLC's James Bevel and his wife, fellow Nashville student Diane Nash, drew up plans for an all-out attack on segregation in Alabama. Their 'Proposal for Action in Montgomery' advocated closing down Alabama's capital city through a coordinated campaign of nonviolence. Its two principal aims were to register every eligible Alabama black citizen to vote and to remove Governor George Wallace from office. The planned campaign would be run with military-like discipline involving the formation of a 'nonviolent army' of trained volunteers. These volunteers, the Bevels envisaged, would hold mass rallies and go to prison as in past campaigns. Moving beyond those tactics, however, they would also paralyse the state capitol building by forming a physical blockade around it, bombard its telephone lines with calls, refuse to pay taxes, organise a general strike, and lie on 'railroad tracks, runways, and bus driveways cutting off train, bus and rail transportation' to the city.[27] The Bevels presented their plan to Fred Shuttlesworth who suggested a strategy meeting to discuss it with King. When King heard the Bevel plan he was taken aback by its radicalism and greeted it with caution. Nevertheless, several SCLC members took the plan seriously and it received enthusiastic support from SNCC.

While the Bevel plan remained on the table, King, along with Abernathy and local black leaders from Birmingham, met with President Kennedy. King stressed the urgency and seriousness of the situation in Birmingham and suggested two immediate courses of action. Firstly, that Kennedy should send federal troops into Birmingham to stop the violence, and secondly, that Kennedy should look into punishing government contractors who continued to discriminate against black employees. Kennedy remained reluctant to apply such overt military and economic pressure but he did concede the need for some form of federal action, not least to forestall the Bevel plan, which greatly alarmed the administration. Favouring a local settlement to the problem, Kennedy sent two representatives to Birmingham, Kenneth Royall and Earl Blaik, to hold talks with local leaders. He also summoned a group of Birmingham's white businessmen to the White House to exert pressure on them to live up to their previous agreement to initiate plans for racial progress in the city.

At the SCLC's convention in Richmond, Virginia, on 28 September, there was much discussion about the organisation's next move. A great deal of press attention focused on the Bevel plan, since the details had by now become public knowledge. King refuted talk of such a campaign, however, stating that an SCLC campaign in Danville, Virginia, or Birmingham was far more likely. Yet within the SCLC the Bevel plan remained uppermost in many minds, although there was some indecision about whether Montgomery or Birmingham should be the focus of activities. Wyatt Walker advocated some form of economic action, perhaps even a national work stoppage or national black boycott of goods. Taking on board these respective views, at the end of the conference King announced that Birmingham would be the SCLC's priority target. He decided that an economic boycott of goods and services produced in or benefiting Birmingham would begin at Christmas and would continue indefinitely. Further, the SCLC laid down four specific demands to leaders in Birmingham: to hire black policemen, to issue a call for law and order, to withdraw Alabama state troopers from the streets, and to begin negotiations with the black community. If these demands were not met, King threatened to return to Birmingham to lead mass demonstrations.

In essence, however, King's threat to return to Birmingham was just that: a threat. A large portion of SCLC's finances was already tied up in bail bonds in Birmingham and the organisation simply did not have the requisite funds to sponsor another full-scale campaign there. Moreover, going back to Birmingham risked turning a perceived victory into a defeat. King banked on the city having little stomach for a return battle after the damage that the Easter campaign had inflicted, and he believed that it would capitulate to demands simply at the threat of further demonstrations. On 7 October, King went to Birmingham to make his pitch. He told white authorities that the city must hire 25 black police officers and begin negotiations with the local black community over downtown hiring practices within two weeks or demonstrations would be revived. Two days later, Mayor Albert Boutwell and the City Council turned down King's demands. King headed a rally in Birmingham on 14 October and called upon the black community to press for the hiring of black policemen and to reinstate an economic boycott in the city. On 21 October, local blacks voted to renew demonstrations. The following day, the City Council again refused to entertain the movement's demands.

King was desperate to claim victory in Birmingham, realising that defeat in a place that had become a symbol of his and the movement's success to date would be a major blow. However, one lesson King had learned from campaigns in Albany and in Birmingham was the need to understand when to cut his losses in order to avoid a damaging protracted defeat. His bluff had been called in Birmingham and there was little he could do about it. The local black community was also divided about the revival of demonstrations, with many black middle-class leaders directly opposed to them. King therefore announced that he was withdrawing his demand for the appointment of police officers. In an attempt to save face, he asserted that such demands were an obstacle to progress and that the public deadline was limiting the City Council's room for manoeuvre. King said he believed that if the movement relieved the immediate pressure on the City Council, it would be more responsive to its demands. King still threatened a revival of demonstrations if nothing were done. Yet even as King made these new threats he knew that they were totally unfounded. Both blacks and whites in Birmingham understood that King was in fact instigating a tactical retreat rather than staying around to face defeat.

The climbdown in Birmingham meant that King and the SCLC needed to again quickly turn around their fortunes if they were to keep up momentum for change. Before the Sixteenth Street Baptist Church bombing, Danville, Virginia, seemed to be the most likely place for the SCLC's next campaign, and it was to there that attention now turned. C.T. Vivian, the SCLC's affiliates director, and other SCLC staff workers went to Danville in the first week of November only to find the Danville

Christian Progressive Association (DCPA) at loggerheads with the local NAACP over the need for outside help in the local movement. When talks with white city representatives collapsed, the SCLC readied itself to launch a full-scale campaign. The threat of action prompted new talks with members of the City Council, which led to an agreement over a policy of non-discriminatory job hiring and future biracial dialogue. When King arrived on 15 November, he announced that demonstrations would be held in abeyance while negotiations continued. SCLC staff workers continued to organise and to mobilise community support ready to launch a campaign if those negotiations failed.

Just as preparations were being made for an SCLC campaign in Danville, however, another event knocked those plans sideways. On 22 November, President Kennedy was assassinated in Dallas, Texas. King watched the unfolding events on his television screen at home with his wife Coretta. 'This is what is going to happen to me,' King told her. 'I keep telling you, this is such a sick society.'[28] Kennedy's assassination brought home more than ever the risks of public leadership. King often spoke of his own impending death, both in public and in private. Some saw this as simply a rhetorical device to stir the passions of audiences and to exert moral suasion over colleagues about the risks he personally endured for the sake of the movement. In some quarters, there was even talk of a self-aggrandising 'martyr complex', something that King stridently denied. Others saw King's talk of death as a morbid obsession that betrayed his innermost thoughts, fears and genuine anxieties about where the leadership of the movement was taking him.

The Kennedy assassination put paid to the evolving Danville campaign as King announced a month's moratorium on all civil rights demonstrations while the nation mourned the death of the president. As the self-imposed quiet ended in late December, there was little for King and the SCLC to return to. In many places where there had been a burst of black activism over the summer, there was now either exhaustion or defeat. The new college and school years diminished the number of student demonstrators available. Nonviolent campaigns moved into winter hibernation, to be replaced by a concentration on economic boycotts and voter registration. Yet underlining just what an important year it had been for the movement in general, and for King in particular, King received the personal accolade of being awarded *Time* magazine's 1963 'Man of the Year Award'.

At the beginning of 1964, King arranged a three-day retreat for senior SCLC staff members at Black Mountain, North Carolina. Two plans germinated at the retreat. Firstly, with regard to the passage of the civil rights bill, Wyatt Walker suggested focusing a nonviolent, direct-action campaign on Washington, DC, accompanied by a Gandhi-like fast by King to counterpoint a possible filibuster by southern politicians.[29] When the idea of a fast was put to the SCLC board in April, King told them that he had 'not yet decided how far I will go – whether unto death'.[30] Secondly, the Bevel proposal for a nonviolent assault on Alabama, appropriately toned down and with an increased emphasis on voter registration, met with favour. Bevel worked on drawing up detailed plans for the campaign, which were approved at the Alabama SCLC affiliates meeting in Montgomery on 4 and 5 March. At a 4 May meeting in Atlanta, the SCLC's executive staff discussed the Bevel plan, along with plans for nonviolent, direct-action campaigns in Washington, DC, and St. Augustine, Florida.

The final decision over which course of action the SCLC should take rested, as always, with King. Although supportive of the Bevel plan, King felt that complications still existed about how it could be effectively implemented. To make the proposal work the SCLC needed an effective base from which to mobilise support, but this was not the case in Alabama. The SCLC could not risk going back to Birmingham, having already retreated from there once. There was little support in Montgomery, where more conservative black leaders now dominated the MIA and the black population showed little enthusiasm to revisit the mass activism of the bus boycott. Selma was a possible target, but SNCC was already heavily involved in that community and a campaign of the magnitude suggested by Bevel could not risk interorganisational conflict. With conditions in Alabama still stalling the Bevel plan, and with plans for demonstrations in Washington, DC, still being formulated, King opted to concentrate the SCLC's immediate attention and resources on initiating a civil rights campaign in St. Augustine, Florida.

The St. Augustine Campaign

The SCLC campaign in St. Augustine was instigated to keep the movement's demands for racial justice in the headlines and to thereby keep attention focused on the need to pass the civil rights bill currently before Congress. The campaign also sought to build momentum for demonstrations planned later that year to enforce the new law if, as expected, the bill was passed. St. Augustine looked like a promising target for such a campaign. Although the city government was deeply committed to segregation, there was also a spirited protest movement in existence, led by Robert Hayling, a black dentist and adviser to the local NAACP Youth Council. Moreover, local black activists were eager to enlist the SCLC's help. Importantly, the city was susceptible to the type of nonviolent campaign run by the SCLC. Billing itself as 'America's Oldest City', St. Augustine was gearing up for its quadricentennial celebrations in 1965 and was looking for federal grants to help restore its old buildings in expectation of a bumper tourism bonanza for local businesses. With the city wishing to promote tourism, to lure federal funds, and to extend a welcome to visitors from the north, the last thing that it wanted was racial unrest and national headlines that would bring adverse publicity.

There were, however, potential problems with running a campaign in St. Augustine. Robert Hayling was a dedicated but controversial black leader who did not have extensive support in the local black community. Complicating matters further was the fact that Hayling was a determined advocate of black armed self-defence who promised to 'shoot first and ask questions later' if harassed by whites.[31] Hayling's stance, coupled with an active Ku Klux Klan in the area, was a potentially explosive mix. In September 1963, Hayling and three other blacks were severely beaten while trying to observe a Klan rally. Four weeks later, when armed whites rode through a black neighbourhood late at night, a shot rang out and killed one of them. The finger of guilt was pointed at Hayling's NAACP compatriot Goldie Eubanks, who along with three other blacks was indicted for murder. Although not convicted, Eubanks, along with Hayling, was forced to resign from the NAACP. The violence led to Florida governor C. Farris Bryant sending state highway patrolmen into St. Augustine to restore and to maintain law and order, and the setting up of a Grand Jury to investigate events. The Grand Jury report was critical of the role played by Hayling, but it recommended the establishment of a biracial committee to address persistent racial problems in the city. Despite these measures, white attacks on the black community continued.

The SCLC's first reconnaissance trip to St. Augustine came early in 1964. Over Easter, members of the SCLC-affiliated Massachusetts Christian Leadership Conference engaged in demonstrations organised by SCLC staff members Hosea Williams and Bernard Lee. This outside help, in turn, stimulated greater efforts from the local black community. From Saturday, 28 March, through to Monday, 30 March, demonstrations and arrests escalated in the city. One particularly newsworthy event was the arrest of Mrs Malcolm Peabody, a 72-year-old demonstrator who was the mother of Massachusetts governor Endicott Peabody. 'The Peabody arrest', notes historian of the St. Augustine movement David Colburn, drew the 'nation's attention to racial conditions [in St. Augustine] as no other incident had.'[32] The high-profile arrest brought front-page coverage in the *New York Times* and a report on the *Today* television show. Though the initial foray was simply meant as a quick strike on segregation, it brought an unwelcome notoriety to St. Augustine. Ominously, however, the city's white power structure remained unmoved by events. Mayor Joseph Shelly declared that 'people like the Peabodys live in exclusive suburbs. They don't practice what they preach. They are hypocrites.'[33] Interviewed on the *Today* show, Shelly complained that St. Augustine had been 'picked on because we were celebrating our four-hundredth anniversary'.[34]

SCLC assistant programme director John Gibson subsequently went to St. Augustine to draw up plans for a more extensive campaign there. Since his initial report back to Wyatt Walker met with little enthusiasm, Gibson took his plan straight to King, who was more impressed with the city's potential for demonstrations. King described St. Augustine as a 'small Birmingham'.[35] When Walker was sent to St. Augustine to investigate, performing one of his last tasks for the SCLC before moving on to a new post in New York, he became more excited about a campaign in the city. The enthusiasm of local activists and the vulnerability of St. Augustine because of its dependency on tourism both augured well, but, Walker warned, there was a need for more discipline and a greater emphasis on nonviolence in the local movement. It was also unclear exactly how white city officials would react to demonstrations, and Walker warned of the need to tread carefully to see what kind of opposition might develop.

King launched the St. Augustine campaign on 26 May 1964, telling movement supporters that the SCLC planned a 'long, hot, nonviolent summer' for the city.[36] Afterwards, a march was held to the old slave market downtown, a highly symbolic site of many of the SCLC's demonstrations in St. Augustine. Another march followed the next night. The idea of marching at night was an innovation proposed by Hosea Williams, who had pioneered the tactic as a local movement leader in Savannah before being recruited on to the SCLC's staff. The night setting in the old, winding and darkened streets of St. Augustine increased the likelihood of a confrontation with the Klan, setting up a dramatic point of conflict to expose the ugly face of white racism in the city. Though hostile whites gathered to jeer the marchers, the local police managed to maintain order.

However, at a third march, on 28 May, a more hostile situation developed and the Klan attacked several white news reporters covering events. Later that night, bullets ripped through the cottage hired for King during his stays in St. Augustine, although he was out of the city at the time. King's white administrative aide Harry Boyte had the back window of his parked car shattered by a bullet. King sent a telegram to President Johnson, who as Kennedy's vice president had succeeded him in office, informing him that 'all semblance of law and order has broken down at St. Augustine, Florida . . . we have witnessed raw and rampant violence even beyond much of what we have experienced in Alabama and Mississippi.' He requested immediate federal protection.[37] The following night, local police turned back an SCLC march. Movement attorneys headed for the courts, petitioning federal district judge Bryan Simpson to protect the constitutional rights of the marchers to peacefully assemble, and to investigate complaints about the collusion of local law enforcement officers with members of the local Ku Klux Klan.

At the federal court hearing on 1 June in Jacksonville, Florida, Judge Simpson pressed Sheriff L.O. Davis about allegations of Klan involvement in St. Augustine's law enforcement. The judge was especially interested in the role of Holstead 'Hoss' Mauncy, leader of the 1,500-strong 'Ancient City Gun Club', whom Davis had deputised into police service. Though Mauncy told the court he thought that the Klan was a 'wonderful organ-ization', he denied any direct affiliation with it. Still, he insisted, 'We're better organized than the niggers and the niggers know it.'[38] When the hearing ended on 3 June, Simpson asked movement attorneys if the SCLC would suspend their night marches until he handed down his ruling. The SCLC agreed. The following day, King spoke at a rally in St. Augustine and vowed that demonstrations on a much larger scale would be held if the city continued to refuse to act to better racial conditions. He declared that 'Soon the Klan will see that all of their violence will not stop us, for we are on the way to freedom land and we don't mean to stop until we get there.'[39] After King departed, a fire gutted his rented cottage. In anticipation of more trouble, Robert Hayling began arming his followers. King was deeply disturbed at the news of Hayling's activ-ities, but with threats on his life circulating in the city, an armed guard remained close by him every night he spent in the town.

On 9 June, Judge Simpson ruled in favour of the SCLC, stating that movement marches should be allowed and that it was the job of the local police to provide protection for them. At the news of the ruling, King announced that 'We are determined the city will not celebrate its quadri-centennial as a segregated city. There will be no turning back.'[40] That night, SCLC programme director Andrew Young led a march of three hundred people downtown. Twenty whites broke through police lines to attack the demonstrators. King again implored President Johnson to act.

Johnson's aide Lee White received assurances from Governor Bryant that the situation was under control. The news was passed on to movement representatives in St. Augustine. Yet when Young and C.T. Vivian led two hundred marchers downtown the night of 10 June, they met a waiting crowd of six hundred whites and faced a hail of rocks. Florida highway patrolmen used tear gas to disperse the white mob.

The following day, King, Abernathy and Bernard Lee were arrested at the segregated Monson Motor Lodge for refusing to leave the premises when asked to do so. After his arraignment the next day, King secretly testified before a Grand Jury set up to investigate the racial conflict in St. Augustine. King's appearance, at the initiative of state circuit attorney Dan Warren, was an attempt to get the Grand Jury to act in appointing a biracial committee to meet one of the movement's central demands and to bring the marches to a halt. After spending a night in jail, King was released on bail on Saturday, 13 June.

As King was released from jail, the shortcomings of St. Augustine as a site for an SCLC campaign were becoming apparent. The strength of the local Ku Klux Klan deterred many local black volunteers from participation in demonstrations. The dependency of large numbers of blacks on the local white population for their jobs in the unskilled and low-paid sectors of the tourist industry also prohibited much public local black support for the movement. This reticence mattered acutely in St. Augustine, where the black population, standing at only around 5,000 out of a total population of around 20,000, was relatively small anyway. Moreover, there were doubts among local blacks about Hayling's leadership of the movement, and the SCLC's tactics, which some saw as needlessly provoking Klan violence. All of this meant that the movement in St. Augustine was relying disproportionately on the SCLC's outside help.

Judge Simpson once again came to the SCLC's aid. On 15 June, he rejected a request from Florida's attorney general to ban marches and reaffirmed his earlier ruling that it was the duty of the state to protect march participants. Governor Bryant, prompted by this rebuke, placed local law enforcement officials under the control of the Florida state highway patrol. Marches on the nights of 16 and 17 June passed without violence. It seemed that the appointment of a biracial committee by the Grand Jury was imminent, with the SCLC and local white businessmen both endorsing the measure. However, on the afternoon of 18 June, when the Grand Jury's recommendations were set to be handed down, an integrated group of seven demonstrators held a 'swim-in' at the Monson Motor Lodge swimming pool, infuriating owner James Brock. Brock poured pool-cleaning chemicals into the water in an attempt to remove the demonstrators. They only finally left when an off-duty city policeman jumped into the pool to physically remove them. One report stated that King, watching the swim-in from across the street, had declared that 'we are going to put the Monson out of business'.[41] Exactly why the seemingly ill-timed demonstration took place is unclear, although it may have related to the previous day's news that the civil rights bill had finally passed through Congress and was now just awaiting the president to sign the bill into law. Under those circumstances, King may have felt that the movement could hold out for more concessions in St. Augustine.

Florida senator Verle Pope told reporters that 'We can't understand why they hit us like this when we were working sincerely on the thing.'[42] The Grand Jury rewrote its recommendations in a much less favourable light. It insisted that King and the movement call a 30-day cessation to demonstrations to prove their commitment to seeking a solution to the city's problems before a ten-member biracial committee was formed. King found these terms unacceptable. He felt that it asked 'the Negro community to give all and the white community to give nothing'.[43] King knew full well from previous experience that calling off demonstrations with only the promise of future action risked completely undermining a campaign. Instead, King offered to cease demonstrations for one week if a biracial committee was appointed immediately. The Grand Jury rejected his proposal. On the evening of 19 June, two hundred people marched downtown and Andrew Young, C.T. Vivian and Hosea Williams were arrested. In response, Governor Bryant issued an Executive Order banning marches from taking place between 8.30 p.m. and sunrise, in the hope of putting an end to the disruptive night marches.

As the movement challenged the order in the courts, it took its campaign to the beaches. Since St. Augustine's beaches were already desegregated, this placed further responsibility for upholding the law on the state and caused a great deal of disruption. The tactic also helped depleted movement funds by saving the bail money that would be needed for the inevitable arrests if segregated downtown facilities were targeted. When whites gathered at the beach to attack black bathers, highway patrolmen were forced to wade into the water to prevent violence. This was made more difficult by the fact that some whites 'greased-up' their bodies to evade the clutches of the law. Before long, clubs were being used by the lawmen to prevent white attacks. 'Those finks!' cried one white woman, criticising the highway patrolmen. 'They didn't even beat the niggers at all.'[44] As a later Florida legislative investigation into events noted, the demonstrations were 'a planned and stage-managed propaganda production for nationwide consumption', much like a 'good T.V. show'.[45] The observation was meant as a criticism. For the movement it was a compliment, since this is exactly what the demonstrations were attempting to achieve. The new spate of activism came to a head on 24 June, when the Ku Klux Klan held a rally in downtown St. Augustine. Movement participants marched towards the rally, resulting in pitched battles between highway patrolmen and the Klan.

The new clashes led to a new round of talks. As Judge Simpson began his hearings over the ban on marching imposed by Governor Bryant, the governor was engaged in talks with St. Augustine banker Herbert Wolfe to try to put an end to demonstrations. Florida senator George Smathers called the two men to impress upon them the view from Washington, DC, that a biracial committee should be formed. King enlisted the help of four of his former Boston University professors to help with negotiations and they were busy talking with state circuit attorney Dan Warren in Jacksonville. Warren was still put out by King's rejection of the Grand Jury's earlier proposals, but agreed to meet with him in secret. According to Warren, King told him, 'I want out of St. Augustine, but I can't go out of here a loser.'[46] With the civil rights bill passed by Congress, King and the SCLC had achieved their goal in St. Augustine and they were ready to leave. However, they felt that they could not do so without securing some tangible local gains. The appointment of a biracial committee, King indicated, would ensure the SCLC's departure.

Efforts to form a four-member biracial committee continued over the weekend and looked to be making progress. However, the recalcitrance of some local officials, especially Mayor Shelly, who had opposed the formation of a biracial committee all along, threatened the whole plan. Shelly called Bryant, adamant that he would not make any concessions to demonstrators. The next morning, local officials brought charges against Hayling, King and John Gibson for contributing to the delinquency of minors by recruiting students for their demonstrations.

Just as the struggle in St. Augustine looked set to escalate, Governor Bryant announced that a four-member biracial committee had been formed. He said that the committee would serve for 30 days until the Grand Jury could appoint a larger, more representative body. All four members of the committee, Bryant told reporters, had agreed to serve. Heartened by the news, Hayling and King agreed to suspend demonstrations for two weeks to allow negotiations to get under way. Mayor Shelly called Bryant, fuming at the governor's apparent subterfuge. Eventually, Bryant confided that in fact no committee existed, but that the false announcement was the easiest way out of the current situation.

Historian David Colburn insists that King knew full well that the 'biracial committee was a fraud', but that King, like Bryant, was driven by an eagerness to resolve the ongoing crisis.[47] King was due at the signing ceremony of the 1964 Civil Rights Act at the White House, and plans to test the new law in Alabama were already well advanced. What had been intended as short-lived campaign in St. Augustine was promising to drag on without resolution and drain the SCLC's resources with little return. King therefore played along with Bryant's ruse. The movement dropped its complaints against Bryant and other officials. King told reporters that he was hopeful about the situation and that he would be back to lead demonstrations if things did not progress.

Exactly what King and the SCLC achieved in St. Augustine is a matter of debate. Though King claimed otherwise, there was little evidence that the campaign swayed any votes in Congress with regard to the civil rights bill. Locally, the SCLC brought Klan activity in St. Augustine out into the open, resulting in state if not federal intervention, with Governor Bryant and Judge Simpson moved to lend protection to the black community. The pressure helped soften the attitudes of the white business community, which eventually voted to comply with the terms of the 1964 Civil Rights Act, although pointedly only after King and the SCLC left. Yet the shortcomings of the campaign were also evident. King and the SCLC had failed to secure the federal intervention they desired. Moreover, the SCLC had provoked Klan violence but had failed in its efforts to build a strong local black movement, leaving the black community in St. Augustine vulnerable to recriminations after the SCLC's departure. Even the eventual desegregation of public facilities did little to address the core economic problems of a local black population that remained 'poor, dependent and oppressed'.[48] 'If there is the suggestion that SCLC exploited the local Birmingham situation, the suggestion was even stronger in St. Augustine,' wrote journalist Pat Watters. King's explanation that 'Some communities, like this one, have to bear the cross' to win national and regional gains for the movement did little to placate local blacks. When King offered to return to St. Augustine in 1965 for demonstrations to coincide with the quadricentennial celebrations, local blacks told him not to bother. As one local black leader put it, 'I don't want him back here now. He left us with a sick city and his coming back would kill it.'[49] As King and the SCLC perfected their technique of forcing national concessions through local campaigns, more people in the civil rights movement became concerned that as an increasingly national-oriented leader, King was neglecting the needs of local communities and of local people. For King, the balancing act between the needs of the national civil rights movement and the needs of local civil rights movements was becoming ever more difficult to maintain, as events later that year highlighted.

The 1964 Civil Rights Act, the Mississippi Freedom Democratic Party (MFDP) and the Nobel Peace Prize

On 2 July, King attended the signing ceremony of the 1964 Civil Rights Act that contained the crucial clause providing for the desegregation of public facilities and accommodations. At the signing ceremony, President Johnson made it clear to civil rights leaders that, particularly with a presidential election in the offing in November, he expected the Civil Rights Act to put an end to mass demonstrations since blacks could now pursue desegregation through the courts. Seemingly ignoring Johnson's request, King met with SCLC staff members and the SCLC's Alabama affiliates in Birmingham on 6 July, intent upon implementing a revised Bevel plan to test public facilities in the state. Yet, despite the expected resistance to the new law in Alabama, when the testing of facilities got under way there was a surprising amount of compliance in many places. Only Tuscaloosa and Selma offered significant resistance.

With the 1964 Civil Rights Act appearing to make its intended impact, King's attention turned to the forthcoming presidential elections. It was clear that the outcome of the election would be important for the continuing success of the civil rights movement. Since the outburst of black activism following the Birmingham campaign in the summer of 1963, a 'white backlash' to civil rights demonstrations had been gathering. Harnessing this latent, deeply conservative national racial sentiment among some sections of the population, Alabama governor George Wallace ran a campaign for nomination as the Democratic Party's presidential candidate. Although the possibility of defeating incumbent Lyndon Johnson seemed unlikely, Wallace polled a significant number of votes in the presidential primary elections in many states. Encouraged by this, the Republican Party sought to exploit the same constituency of voters that Wallace had tapped. Right-wing Arizona senator Barry Goldwater emerged as the Republicans' favoured candidate. Goldwater had voted against the 1964 Civil Rights Act and was preparing for an election battle against Johnson on an anti-civil rights platform. On 7 July, King appeared before the platform committee of the Republican National Convention to put forward his case for a more enlightened civil rights policy. His plea fell on deaf ears. The Republicans chose Goldwater as their presidential candidate regardless. King made no bones about his feelings for Goldwater, labelling the Republican choice 'unfortunate and disastrous', and warning that from the civil rights movement's point of view, Goldwater's candidacy was 'morally indefensible and socially suicidal'.[50]

One of the most important civil rights initiatives during the 1964 presidential election year was the 'Freedom Summer' in Mississippi. While the SCLC concentrated on launching a campaign in Alabama, SNCC, the dominant organisation in the Council of Federated Organizations (COFO) coordinating the Mississippi campaign, concentrated its field staff in Mississippi where, aided by an influx of white student volunteers from northern colleges, it embarked upon a massive voter-education and voter-registration campaign. As historians John Dittmer and Charles Payne have noted, in doing so SNCC built upon a long and rich indigenous tradition of civil rights activism and community organising. Many people in the movement saw Mississippi as the epitome of white resistance to racial progress in the South, and SNCC encountered violent opposition in its efforts to build black political power in the state. Freedom Summer captured the national headlines in June 1964 with the disappearance of three young civil rights workers, two white New Yorkers, Michael Schwerner and Andrew Goodman, and black Mississippian James Chaney. The discovery of their burnt-out car in a Mississippi swamp confirmed the movement's worst fears that the three had been murdered. President Johnson ordered the FBI to investigate. SNCC continued its efforts to create a Mississippi Freedom Democratic Party (MFDP). Insisting that the regular Mississippi Democratic Party was illegitimate because of electoral corruption in the state, which included the widespread denial of black voting rights, SNCC held its own more inclusive 'Freedom Vote' to elect a different slate of delegates from Mississippi to attend the 1964 Democratic National Convention.

On 21 July, King began a five-day tour of Mississippi in a show of support for SNCC's efforts there. Threats against King's life hung over his visit. Though such threats were ever-present, they were taken seriously enough in Mississippi for President Johnson to order personal FBI protection for King while he was there. King called Freedom Summer 'one of the most creative attempts I had seen to radically challenge the oppressive life of the Negro'.[51] After a successful tour of Mississippi, King responded to a call from New York mayor Robert Wagner to help quell the racial violence that had erupted in the city after the shooting of a black youth by a white policeman. Talks with the mayor produced little progress. As yet, King and the SCLC only possessed a rudimentary grasp of the issues effecting blacks in the north. It was not until the SCLC's

1966 Chicago campaign that they became more aware of the fact that the north was in many ways a very different proposition, in terms of the struggle for civil rights, from the South.

More problems arose on 29 July, when King met with other civil rights leaders at a meeting arranged by the NAACP's Roy Wilkins in New York. Wilkins, following up on the earlier remarks of President Johnson, proposed a cessation of demonstrations until after the presidential election. Doing this, Wilkins argued, would prevent handing Republican presidential candidate Barry Goldwater ammunition to use against the pro-civil rights Johnson. King, along with Bayard Rustin, A. Philip Randolph and Whitney Young of the National Urban League, all agreed with Wilkins. CORE's James Farmer and SNCC's John Lewis both refused to endorse the plan. After the New York meeting, King's attention focused on the Democratic National Convention at Atlantic City, New Jersey, and attempts to seat the MFDP delegation. King was hopeful of a personal meeting with Johnson to discuss the convention, but when his request eventually evolved into a general audience with civil rights leaders he declined to attend. His decision turned out to be the right one. At the meeting on 19 August, Johnson browbeat the black delegation, refusing to discuss the convention and instead delivering a monologue on his administration's civil rights achievements. King's decision not to attend left him able to oppose Johnson's wishes for muting civil rights issues at the convention without a prior direct confrontation.

Just before the start of the 1964 Democratic National Convention, on 20 August 1964 Congress passed the Economic Opportunity Act (EOA), the centrepiece of Johnson's planned War on Poverty and an integral part of the president's desire to create a Great Society in the United States. Building upon and extending the programmes already initiated by the Kennedy administration to tackle poverty, the EOA, passed in the face of stiff Republican opposition, created the Office of Economic Opportunity (OEO) to coordinate various local and state anti-poverty programmes in areas such as social services, health services, education and employment. The anti-poverty programmes were required to promote 'maximum feasible participation' by the poor in them, a term that appeared to borrow much from SNCC's grassroots organising philosophy. The anti-poverty programmes proved highly controversial in terms of the amount of money spent on them, their administration and their overall effectiveness. Yet clearly, given the problems of poverty that disproportionately affected blacks in the United States, the federally funded programmes held out at least the promise of a better life and raised black expectations. Ultimately, however, the War on Poverty would only fuel black frustration and anger when anti-poverty programmes proved to be chronically underfunded, in part because of the escalating cost of fighting the Vietnam War. Despite its eventual shortcomings, the passage of the EOA indicated that Johnson was a socially progressive president and therefore a potential ally of the civil rights movement – certainly more so than Republican presidential candidate Barry Goldwater. Yet the conservative opposition to the EOA in Congress underlined just how politically delicate passing such legislation and supporting such a programme was. As a wily politician, Johnson understood the need to cultivate enough conservative support to win re-election and to be able to pass such legislation in Congress. It was within this conflicted political context that the 1964 Democratic National Convention unfolded.

The MFDP challenge to be seated at the convention instead of the regular Mississippi Democratic Party delegation began when the Democratic Party Credentials Committee held a hearing on the matter on Saturday, 22 August. The MFDP's 68 delegates, four of them white, included a representative sample of 'black, white, maids, ministers, carpenters, farmers, painters, mechanics, schoolteachers, the young, [and] the old' in Mississippi.[52] In front of the Credentials Committee, MFDP leaders, their white Washington, DC, attorney Joseph L. Rauh Jr and King, all argued for the seating of the MFDP delegation in the face of the discriminatory practices that had allowed the regular all-white state delegation to be elected. King told the Credentials Committee that 'if you value the future of democratic government, you have no alternative but to recognize, with full voice and vote, the [MFDP]'. MFDP delegate Fannie Lou Hamer gave an emotional account of the brutalities taking place against blacks in Mississippi that was broadcast live to the nation on television. She asked the Credentials Committee, 'Is this America, the land of the free and the home of the brave, where we have to sleep with our telephones off the hooks because our lives are threatened daily, because we want to live as decent human beings, in America?'[53] The Johnson administration hastily arranged a televised presidential press conference to remove Hamer's powerful testimony from the airwaves.

On Sunday, 23 August, Oregon congresswoman Edith Green proposed a solution to the problem by offering to seat any member of either of Mississippi's two delegations if they first swore a loyalty oath to the Democratic Party and its presidential ticket. The proposal highlighted the manifest irony of the situation. The MFDP delegates were all able to accept these terms since they supported Johnson, as a civil rights advocate, to stand against Republican Goldwater in the general election. None of the all-white Mississippi delegation could accept these terms since they supported Goldwater and his opposition to civil rights and they were fully prepared to back the Republican candidate in the general election rather than a pro-civil rights Democratic Party candidate. Yet such were the convoluted politics of the time that Johnson believed seating the MFDP delegates would be too clear a sign of his support for civil rights, which would boost Goldwater's anti-civil rights appeal and risk alienating southern Democratic congressmen and white southern voters.

The MFDP needed the votes of eleven Credentials Committee members to take their case to a vote before the whole convention. Pro-MFDP forces campaigned to win these crucial votes while Johnson's aides tried to swing committee members around to their way of thinking. SNCC worker Courtland Cox recounts the pressure placed on the Credentials Committee by the Johnson administration as 'something unbelievable. Every person on the list, every member of that Credentials Committee who was going to vote for the minority, got a call. They said "Your husband is up for a judgeship, and if you don't shape up, he won't get it. You're up for a loan. If you don't shape up, you won't get it."'[54]

As Johnson's people worked at undermining the Green proposal, they approached the MFDP with a compromise of their own. The proposal was to seat two out of the 68 MFDP delegates and to give them 'at large' convention votes (that is, they would be allowed to vote, but not as Mississippi delegates). The rest of the MFDP delegates would be seated as guests of the convention but would not be allowed to cast votes. Furthermore, only those in the all-white delegation who took a loyalty oath would be allowed to cast their votes and the Democratic Party would undertake to eliminate all discrimination in delegate selection procedures by the 1968 Democratic National Convention. Although the MFDP delegation refused to accept the compromise and continued to lobby for the preferred Green proposal, it was Johnson's plan that the Credentials Committee voted through over the protests of the MFDP and their attorney.

The outcome of the vote narrowed the MFDP's options considerably. There was now only one decision to be made. They could either accept the two-seat compromise offered by Johnson or withdraw from the convention altogether. King was placed in a difficult situation on Tuesday, 25 August, when he discussed the situation with supportive members of the Credentials Committee, Bayard Rustin, SNCC's James Forman, MFDP attorney Joseph Rauh and MFDP leaders. Reflecting on the hard-learned lessons of the past about the need for compromise, many in the SCLC, along with Rustin and Rauh, were ready to counsel the MFDP to accept the Johnson proposal as a victory of sorts, even though it by no means granted everything that the MFDP had set out to achieve. MFDP delegates opposed any compromise on the grounds that they would be betraying the ideals of all those who had worked for, voted for, and in some cases had even given their lives for, the MFDP cause. King was torn between the arguments of political pragmatism that as a national leader he fully understood, and the political idealism of grassroots activists with which he also strongly empathised. King awkwardly told MFDP leaders that as a national black leader he wanted them to accept the compromise, 'but if I were a Mississippi Negro, I would vote against it'.[55] He thereby left the difficult decision to MFDP delegates.

Others were less equivocal than King in their insistence that the MFDP delegation should accept the compromise. The heated arguments that flew around the room only served to highlight growing movement divisions between national leaders with national goals and local leaders who were committed to fighting for change in their own communities. The debate also brought to the fore class divisions in a movement with a largely black middle-class national leadership but with a largely black working-class, grassroots constituency. As usual, the most blunt of all the national leaders was the NAACP's Roy Wilkins, who told MFDP delegates that 'You all are ignorant. You have put your point across. You should just pack your bags up and go home.'[56] Fannie Lou Hamer, speaking for the Mississippi grassroots membership, criticised black middle-class leaders like Wilkins, declaring, 'Give em two dollars and a car and they think they're fine . . . [but] we didn't come all the way up here to compromise for no more than we'd gotten here . . . We didn't come all this way for two seats.'[57] SNCC's James Forman felt that Wilkins's speech was typical of what he called the NAACP's 'fuck-the-people' stance.[58] Forman further criticised SCLC leaders like King and Andrew Young, telling them that 'While you niggers been staying in fancy hotels eating chicken, we been sleeping on floors in Mississippi . . . Y'all come through with nice cars, make a speech and run back to your fancy churches in Atlanta. It's bullshit!' Andrew Young urged the MFDP to choose pragmatism over idealism, adopting Forman's earthy language to tell him that 'If you win a seat for every nigger in Mississippi at this convention and Goldwater gets elected in November, you have gained nothing.'[59]

One of the things that rankled with the MFDP was the fact that the Johnson proposal dictated very specific terms. The proposal insisted that the MFDP could have just two delegates seated and it explicitly named who those two delegates would be: black MFDP chair Aaron Henry and white college chaplain Edwin King. In an effort to modify this proposal, and to stamp some authority on proceedings, MFDP leaders including Aaron Henry, Edwin King and Robert Moses, along with King and Andrew

Young of the SCLC, met with potential vice-presidential nominee Hubert Humphrey and United Auto Workers' president Walter Reuther to discuss alternative arrangements. Two proposals put forward were the seating of all 68 delegates and then giving each of them a fraction of a vote, or seating four delegates with half a vote each. Hubert Humphrey warned Rustin that in the light of her earlier impassioned speech, under no circumstances would 'The President . . . allow that illiterate woman [Fannie Lou Hamer] to speak from the floor of the convention.'⁶⁰ With discussions still continuing, the Democratic National Convention chair, Rhode Island senator John Pastore, appeared on the television screen that was broadcasting events live from the convention floor. Pastore falsely announced that the MFDP had already accepted Johnson's proposed two-vote compromise. Robert Moses stormed out of the meeting with Humphrey and Reuther, pausing only to turn to Humphrey to tell him, 'You cheated.'⁶¹

Johnson's duplicity enraged the MFDP delegates, who the following day voted to reject the two-seat compromise and left Atlantic City. That evening, Johnson received his party's nomination to stand for the presidency and Hubert Humphrey made up the Democratic ticket as the party's nominee for vice president. For SNCC, the events of the convention left a bitter aftertaste. Having worked through legitimate democratic channels to make their voices heard, only to then have their efforts undermined by political skullduggery, marked the final disillusionment with 'the system' for many in SNCC. Ella Baker, who had been in Atlantic City with the MFDP delegation, recalls that these events 'settled any debate [about] the possibility of functioning through the mainstream of the Democratic Party'.⁶² Many felt that the movement's white liberal supporters in the Democratic Party had betrayed them. Equally, many in SNCC and the MFDP felt that they had been betrayed by national black leaders and particularly by King's failure to back their demands strongly. Many commentators have pointed to the episode as a turning point in SNCC's radicalisation, which led to its later embrace of the 'Black Power' slogan.

Ironically, the MFDP's efforts turned out to be more of a victory than was apparent at the time. If the MFDP did not get to take their seats at the delegation, then neither did the all-white Mississippi regulars, who refused to take the required loyalty oath and also walked out of the convention. At the 1968 Democratic National Convention, the Democratic Party kept its promise to instigate reform and barred the all-white regular delegation in favour of seating MFDP delegates. Yet although such victories were important, they did not address the immediate frustrations of grassroots activists in 1964. Events in Atlantic City only served to highlight the very different frameworks within which national and local civil rights movements increasingly operated.

King's activities over the following months only exacerbated the apparent distance between himself and the rank and file of the movement. As a downtrodden SNCC and MFDP headed back to Mississippi to pick up the pieces of the struggle there, King toured Europe with his wife Coretta and Ralph Abernathy, meeting with Berlin mayor Willy Brandt and attending a personal audience with Pope Paul VI in Rome. In October, King was awarded the 1964 Nobel Peace Prize in the Norwegian capital of Oslo. Of course, King's tour was designed to publicise and to benefit the movement as a whole. He accepted the Nobel Prize on behalf of the movement's collective achievements and donated all of the prize money that came with it back to the cause. Yet although King was part of the same movement as SNCC and the MFDP, his activities took him into a very different world where the rewards and glamour appeared far more tangible than the day-to-day struggle at the local level. Under these circumstances, it was difficult for many to believe that King could any longer truly identify with the civil rights movement at the grassroots level. This was further emphasised when King returned from his tour to campaign for Lyndon Johnson, the very man who many black activists believed had betrayed the movement in Atlantic City, in the 1964 presidential election. However, King rightly believed that Johnson's candidacy was far more appealing than the hostility to civil rights demonstrated by Republican presidential candidate Barry Goldwater. On 3 November, Johnson was returned to office with a landslide victory.

King and the FBI

Hard on the heels of the 1964 presidential election, King found himself at the centre of a heated controversy with FBI director J. Edgar Hoover. On 18 November, Hoover labelled King 'the most notorious liar in the country' in an interview with women journalists.[63] Hoover cited complaints from King over the FBI's conduct in Albany as the reason for his comments. However, Hoover's off-the-record utterance afterwards that King was 'one of the lowest characters in the country' revealed a much more deep-seated personal dislike of King.[64] As early as 1962, Hoover had made up his mind that 'King is no good' and often referred to him derogatorily in private as the 'burrhead'.[65] King replied to Hoover's comments at the press conference with a telegram that attempted to kill Hoover's comments with kindness while defending King's own earlier comments. King said he believed that Hoover must have been 'under extreme pressure' to make such a statement and expressed 'nothing but sympathy for this man who has served his country so well'. Nevertheless, King pointed out the numerous shortcomings of the FBI's civil rights record that seemed more than ample justification for any past complaints. In private, FBI wiretaps picked up King's true feelings that Hoover was getting 'old and senile' and that he should be 'hit from all sides' by an SCLC publicity counteroffensive.[66] In a meeting with President Johnson the day after the story broke, all the other major civil rights leaders defended King against Hoover's accusations. This did not prevent Hoover, at a speech on 22 November at Loyola University in Chicago, referring to certain 'pressure groups' headed by 'Communists and moral degenerates'.[67]

King's closest advisers were divided about how to respond to Hoover's attack. Some counselled a forceful counter-attack while others cautioned him about the potential for a public battle with Hoover to do more harm than good. King eventually took Stanley Levison's advice for a third solution of setting up a meeting with Hoover to discuss their differences face to face. With the help of Acting Attorney General Nicholas Katzenbach (Robert Kennedy had vacated the post to run for a US Senate seat in New York), a meeting was arranged. On 31 November, Andrew Young, Ralph Abernathy and Walter Fauntroy, a Washington, DC, pastor who often served as the SCLC's contact in the city, accompanied King to the meeting. Given the circumstances surrounding it, the meeting proved quite amicable. One of Hoover's assistant directors, Cartha 'Deke' DeLoach, labelled it a 'love feast'.[68] King started the meeting on a conciliatory note, stating that many of his reported criticisms of the FBI were false and that he acknowledged the importance of having a good working relationship with Hoover and his agents. Hoover's response was an almost hour-long ('You know, he talks a hell of a lot, J. Edgar Hoover,' Robert Kennedy once noted), rambling account of all the FBI's efforts on behalf of the movement.[69] King only interjected once to inform Hoover of the SCLC's planned campaign in Selma, Alabama, scheduled for the beginning of 1965.

The meeting ended with an agreement on both sides not to reveal the contents of their discussion to news reporters. However, the pleasantries achieved very little since they failed to address the core disagreements between the two men. Neither did the meeting bring any let-up in the efforts of the FBI to besmirch King's name. Indeed, even as the two men spoke the FBI had already hatched its most devious plot yet against King. On 2 November, FBI assistant director William C. Sullivan ordered a taped compilation of the 'highlights' of the FBI's covert surveillance, which allegedly contained 'dirty jokes and bawdy remarks ... plus the sound of people engaging in sex' – presumably including King – to be sent to the SCLC headquarters. The package contained a note that invited King to 'look into your heart. You know you are a complete fraud and a great liability to all of us Negroes' (Sullivan was, of course, white), and ended with a thinly veiled threat to make the tape's revelations public if King did not commit suicide or withdraw from public life before Christmas.[70] The package was not opened until Coretta discovered its contents at their family home in Atlanta on 4 January 1965. Neither Coretta, who later dismissed the tape as 'just a lot of mumbo jumbo', or friends pressed King on the tape's contents.[71] Still, the tape succeeded in rattling King, who confided to a friend that he believed the FBI were 'out to get me, harass me, break my spirit'.[72] Efforts to confront the FBI over the material met with flat denials about the organisation's involvement.

Subsequent revelations about King's sex life by both historians and SCLC contemporaries, notably Ralph Abernathy, alleging that he had mistresses in several cities and a long string of casual affairs, seem to indicate the possible authenticity of the FBI tape. The FBI also appears to have offered salacious stories about King to several newspaper editors at the time, only to have them refused. Living in an age when the media shows less restraint, the question of whether King's leadership could have survived such revelations if his career had unfolded today is an intriguing one. Certainly, the revelations have been used since King's death to raise questions about his personal integrity. There are ready explanations and excuses for King's actions from his supporters: he was on the road away from his family most of the time; as a handsome and charismatic figure, he had no shortage of temptation placed in his way; and he was under constant stress and strain from movement pressures that were relieved by physical intimacy. Yet King fully understood that his actions were at odds with his own values as a minister and a committed Christian. As such, they caused him personal pain and anguish that sometimes seemed to slip into his public utterances and reflections. 'In our individual and collective lives are a disturbing incompleteness and agonizing partialness,' King ruminated in one sermon. 'Very seldom are we able to affirm greatness in an unqualified sense. Following almost every affirmation of greatness is the cognitive "but." Naamon "was a great man" says the Old Testament, "but – ." That "but" reveals something ... disturbing. "But he was a leper." How much a man's life can be so described!'[73] 'Each of us has two selves,' King mused on another occasion. 'And the great burden of life is always to try to keep the higher self in command. Don't let the lower self take over.'[74] Later,

King suggested that 'God does not judge us by the separate incidents or separate mistakes that we make, but by the total bent of our lives . . . You don't need to go out saying that Martin Luther King is a saint, oh no; I want you to know this morning that I am a sinner like all God's children, but I want to be a good man.'[75] However individuals might view the revelations about the intimate details of King's sex life, perhaps what is ultimately most revealing about them is the reminder that, like most leaders, and like most people, King continually struggled with his own personal and private demons in the midst of his day-to-day battles in his public life.

Chapter 5

A Movement in Transition, 1965–6

King and the SCLC's 1965 Selma campaign marked the culmination of its southern-based Birmingham strategy, which it had developed since 1963. Working alongside SNCC and local people, King and the SCLC ran nonviolent, direct-action demonstrations that led to confrontation and conflict with Alabama state troopers. The violence used against the demonstrations prompted federal intervention in the form of troops on the ground and federal legislation with the introduction of the voting rights bill to Congress, which was later passed as the 1965 Voting Rights Act. The Selma campaign brought more public sympathy, support from northern whites and action from the federal government than any other event in the civil rights movement.

Yet Selma gave way to a period of transition that signalled the drawing to a close of one phase of the civil rights movement and the beginning of another. With two of the central demands of the movement met – the 1964 Civil Rights Act ending segregation in public facilities and accommodations, and the 1965 Voting Rights Act removing obstacles to black voting rights – King, the SCLC and others in the civil rights movement faced the question of what their future goals should be.

As King and the SCLC reflected upon what to do next, it was developments elsewhere that shaped their response to that question. Just five days after President Johnson signed the 1965 Voting Rights Act, one of the worst race riots of the post-war era broke out in Watts, Los Angeles. There had been racial disturbances in several cities the year before and Watts presaged a number of riots that rocked urban areas, particularly in the west and north of the United States, over the following years. Partly as a result of the Watts riot, King and the SCLC launched their first northern-based campaign in Chicago, where they attempted to modify their Birmingham strategy to address the multitudinous problems of the northern black ghetto. While the Chicago campaign was under way, the slogan of 'Black Power' was popularised by new SNCC chair Stokely

Carmichael on the James Meredith-inspired March Against Fear through Mississippi. The slogan quickly gained currency, particularly among militant black youth groups. The outbreak of urban rioting and the emergence of black power highlighted black constituencies that King and the SCLC, by hitherto concentrating on southern small towns and cities, had largely left ignored: the black urban poor and powerless in America's major cities and the black rural poor and powerless in isolated southern communities. Both these groups felt increasingly neglected by the civil rights movement. Indeed, many of those people began openly to question if the goals and tactics of the civil rights movement as King and the SCLC articulated them were, in fact, relevant to them at all.

The Selma Campaign

'Selma, Alabama, was to 1965 what Birmingham was to 1963,' King later reflected.[1] Just as Birmingham represented one of the South's most violent and segregated cities in 1963, Selma was a glaring example of the South's continual widespread denial of black voting rights in 1965. Whites accounted for 99 per cent of the electorate in Selma although they made up only approximately half of the city's 28,500 population. Complicated forms and tests were used to prevent black voter registration. Moreover, voter registration took place on only two days each month. White election officials administered the whole process with extreme racial bias. As a result, pointed out Attorney General Nicholas Katzenbach (appointed on a permanent basis to the post by President Johnson to succeed Robert Kennedy), 'You had black Ph.D.s who couldn't pass a literacy test and you had whites who could barely write their name who had no problem registering to vote.'[2] Outside Selma, in adjacent counties such as Lowndes and Wilcox, the situation was even worse. There, blacks outnumbered whites two to one, but not one single black person was registered to vote.

In conjunction with long-standing local civil rights organisations such as the Dallas County Voters League (the county in which Selma was located) and the more recently founded Dallas County Improvement Association, beginning in February 1963 SNCC had organised two 'Freedom Days' in an effort to register black voters. These efforts had met with staunch white resistance. Police arrested prospective black voters on a variety of charges and state circuit judge James A. Hare issued an injunction against the local movement that virtually outlawed all forms of civil rights activism.

White Selma's stand was not surprising. The city was home to Alabama's first White Citizens' Council and one of the southern cities to offer most resistance to the implementation of the 1964 Civil Rights Act. Dallas County sheriff James G. Clark Jr epitomised white resistance to racial change in Selma in much the same way that Bull Connor did in Birmingham. Along with Colonel Albert J. Lingo, commander of the Alabama state troopers, Clark was part of an anti-civil rights corps under the political tutelage of Alabama governor George Wallace that travelled around the state to crush black protest. Clark relished his role as a defender of segregation and made no attempt whatsoever to hide his preference for brutal policing methods. The SCLC's new executive director Andrew Young, who replaced Wyatt Walker, described Clark as a 'near madman' and SNCC's John Lewis found him 'a very strange character'.[3] Even Selma's white mayor, Joseph T. Smitherman, found Clark's militaristic attire somewhat eccentric: 'he had a helmet like General Patton, he had the clothes, the Eisenhower jacket and the swagger stick'.[4] Like Sheriff L.O. Davis in St. Augustine, Clark had a posse of men – later declared illegally constituted and ordered to disband by the courts – to assist with law enforcement. Clark's posse was over three hundred strong. A hard core of about a hundred, recalls SNCC's James Forman, wore 'old army fatigues, helmets, and boots, and the whole posse was empowered to carry weapons and make arrests', giving them a militia-like status.[5]

Another way that the situation in Selma in 1965 echoed Birmingham in 1963 was the white business community's concern over the city's reputation for rampant racism. As in Birmingham prior to 1963, white businessmen in Selma had also taken some steps to address the situation. Fearing an SCLC campaign in Selma, they had held talks with local black leaders resulting in the removal of segregation signs from water fountains at the downtown courthouse. Selma had recently elected a new, young mayor, Joseph Smitherman, who appeared to support efforts to move towards greater racial moderation. Smitherman had appointed a director of public safety, Wilson Baker, to try to restrain Clark and his posse and to handle any civil rights demonstrations.

King and the SCLC knew that for a campaign to succeed in Selma it would need the full backing of the local black community and of SNCC, which had already laid claim to the city as its territory. However, unlike Albany, SNCC was more receptive to SCLC involvement in the local movement at Selma. As SNCC's campaign faltered, local civil rights leader Amelia Platts Boynton, whose husband S. William Boynton had revived the Dallas County Voters League in 1936, approached King and the

SCLC for assistance. The SNCC begrudgingly acquiesced to the request for King and the SCLC's help. As SNCC communications director Julian Bond explains, 'We would sometimes ask King to go someplace, because we knew the attention he drew would be helpful to the local scene, even if it wasn't helpful to us.' Despite this, Bond and others in SNCC remained ambivalent about the need for King's presence, describing it as 'an irritation'.[6]

When King arrived in Selma on 2 January 1965, he spoke to several hundred people at Brown Chapel AME Church, labelling the city 'a symbol of bitter-end resistance in the South'.[7] King's presence helped to bolster a flagging local movement. Local black lawyer J.L. Chestnut recalls that King 'gave the movement in Selma more legitimacy and raised the confidence factor' among local people.[8] On Monday morning, 18 January, King and SNCC chair John Lewis led four hundred blacks to the county courthouse in an attempt to register them to vote. Scrupulously obeying the letter of law, they walked in groups of no more than four or five to avoid breaking the city's parade ordinance. Sheriff Clark, at the behest of Mayor Smitherman and Director of Public Safety Wilson Baker, acted with restraint, asking the black voter-registration applicants to wait in a nearby alley so that they could be called in one at a time to face the voter-registration tests. Several hours later, however, not one black voter had been registered. Disappointed at the lack of a dramatic confrontation with Clark's men and fearing that Albany-style policing might thwart the movement in Selma, King began to think about taking the struggle for voting rights out to other more hostile surrounding counties in search of a showdown.

By the next day, however, Clark's patience had already run out. Clark told Smitherman and Baker that he had had enough and that he 'was gonna arrest every so-and-so that came up here that day'.[9] When a line of blacks waiting to register to vote at the city courthouse refused to move into a side alley as Clark instructed, the *New York Times* reported, Clark grabbed Amelia Platts Boynton 'by the back of her collar and pushed her roughly for half a block into a patrol car'. Boynton later confessed that at the time she 'didn't know whether I should go limp or whether I should turn around and knock him [Clark] out'.[10] In defence of his actions, Clark pointed out that Boynton 'was a tall woman. It may look like she was a tiny woman from the angle of the cameras, and that I was taking advantage of her.'[11] King was in no doubt about the meaning of the event. He described it as 'one of the most brutal and unlawful acts I have ever seen an officer commit'.[12] Clark's men made over 60 arrests that day. Director of Public Safety Wilson Baker lamented that 'they [the movement] could depend upon him [Clark] from now to do anything they wanted him to do [and] they played him like an expert playing a violin'.[13] A further 150 demonstrators were arrested the following day. On Friday, 22 January, 100 black teachers marched on the courthouse to demonstrate against the unfair voter-registration system. The following day, in response to a suit filed by the NAACP, federal district judge Daniel H. Thomas issued a temporary restraining order against Selma and Dallas County law officials from impeding black voter registration. Yet the following week Sheriff Clark continued in his use of heavy-handed policing. The campaign in Selma gathered further momentum as a result.

James Bevel and other SCLC staff members believed that the time was right to bring the demonstrations to a head by having King submit to arrest. On 1 February, King led several hundred volunteers to the court-house. Wilson Baker, who was aware of the movement's plans, made sure that he was on hand to supervise King's arrest rather than leaving it to Clark. Baker's men halted the march before its arrival at the courthouse and made 260 arrests. Later that day, Clark arrested 700 demonstrators at the courthouse. In a first step to expand the movement to surrounding counties, the SCLC organised a march by 600 blacks in Marion, Perry County, 50 miles from Selma. From a Selma jail cell, King kept in close contact with developments, handing detailed instructions to Andrew Young about what the movement should do next and insisting that demonstrations should not be called off until he had been personally consulted on the decision first.

On Thursday, 4 February, Judge Thomas issued instructions to help facilitate the registration of black voters. These included dropping the existing voter-registration tests, ignoring minor errors on application forms, and registering at least a hundred black voters every day. Thomas also ordered Clark to desist from impeding prospective black voters from assembling at the courthouse. Soon after Thomas's order, President Johnson issued a strong public statement in support of black voting rights. The interventions of Thomas and Johnson left King and the SCLC with a difficult choice to make. If they continued with demonstrations they would stand accused of not giving efforts to improve the situation in Selma a chance to work. However, past experience had shown that if they halted demonstrations they risked the local movement losing momentum and even coming to a standstill. Left in charge, Andrew Young equivocated. Initially, he called Judge Thomas's order 'disappointing' since he felt that it did not go far enough to guarantee black voting rights. Later, he told reporters that King needed time to think about the movement's next move. Finally, Young made the decision to suspend demonstrations.

When Young told King that he had suspended demonstrations, King told him that he had made the wrong decision. King insisted that the SCLC should step up rather than step back from demonstrations and that it should keep up pressure for change for as long as it could. 'Don't be too soft,' King told Young. 'We have the offensive ... In a crisis we must have a sense of drama. Don't let Baker control our movement.'[14] The following morning an advertisement appeared in the *New York Times* titled 'A Letter from Martin Luther King from a Selma, Alabama, Jail'. Explicitly drawing a parallel between events in Selma and the earlier 1963 Birmingham campaign, when King had written his 'Letter From Birmingham City Jail', King appealed for financial contributions to help the movement and pointed out that 'THIS IS SELMA, ALABAMA. THERE ARE MORE NEGROES IN JAIL WITH ME THAN ARE ON THE VOTING ROLLS.'[15]

As historian of the Selma movement Stephen Longenecker notes, 'With King in jail, events in Selma increasingly became national rather than local.'[16] King left jail on 5 February, as planned, on the same day that the *New York Times* advertisement appeared. He announced to reporters that he would be going to Washington, DC, to ask President Johnson for voting rights legislation. During their ten-minute meeting, Johnson assured King that he was already preparing to act in the area of black voting rights.

Back in Selma, the movement was going through trying times. In response to Judge Thomas's restraining order, local officials had suggested the introduction of an 'appearance book'. Prospective black voters could sign the book to make an appointment to register to vote and could thus avoid waiting in a long line outside the courthouse. On Monday, 8 February, president of the Dallas County Voters League, the Revd Frederick D. Reese, accepted the proposal. The SCLC's James Bevel overruled him. Although the appearance book made the process of turning up to register to vote more convenient for local blacks, it robbed the movement of an important visible presence in the streets. The needs of the local and the national movement again appeared to be in conflict. To maintain the movement's visibility, Bevel took a small group of prospective black voters with him to the courthouse to publicly defy the appearance book. Sheriff Clark tried to remove them forcibly. When that failed, he arrested them all. On Wednesday, the scene became more violent as Clark and his men drove off prospective black voters with nightsticks and cattle prods.

The first signs of internal movement dissent and the possibility of escalating violence convinced King to wind up the Selma campaign while the movement was still ahead. Drawing upon past experience,

King understood that engineering a timely and successful conclusion to a campaign was an integral part of its perceived overall success. Since the movement in Selma had made significant progress and had already prompted President Johnson to act, King decided that the time had come for the SCLC, in concert with SNCC and local movement leaders, to declare a victory, to leave local people with tangible gains to show for their efforts, and to shift the focus of protest from Selma to outlying areas. The decision was a tacit acknowledgement that local people in Selma had been pushed to their limit. Fatigue was beginning to set in after almost a month of sustained demonstrations. Underscoring just how draining events had been, the following weekend King was hospitalised in Atlanta suffering from exhaustion. The incarcerated James Bevel went down with a fever and was treated at a local Selma infirmary while still chained to his prison bed. Even Sheriff Clark was feeling the strain. He too was hospitalised, with chest pains. 'The niggers are giving me a heart attack,' he told friends.[17] Almost two hundred black Selma school children prayed in the rain outside for Clark's speedy recovery. They even sent flowers. The move highlighted the moral dimensions of the struggle and its stress of love for one's enemies, while no doubt raising Clark's blood pressure even higher.

Both SNCC and local leaders agreed with King that it was time for the movement to shift its attention elsewhere. They targeted nearby Lowndes, Perry and Wilcox counties as the focus of new voter-registration efforts. In doing so, they would at least be aided by the fact that those counties came under the jurisdiction of federal district judge Frank M. Johnson Jr, who was one of the more sympathetic federal judges to the movement. When white city officials discovered King and the SCLC's desire to leave Selma, they agreed to hold talks with local movement representatives. Aided by the federal Community Relations Service (CRS), a body created by the 1964 Civil Rights Act, white city officials and local black leaders reached an agreement to work towards fairer voter-registration procedures. On Thursday, 18 February, as part of the movement's new wave of demonstrations, the SCLC's C.T. Vivian led local blacks in Marion, Perry County, down to the local courthouse. Local police, assisted by state troopers, attacked the demonstrators. One young black participant, Jimmie Lee Jackson, was shot and wounded by a state trooper while attempting to shield and protect his mother from attack. On 26 February, Jackson died in his hospital bed, the first person ever to be killed in demonstrations directly linked to an SCLC campaign. Jackson's death reversed the movement's plans for a cooling-off period of recuperation in Selma. Instead, King announced plans to dramatise the situation over the denial of black voting rights in Alabama, and to protest against Jackson's death, by organising a mass motorcade from Selma to Alabama's seat of government at Montgomery. Later, at the suggestion of local Marion woman Lucy Foster, King and the SCLC decided that movement participants should walk the route from Selma to Montgomery, starting on Sunday, 7 March.

Bloody Sunday

As the date for the march approached, both blacks and whites pondered its logistics. Taking a group of blacks on foot through 54 miles of some of the most racist territory in the South was a hazardous, not to mention a physically arduous, undertaking. It was the symbolic intent of the march rather than its speedy completion, however, that was the most important concern of the movement. As SNCC's John Lewis understood it, the best that the movement realistically hoped for was to 'march outside of Selma that night and then come back, and then we would continue' on the following day.[18] King and the SCLC believed they would not even be allowed to travel that far and they fully expected the march to be stopped before it left Selma. Initially, Governor George Wallace and his aides contemplated calling the movement's bluff and allowing the march to proceed, knowing full well that it was hastily arranged, that the movement was not fully prepared to make the trek, and that movement leaders expected to be halted. Yet with death threats against King already circulating in rural counties, Wallace and his aides ultimately decided that it was too risky to let the march take place. More civil rights martyrs, they decided, would bring even more unwanted national attention to Alabama. Wallace therefore instructed state troop commanders not to allow the march to proceed and to turn it back before it left Selma.

With Wallace declaring his intent to halt the march, King and the SCLC considered their response. One option was to seek a court order that expressly permitted the march and compelled the state authorities to let them proceed. Another option was to go ahead with the march, wait for a stand-off with state troopers to develop, and then either stand their ground or poignantly pause before turning back. SNCC opposed the march on the grounds that it would lead to local people being placed in danger for the sake of what they felt was little more than a publicity stunt on the part of King and the SCLC. Although this was SNCC's official line, SNCC chair John Lewis and several other SNCC members felt an obligation to support the march, since they had been involved with the Selma movement for some time and they did not want to abandon local people to potential danger. Thus SNCC agreed, Lewis explained, not to officially endorse the march, but 'that if any individual staff member wanted to march, they should feel free to participate'.[19]

King and SCLC staff members pondered the question of whether or not King should personally lead the march. Threats against King's life were being taken seriously enough to elicit warnings from the FBI and Attorney General Nicholas Katzenbach. There were also more practical matters to take into account. The likely prospect of the march being halted and of the participants being arrested would put King out of commission when his influence as a national lobbyist for voting rights legislation might be most needed. King considered delaying the march because of this, but both James Bevel and Hosea Williams stressed that a delay would weaken its impact. King therefore tentatively agreed that the march should go ahead in his absence.

On the day of the march, with six hundred movement supporters already gathered at Brown Chapel, SCLC staff remained uncertain of their exact plans. As expected, state troopers had been deployed across Edmund Pettus Bridge to block the march route to Montgomery. Some SCLC staff suggested that they should take a different route to avoid the state troopers. Others insisted that they should not back down from a confrontation. From Brown Chapel, Hosea Williams called Ralph Abernathy in Atlanta, who in turn called King. King relayed a message back that the march should proceed along the planned route. SCLC staff drew lots to see who would lead the march in King's absence. Hosea Williams won the dubious honour, and SNCC chair John Lewis took his place alongside him at the front of the march. The marchers set off through Selma's streets before finally arriving at Edmund Pettus Bridge. As they reached the crest of the bridge they could see the state troopers lined up across the road at the end of the bridge waiting for them.

When the marchers reached the state troopers, troop commander Major John Cloud halted them. 'This is an unlawful assembly,' Cloud told the marchers. 'Your march is not conducive to public safety. You are ordered to disperse and go back to your church or to your home.' Three times Hosea Williams asked to speak with the major. Three times Cloud replied that 'There is no word to be had.' Cloud then told the marchers, 'You have two minutes to turn around and go back to your church.' Approximately one minute later, Cloud shouted, 'Troopers, advance.'[20]

The state troopers charged at the marchers. John Lewis, at the front of the march, later remembered, 'The troopers came toward us with billy clubs, tear gas, and bullwhips, trampling us with horses.'[21] Eight-year-old

Sheyann Webb, King's 'smallest freedom fighter' in Selma, was one of the marchers.[22] 'I saw these horsemen coming toward me and they had those awful [gas] masks on; they rode right through the cloud of tear gas,' she recalls. 'Some of them had clubs, others had ropes or whips, which they swung about them like they were driving cattle ... People were running and falling and ducking and you could hear the horses' hooves on the pavement and you'd hear people scream and hear the whips swishing and you'd hear them striking the people. They'd cry out; some moaned.'[23] As Webb was retreating, Hosea Williams picked her up and put her under his arm to carry her to safety. Local black attorney J.L. Chestnut later described the scene as one of 'utter confusion, blood, people lying down. It looked like a battlefield.'[24]

Cloud's men forced the marchers right back to Brown Chapel, located in the heart of the black community. The white invasion of the black neighbourhood brought black residents out into the streets, most of whom were not involved with the local movement or trained in nonviolence. A number appeared with 'shotguns and rifles and pistols'.[25] Fearing a bloodbath, Andrew Young did his best to persuade black residents to 'Get back into the house with those weapons ... we're not going to have any weapons out.'[26] By the time the conflict ended there were over 70 hospitalisations due to 'fractured ribs and wrists, severe head gashes, broken teeth', and the suspected fractured skull of John Lewis.[27] Before being carted off to hospital, a concussed Lewis told the audience at Brown Chapel, 'I don't understand it why President Johnson can send troops to Viet Nam ... and cannot send troops to protect people in Selma, Alabama, who just want to vote.'[28]

Television footage of events made sensational viewing for the nation that evening. The American Broadcasting Company (ABC) interrupted its feature film *Judgement at Nuremberg* to show coverage of events at Selma. Andrew Young later wryly noted that '[M]any viewers apparently mistook those clips for portions of the Nuremberg film.'[29] The photographs of events in Selma that appeared on the front pages of national newspapers the following morning reinforced the national outrage at the events.

King was stung by the subsequent criticism about his absence from the march. He insisted that he had fully expected that the police would 'arrest ... all of the people in the line. We never imagined that they would use the brutal methods to which they actually resorted to repress the march.' Nevertheless, King felt pangs of guilt over his absence, recalling later, 'I shall never forget my agony of conscience for not being there when I heard of the dastardly acts perpetrated against nonviolent demonstrators.'[30] King appealed to movement supporters nationwide to bombard the president and Congress with telegrams to protest against events in Selma and for them to converge on the city for a second attempt to march from Selma to Montgomery the following Tuesday. This time, King insisted, he would be there at the front to lead the march. SCLC attorneys went to federal district judge Frank Johnson to ask him to prevent any interference with Tuesday's march. In Congress, there was widespread condemnation of the events in Selma. Minnesota senator Walter Mondale asserted that 'Sunday's outrage in Selma, Alabama, makes passage of legislation to guarantee Southern Negroes the right to vote an absolute imperative for Congress this year.'[31] Attorney General Nicholas Katzenbach later told Selma's Director of Public Safety Wilson Baker that 'You people [in Selma] passed t[he 1965 Voting Rights Act] on that bridge that Sunday.'[32] Katzenbach met with President Johnson to discuss the problems posed by Tuesday's planned march and the ways in which the federal government might help. Back in Alabama a furious Governor Wallace bawled out state lawmen for letting the situation get out of hand and for achieving exactly the sort of debacle that the state had wanted to avoid.

King's 'Tuesday Turnaround'

When King arrived in Selma on the Monday evening before the march, he was greeted with the news that Judge Johnson wanted the march delayed so that he could hold hearings about issuing a restraining order against interference with it. Judge Johnson told movement officials that if they went ahead with the march irrespective of his wishes, he would issue an order to expressly forbid it from taking place. This new development divided opinion within the movement. CORE's James Farmer thought the movement should obey the judge's wishes. The SCLC's Hosea Williams urged that the march should go ahead because of an obligation to local people. SNCC's James Forman, who had adamantly opposed the first march, now backed Williams by insisting that the second march must go ahead. King was inclined to postpone the march to stay on the right side of the law, but when he later addressed a mass rally at Brown Chapel, he reluctantly declared that the march would go ahead. King feared that if he cancelled the march the anger simmering in the local black community might spill over into violence. Going ahead with the march offered a constructive and, importantly, a nonviolent way for local people to vent their anger. 'It was one of the most painful decisions I ever made,' King later recalled. '[T]o try on the one hand to do what I felt was a practical matter of controlling a potentially explosive situation, and at the same time, not to defy a federal court order.'33

Movement attorneys and Assistant Attorney General John Doar, President Johnson's representative in Selma, were confused by King's apparent change of heart. They believed that they already had a tacit agreement with King to delay Tuesday's march in return for an eventual restraining order against interference with it. President Johnson dispatched CRS director LeRoy Collins and his staff member A.M. Secrest to Selma to negotiate a solution. On Tuesday morning, Collins, Secrest, two fellow CRS workers already on the scene, and John Doar, went to visit an unrepentant King. Desperate to avoid a repeat of the scenes witnessed the previous Sunday, the federal representatives suggested a compromise. Under the compromise agreement, the march would begin as planned. However, when the marchers reached state troopers on Edmund Pettus Bridge, the marchers would turn around and go back to Brown Chapel to wait for the court's restraining order to be handed down. When that court order had been handed down the march would then be able to proceed lawfully and unhindered. The federal representatives hoped that this would satisfy movement demands for the march to go ahead while at the same time placating Judge Johnson. Indeed, NAACP attorney Jack Greenberg had earlier suggested a similar plan. King was agreeable to the plan, but expressed doubts over whether SNCC or the state troopers could be persuaded to back down if the seemingly inevitable confrontation between them arose. King agreed to talk over the plan with SNCC and local movement leaders and Collins agreed to work on the state troopers to uphold their end of the bargain not to attack demonstrators.

Later, as King waited at Brown Chapel to begin the march, news came through that Judge Johnson had issued an order banning it. King had never broken a federal court order before. He conferred with his advisers about the latest development. Bayard Rustin advised King to proceed as planned. NAACP attorney Jack Greenberg counselled against marching and advised an appeal of Judge Johnson's ban in the courts first. After weighing the two arguments carefully, King decided to proceed with the march. Many people from across the country, black and white, had responded to the SCLC's call for help and had arrived in Selma to join the march. To tell them the march was cancelled, King reasoned, would be a serious blow to the movement's prestige nationally as well as locally. Added to this, SNCC had already decided that the march was going to go ahead with or without King. If King participated he could at least exert some degree of control over events. Around two thousand marchers had already set off by the time CRS director LeRoy Collins caught up with

King at the head of the column. Collins told King that those in charge of the state troopers had agreed to the 'turnaround' plan. King replied that he would do his best to get the marchers to comply.

As the marchers reached Edmund Pettus Bridge a US marshal, H. Stanley Fountain, stopped King and read out Judge Johnson's order banning the march. After listening to Fountain, King and the marchers proceeded over the bridge to face the Alabama state troopers. When King and the marchers reached them, King stopped, knelt down and held prayers. After rounding off prayers with the song that had become the movement's anthem, 'We Shall Overcome', King turned around to lead the marchers back to Brown Chapel. At the precise moment that King turned around, however, the state troopers blocking the road ahead to Montgomery moved aside, inviting the marchers to proceed. It was a calculated act designed to embarrass King. Nevertheless, King stuck to his word and led the marchers back to Brown Chapel.

To those not privy to the agreement made by King, Collins and Alabama lawmen – which included most march participants and most march spectators – King's decision to turn around when confronted by an open road was a baffling loss of face. Back at Brown Chapel, King had to tread a delicate line. He did not want to admit to a deal with Collins since he feared the inevitable SNCC charge that, as usual, he had sold out the local movement – 'treachery against the people' was how SNCC's James Forman later described King's decision. At the same time, King did not want to deny that a deal had been done, since it offered a potential future defence against a contempt of court citation from Judge Johnson. When confronted about his actions, King waffled evasively, seeking to escape questions altogether by keeping himself in seclusion. Later, he explained away what SNCC dubbed the 'Tuesday Turnaround' by insisting that it had been instigated 'because we felt we had made our point, we had revealed the continued presence of violence'.[34]

That evening, as supporters of the movement continued to flood into Selma, local whites at the Silver Moon Café attacked white Boston minister the Revd James B. Reeb as he was walking back from downtown with two other ministers. Two days later, Reeb died from his injuries, becoming the second fatality of the Selma campaign. Nationwide, marches in many of the United States's major cities demonstrated widespread support for the local movement in Selma. Congressmen lined up to condemn events in Alabama and President Johnson hurried efforts to frame voting rights legislation. When Judge Johnson's hearing on the events began on Thursday, King finally admitted that he had brokered a deal with Collins to turn the march around.

On Friday, Governor Wallace requested a meeting with President Johnson to put forward the case for Alabama. When the two men met in the White House the next day, Wallace insisted that it was King, the SCLC and SNCC that were the real troublemakers. In no uncertain terms Johnson told Wallace that he was wrong. Johnson pointed out that it was Wallace's duty as a state governor to uphold the constitutional right to peaceful assembly and to allow blacks to vote. At a press conference afterwards, Johnson told reporters that 'It is wrong to deny any person full equality because of the color of his skin.'[35] On Monday, President Johnson gave a special televised address to Congress in which he unequivocally threw his support behind black voting rights and behind the civil rights movement. Poignantly, Johnson used the movement's own words to insist to the nation that 'We Shall Overcome'. King, in Selma for James Reeb's memorial service, watched the speech on television. It brought tears to his eyes. The NAACP's Roy Wilkins was similarly moved, recalling that 'I had waited all my life to hear a President of the United States talk that way.'[36] 'I almost went limp, I was weak,' remembers Selma's Mayor Smitherman, on hearing Johnsons's speech. 'When he said "We Shall Overcome" it was just as though somebody had just stuck a knife in your heart.' Smitherman felt that 'it's over with now . . . our President's sold us out.'[37]

The Selma to Montgomery March, the 1965 Voting Rights Act and the Chicago Campaign

On Wednesday, 17 March, President Johnson introduced his voting rights bill to Congress. Its central proposal was to provide the US attorney general with the power to cancel all literacy and voting rights tests and to appoint federal registrars to actively assist black voters. This applied to all areas where less than 50 per cent of the population had been registered voters, or where less than 50 per cent of the population had actually cast ballots, in the previous presidential election. The formula covered Alabama, Georgia, Louisiana, Mississippi, North and South Carolina and Virginia, although it left out Arkansas, Florida, Tennessee and Texas. The bill met with swift action in the US Senate but in an indication of the power of the southern states in the US House of Representatives – not inconsequentially, a power that was itself a product of the corrupt voting rights practices that the bill sought to abolish – the bill did not become law until August 1965.

On the same day that the voting rights bill was introduced to Congress, Judge Frank Johnson concluded his hearings in Montgomery about the disturbances in Selma. Echoing President Johnson's previous remarks, Judge Johnson condemned the actions of law enforcement officials and upheld the right of the movement to peaceful assembly. Moreover, Judge Johnson approved the SCLC's specific proposal submitted to the court for a new march from Selma to Montgomery. He also ordered that the state must provide the marchers with adequate protection on the march.

After the hearing, King and the SCLC announced that the new march would begin on Sunday, 21 March. Governor Wallace went on state television to denounce Judge Johnson's findings and to insist that Alabama did not have the resources to provide protection for the marchers. After failed court appeals against Judge Johnson's decision, Wallace claimed that the state simply could not afford to call the Alabama National Guard into service to protect the marchers. President Johnson responded by issuing an Executive Order federalising 1,800 members of the Alabama National Guard. Johnson also sent federal troops, US Marshals and the FBI to monitor the march, and named Deputy Attorney General Ramsey Clark as coordinator of federal operations.

Since the voting rights bill had already been introduced to Congress, and the courts had already affirmed the right of the march to proceed, and the federal government had already arranged protection for the marchers, the march from Selma to Montgomery became a victory parade rather than a demonstration. King led the march, which culminated at Montgomery on Thursday, 25 March. In a rousing speech from the steps of Alabama's state capitol building, King told the crowd, 'We are on the move now . . . Like an idea whose time has come, not even the marching of mighty armies can halt us.'[38] The occasion marked a homecoming of sorts by bringing King back to the site of the Montgomery bus boycott, which he had led as president of the MIA almost ten years previously. Contemporary events underscored just how far the movement had come in such a relatively short space of time. King later wrote that, 'As I stood with the [other marchers] and saw white and Negro, nuns and priests, ministers and rabbis, labor organizers, lawyers, doctors, housemaids and shop-workers brimming with vitality and enjoying a rare comradeship, I knew I was seeing a microcosm of the mankind of the future in this moment of genuine and luminous brotherhood.'[39] Yet despite King's elation, the day witnessed the third fatality of the Selma campaign. White Detroit housewife Viola Gregg Liuzzo was shot and killed by Ku Klux Klan members in Lowndes County as she ferried movement workers back to Selma from Montgomery.

'With Selma and the Voting Rights Act one phase of development in the civil rights revolution came to an end,' reflected King in 1967. 'A new phase opened, but few observers realized it or were prepared for its implications.'[40] In truth, King only understood this with the benefit of hindsight. At the time, King and the SCLC were as perplexed and divided as everyone else over where the civil rights movement should head next. 'When the 1965 SCLC convention took place in August in Birmingham,' admits SCLC's Andrew Young, 'we really didn't know what our direction should be after Selma.'[41] A. Philip Randolph termed the movement's condition a 'crisis of victory'.[42] When the 1965 Voting Rights Act passed in August 1965, the movement had succeeded in gaining federal legislation in response to two of its central demands, the desegregation of public facilities and accommodations and the enforcement of black voting rights. The Selma campaign had witnessed an unprecedented degree of public support, manifest both in opinion polls and in the number of whites actually willing to participate in civil rights marches and demonstrations. The federal government had provided the movement in Selma with more assistance than at any time in the past. The challenge for the movement now was to devise a programme that could tap latent support for civil rights and take the movement on to its next stage of development.

Those closest to King provided him with very different answers to the question of what that development should be. Bayard Rustin advocated widening the movement's base with a switch, as he put it, from 'protest to politics'.[43] Rustin urged King to form a coalition with labour unions and other white movement allies that could move beyond issues of civil rights. Economic issues, Rustin argued, were now at the heart of impediments to black advancement. These problems could not be tackled by blacks alone but must involve a biracial political movement that sought a fundamental restructuring of American society. Only this, he insisted, would lead to a more equitable allocation of resources and wealth. Stanley Levison, who King decided to bring back from exile into the SCLC fold after the Selma campaign, cautioned against Rustin's far-reaching ambitions. Levison likened the circumstances of the movement to those faced by New Deal liberals in the 1930s. They, like the movement activists of the 1960s, Levison argued, had successfully managed to win significant reforms in a sympathetic political climate. However, their success had been based on pragmatic, limited reform, rather than on a platform for social and economic revolution. The support that the civil rights movement currently enjoyed was similarly based upon limited goals that sought reform in relation to very specific demands. Levison warned that attempts to move beyond an agenda for limited reform might derail support for any further change at all.

SCLC staff members also offered competing views over what programmes the organisation should develop next. James Bevel put forward a proposal to expand the remit of nonviolent direct action by using the Selma campaign as a launch pad to revisit his idea for a full-scale assault on segregation in Alabama. Bevel called for demonstrations in localities across Alabama coupled with a nationwide economic boycott of the state's goods to put pressure on white leaders to comply with the new voting rights legislation. Hosea Williams put forward a proposal to concentrate on a voter-registration campaign to build upon and to help implement the provisions of the 1965 Voting Rights Act. Williams's plan for a Summer Community Organization and Political Education Project (SCOPE) involved enlisting 1,000 northern students to work in up to 120 black belt counties to organise black voter-registration drives. Undecided, King backed both Bevel's and Williams's proposals. Neither project fared well. Bevel's proposal for a nationwide boycott of Alabama goods drew a storm of criticism from northern white supporters of the civil rights movement and from the Johnson administration. In Alabama, division and dissent, both within local movements and between local movements and the SCLC, hampered the project. The campaign withered away until it was finally dropped altogether. Williams's SCOPE project engaged less support, encountered more opposition, and cost far more than initially anticipated. Ultimately, the SCOPE project revealed that the SCLC was simply not equipped with the resources to embark upon such a demanding and ambitious region-wide campaign that spread its limited resources far too thinly.

Despite the competing proposals vying for King's attention, it was external events rather than internal initiatives that shaped King and the SCLC's next major campaign. On 11 August 1965, just five days after President Johnson signed the Voting Rights Act into law, a riot broke out in Watts, a predominantly black district of Los Angeles, after an altercation between local black residents and a white state highway patrolman. The riot, which lasted for six days and resulted in 35 deaths, was the most serious outbreak of race-related violence in the United States since the civil rights movement had begun. Racial disturbances in New York, Philadelphia and Rochester the previous year were forewarnings of the potentially explosive mounting black frustration and anger in America's cities. After some hesitation about becoming involved, King finally accepted the invitation of black clergymen in Los Angeles to visit the city. Accompanied by Bayard Rustin and the SCLC's Bernard Lee, King was appalled on arrival by the devastation caused by the riots and by the desperation of the local black population living in squalid urban conditions. Yet King found few blacks in Watts willing to listen to his message of nonviolence. Instead, local residents put forward their own 'Watts Manifesto' of 'Burn, Baby, Burn'. One local black resident told Rustin, 'We won.' When Rustin questioned how burning down their own neighbourhood could be considered a victory, he met with the reply, 'Well, I'll tell you how we won. We were for years telling those white folks peacefully what was needed. They didn't come. We tried to get some war on poverty. It didn't come. But after our manifesto, daddy, the Mayor, the Governor, your Dr. King, everybody came.'[44] In other words, the riot demonstrated that the problems faced by urban blacks could no longer be ignored without consequences. King found white officials equally unreceptive to his entreaties. Rustin reported a heated discussion between himself, King and Los Angeles mayor Sam Yorty as 'The biggest confrontation I've ever seen with King . . . [Yorty] ordered us to get the hell out.'[45] King later reflected that 'The situation in Watts erupted in volcanic form, because the people there knew or felt that their deep troubles were interlaced with manifest injustice. And this eruption potential is just below the surface in portions of almost every large city in the U.S.'[46]

King came away from Watts convinced that the SCLC must now turn its full attention to the plight of urban blacks in America's major cities that had been largely neglected in a movement that had till now concentrated on small southern towns and cities. Significantly, King took the decision to take the SCLC north against the advice of his closest advisers and over the reservations expressed by several SCLC staff members. Stanley Levison warned King that a northern campaign would run the risk of alienating the support of white liberals there, which in turn would severely impact upon the SCLC's financial contributions. Bayard Rustin felt that King would be out of his depth, telling him bluntly that 'You don't know what you are talking about . . . You're going to get wiped out.'[47] King's determination to carry on despite the dissenting voices marked the development of a new independence that would become evident over the following years. On the one hand, this has led some, such as King biographer Peter J. Ling, to see King between 1965 and his death in 1968 as a more heroic figure who was prepared to take more risks and a more radical and idealistic stance on a number of issues.[48] On the other hand, it should be noted that King's actions and statements during these years meant that his movement leadership veered ever further away from the centre ground that he had previously occupied and as a consequence meant that his actual ability to secure tangible victories lessened considerably. King's wife Coretta felt that her husband's award of the Nobel Peace Prize in 1964 had an important influence on his change in direction. She claims that he saw the prize as a mandate for taking a more assertive civil rights and human rights stance. Certainly, in his acceptance speech, King noted that 'I feel as though this prize has been given to me for something that really has *not* yet been achieved. It is a commission to go out and work even harder for the things in which we believe.'[49] Making the final decision to run a northern campaign, King told Rustin that God himself dictated the move and that 'this is where our mission is, we have received a calling.'[50]

Over the summer of 1965, King set out on a People-to-People tour of northern cities including Cleveland, New York, Philadelphia, Washington, DC, and Chicago. Of these places, Chicago emerged as the most promising target. The city appealed for a number of reasons. King called it 'the Birmingham of the North', believing that it symbolised black northern problems in 1965 in the same way that Birmingham had symbolised black southern problems in 1963.[51] King also believed that if the SCLC could tackle the problems blacks faced in Chicago it could provide a blueprint for tackling similar problems faced by blacks in other northern cities, just as the Birmingham campaign had provided a blueprint for black protest in the South. Since the early decades of the twentieth century, Chicago had been one of a number of northern cities that were magnets for southern black migrants in search of perceived better opportunities. By 1960, Chicago was the second biggest city in the USA and over 1 million of its 3.5 million inhabitants were black. However, blacks in Chicago found themselves mired in a pervasive system of racial discrimination. Central to the difficulties that blacks faced was the development of black ghettos to the south and the west of the city that were a cauldron for a whole host of interconnected problems: poor housing, high unemployment, crime, drugs and youth gangs. Despite the existence of these problems, rents and house prices in the ghettos were extortionately high because of collusion between unscrupulous white landlords and city real estate brokers to keep them that way. Blacks who attempted to move into surrounding white neighbourhoods met with violent resistance. What effectively constituted segregated housing in Chicago, enforced in practice if not by law, led to *de facto* segregated schools and other facilities that were located in black neighbourhoods.

Despite these complex and deep-rooted problems, King and the SCLC were optimistic about running a campaign in the city for a number of reasons. Chicago mayor Richard J. Daley fronted an influential local Democratic Party that dominated the city's affairs and was a force to be reckoned with in national Democratic Party politics. Daley had been supportive of the civil rights movement in the past: he had spoken at a civil rights rally in the city in 1963 after the SCLC's Birmingham campaign; the Chicago City Council that Daley dominated had passed a resolution supporting black voting rights in Selma in 1965; and Daley had placed a black director at the head of Chicago's anti-poverty efforts. Given Daley's track record, King believed that if he could persuade the mayor of the need to do more to tackle the problems that his own black constituents faced, Daley might act to implement reform. Chicago's strong white union contingent and the prominent role of the Catholic Church in the city held out the promise of two other potential constituencies of sympathetic white liberal support. In the black community, the existence of a strong local civil rights organisation, the Coordinating Council of Community Organizations (CCCO), which actively welcomed the SCLC's presence, also appeared to be in King and the SCLC's favour. King and the SCLC joined the CCCO, headed by Albert Raby, in an alliance under the banner of the Chicago Freedom Movement (CFM).

The fact that two of the SCLC's most dynamic figures, one old, one new, were based in Chicago gave the city added appeal. James Bevel had taken a leave of absence from the SCLC in 1965 to become programme director of the West Side Christian Parish, an inner-city outreach ministry on Chicago's West Side. Jesse Jackson, a relative newcomer to the SCLC but one of its fast-rising stars, was the SCLC's main contact on the South Side. Jackson became involved with the civil rights movement during 1963 demonstrations in Greensboro, North Carolina, and a year later he moved north to study at the Chicago Theological Seminary. In 1965, Jackson took part in the Selma campaign, and when the SCLC began to turn its attention to Chicago he became involved in its activities there.

Given the scale and depth of the problems of racial discrimination in Chicago, King and the SCLC proposed a different sort of approach to that city from previous campaigns. Before engaging in nonviolent, direct-action demonstrations, King and the SCLC planned a period of fact-finding, community organising and community education in order to get to grips with the problems blacks faced in the city and to try to come up with ways in which they might be addressed. James Bevel liaised with local blacks on the West Side and developed a programme for a 'Union to End Slums' by organising ghetto tenants on a block-by-block basis. Jesse Jackson liaised with local blacks on the South Side, and developed two different programmes. Firstly, he helped to found and then led the Kenwood–Oakland Community Organization in one South Side neighbourhood. Secondly, he helped to enlist the support of Chicago's black ministers. Wary of Bevel's more radical tenant-organising campaign, black ministers were persuaded, under Jackson's direction, to launch

'Operation Breadbasket', which used selective buying campaigns as leverage to elicit better black job opportunities from employers.

Because of the different SCLC approach in Chicago, King's own involvement in its early stages was slight. Andrew Young announced the start of the SCLC's Chicago campaign on 1 September 1965, but it was not until 5 January 1966 that King made his first appearance in the city. Even then, King did not commit to Chicago on a full-time basis, although he did vow to try to spend at least three days a week there. SCLC's Bernard Lee found a run-down apartment on the third floor of a building at 1550 South Hamlin Avenue in Chicago's West Side ghetto for King to move into, in a pointed attempt to illustrate existing slum conditions. Lee signed the contract of residence on behalf of King before the building management was aware of the identity of its new tenant. When the management discovered that King was moving in, it quickly got to work redecorating and repairing the place to try to make it more inhabitable. This prompted one Chicago newspaper to facetiously suggest that if King simply adopted the tactic of moving from apartment to apartment, all the slums would eventually disappear. When King, Coretta and their children moved into their new temporary home on 26 January, however, conditions in the apartment were still extremely poor. '[I]t was grim,' Coretta recalls simply.[52] Ralph Abernathy, who moved into an apartment in the same block as the Kings, remembers that 'The hallways were filled with rotting food and piles of feces and always you could see the rats patrolling.'[53] Abernathy lasted only one night in such conditions before checking into a hotel.

King's first attempt to dramatise the problems of Chicago's slums came when he seized an apartment building at 1321 South Homan, in what he termed a 'supralegal trusteeship' of the building.[54] Arrangements were made for the tenants to withhold rent money and to pool funds for repairs to the building instead. Questioned about the legality of the move, King replied that 'the moral question is far more important than the legal one'.[55] However, the ploy soon backfired. The Chicago press condemned the seizure of property and Chicago's Cook County Welfare Department withheld its rent subsidy to the tenants. Even the SCLC's Stanley Levison complained that the takeover made the organisation look like a 'gang of anarchists'.[56] Things were made even worse when it turned out that the owner of the building was John Bender, a white, poor, sick, 81-year-old, who was hardly the epitome of the slum landlord that King had hoped he would be. 'I think King is right,' Bender told reporters. 'I think his intentions are right and in his place I'd do the same thing.'[57] The city charged Bender with 23 housing code violations. Three months later the courts ordered the building to be returned to its owner. Bender died shortly afterwards. During their period of occupation, the SCLC spent $2,000 on repairs and collected only $200 in rent. The whole episode was a public relations disaster.

Almost eight months after Andrew Young had announced the beginning of the SCLC's Chicago campaign, the organisation had precious little to show for its efforts. It was not that the campaign was an abject failure: Bevel and Jackson were making steady progress in their respective projects and other SCLC staff members were hard at work. It was more that the SCLC's approach to the Chicago campaign was highlighting exactly why King and the SCLC had made the type of contribution to the civil rights movement that they had in the past: short-term, black community mobilising in a nonviolent, direct-action campaign was what they were most suited to and what they did best. In trying to run an SNCC-like campaign of community organising in Chicago, the SCLC discovered that its inexperience in such a campaign and its lack of human resources to run it militated against success. In certain respects, King and the SCLC were also hostages to their own fortune. The drama and spectacle of each past campaign set a benchmark and raised expectations for the next. The newsworthiness of King and his national prestige were in many ways the SCLC's main asset. The day-to-day trudge of community organising lacked the glamour and excitement that could attract the media and focus attention on King. There was a dawning realisation in the SCLC that it needed to return to the type of campaign that it had run in the past, which best played to its strengths. It had to simplify and to focus the issues of the campaign much better in order to dramatise them and to put King at the forefront once more. Plans were made to launch a nonviolent, direct-action campaign that would concentrate attention on the inability of blacks to escape the ghetto by bringing that problem quite literally to the doorsteps of whites in a number of 'open housing' marches through white neighbourhoods. Before that new phase of the campaign began, however, King's attention was drawn elsewhere.

The Meredith March Against Fear and the Rise of Black Power

On 5 June 1966, James Meredith set out from Memphis, Tennessee, on a 'Walk Against Fear' through Mississippi to the state capital of Jackson. Meredith had integrated the University of Mississippi in 1962 amid a great deal of controversy. White resistance to Meredith's admission to the university had resulted in clashes between a white mob and federal marshals and a federalised Mississippi National Guard. The white mob had wounded 160 federal marshals and killed two people. Meredith's plan to march across Mississippi was essentially a personal protest befitting his reputation as something of a civil rights maverick ('an ego trip by one man' was how the SCLC's Andrew Young described the march[58]). The march would inevitably expose Meredith to personal danger. He was one of the most notorious black activists in Mississippi and planned to walk solo through some of the most hostile rural territory in the South. On the second day of his march, Meredith was felled by two shotgun blasts. Fortunately, the injuries were not too serious but they did mean that the march looked like coming to a premature end while Meredith recovered from his wounds in a Memphis hospital.

King was in an SCLC meeting when he heard the news about the Meredith shooting. There was 'a momentary hush of anger and dismay throughout the room', King recalled, as early reports suggested that Meredith had been killed.[59] Relieved when the news arrived that Meredith had only been wounded, King and other civil rights leaders resolved to continue the Meredith March. On 7 June, King, new CORE national director Floyd McKissick and newly elected SNCC chair Stokely Carmichael met with Meredith in his hospital room. King, McKissick and Carmichael 'spent some time discussing the character and logistics of the march and agreed that we would consult him [Meredith] on every decision'.[60] Meredith gave his blessing for the march to continue. That afternoon, 21 people drove to the spot where Meredith had been shot and resumed the march. They had walked barely 50 yards before Mississippi highway patrolmen forced them off the road, telling participants that they did not have a permit to march and that they would therefore have to walk at the side of the road. After some pushing and shoving as patrolmen physically removed the marchers from the road, King calmed tempers by insisting that it would be better for the march to continue peacefully than not to continue at all. Later, spirits began to lift as the marchers covered six miles to the small town of Coldwater, Mississippi, without impediment.

That night, the marchers returned to Memphis, holding a rally at James Lawson's Centenary Methodist Church. The NAACP's Roy Wilkins and the National Urban League's Whitney Young joined them afterwards to discuss strategy and tactics for the march. They were ready to back the march as a means of focusing national attention on efforts to pass a new civil rights bill currently before Congress, but Carmichael vehemently objected to their presence. He put forward a list of demands that were bound to be unacceptable to them. The march should focus on its original intention of eliminating black fear and not on national legislation, Carmichael said. If there was to be any mention of legislation, it should highlight the shortcomings of Johnson's existing proposals and not support them. Moreover, Carmichael insisted that groups advocating armed self-defence, such as Louisiana's Deacons for Defense and Justice, should be welcome on the march. Carmichael even castigated Wilkins and Young directly, using colourful and abrasive language and making it clear that he believed that the older and more conservative civil rights leaders were completely out of touch with the current direction of the movement. 'We used that opportunity to say to Roy Wilkins what people in our organization had been wanting to say for so long,' recalled SNCC worker Stanley Wise. '[T]hat is, to retire, to teach in a college and write a book about his earlier days.'[61] Irate at Carmichael's onslaught and King's apparent unwillingness to leap to their defence, Wilkins and Young left the meeting and returned to New York.

The departure of Wilkins and Young was part of a carefully contrived strategy by Carmichael. His rise in SNCC reflected a significant shift in the organisation away from its initial emphasis on nonviolence and interracialism, and towards an embrace of black nationalism, black separatism and black armed self-defence. Carmichael had previously helped to found the Lowndes County Freedom Organization in Alabama as an independent expression of black political strength. Disillusioned with coalition politics, Carmichael called for a focus on raising black consciousness and the promotion of race solidarity and race pride. Only when the black community built its own political, economic and cultural institutions, Carmichael believed, could it truly begin to address its position of powerlessness in American society. This new direction marginalised the role whites played in SNCC. By the end of 1966, SNCC had effectively expelled all whites from the organisation. Hand in hand with SNCC's shift in its civil rights objectives was a shift in tactics. Nonviolence began to give way to an advocacy of armed self-defence. To SNCC workers in rural Alabama and Mississippi, the idea of nonviolence seemed increasingly irrelevant in the face of extreme white violence. Though still prepared to entertain nonviolence purely as a tactic, there was no longer the same ideological and moral commitment to it that King and the SCLC held. Carmichael's defeat of John Lewis for the position of SNCC chair in May 1966 both reflected, and acted as a further catalyst for, the shifting orientation of the organisation.

To Carmichael, the Meredith March offered an ideal opportunity to publicise and rally support for the new SNCC regime. Getting rid of Wilkins and Young removed the influence of those conservative civil rights leaders from the march. Exactly why King allowed this to happen is unclear. It has been suggested by some that King let his existing personal differences with Wilkins cloud his judgement on the matter. Others have suggested that King believed that he could control SNCC better by appearing to side with its militancy over more conservative leaders. Whatever his motives, King did not seem to fully appreciate the extent to which Carmichael was manipulating the march for his own ends. Preoccupied with the SCLC's Chicago campaign, King was largely oblivious to the new turn of events within SNCC. Carmichael hoped to use King's kudos to publicise the march and to convince him to adopt a more radical stance.

When King and McKissick held a press conference on Wednesday, 8 June, their march 'manifesto' bore the stamp of SNCC's uncompromising rhetoric. The document highlighted the failures and shortcomings of federal action rather than backing present proposed legislation. The mood of the march when it began echoed those sentiments. 'I'm not for that nonviolence stuff anymore,' one student told King. 'If one of these damn white Mississippi crackers touches me, I'm gonna' knock the hell out of him,' said another. Still others insisted that the movement's signature song should be changed from 'We Shall Overcome' to 'We Shall Overrun'.[62] Over the next few days the number of marchers grew to four hundred. As they came into contact with black communities they encouraged voter-registration efforts and local civil rights activism. Despite their perceived differences with King, some SNCC workers were surprised at how well they got along with him. 'He turned out to be easygoing, with a delightful sense of humor,' noted Cleveland Sellers. 'His mind was open and we were surprised to find that he was much less conservative than we initially believed.'[63] Carmichael had known King for many years and remembered that 'When I went into Atlanta I would go and eat in his house. Our relationship was very strong even where we had political disagreements.'[64] King left the march for Chicago on 10 June, returning briefly to Mississippi on Sunday, 12 June, before leaving again to attend to SCLC business in Atlanta. He rejoined the march at Grenada, Mississippi, on 14 and 15 June, before leaving for Chicago again for the following two days.

King's frequent absences played into SNCC's hands by allowing it to set the tone for and thereby seize control of the march. As King was away in Chicago on 16 June, the march headed to Greenwood, a long-established centre of SNCC activism. That night, when Carmichael and others tried to pitch tents at a local black school, white public safety commissioner B.A. Hammond ordered them to leave. When they refused, they were arrested. Later released on bail, an angry Carmichael went to Broad Street Park where the city had finally allowed the marchers to set up camp. Carmichael told the marchers that 'every courthouse in Mississippi should be burnt down tomorrow so we can get rid of the dirt'.[65] He insisted that black sheriffs should preside in predominantly black counties and that black citizens should hold political power. Then, putting a name to the new mood in SNCC, in a slogan already popularised on the march by SNCC worker Willie Ricks, Carmichael shouted, 'We want black power.'[66] The crowd enthusiastically echoed his chant.

The following afternoon, King returned from Chicago to lead a thousand marchers to the Leflore County Courthouse. After confronting Leflore County sheriff George Smith, march leaders successfully entered the building to hold a twenty-minute meeting on voter registration. At the evening rally in Greenwood, Willie Ricks once again took up the chant 'We want black power.' It was the first time King had heard the slogan, and he immediately found it disconcerting. He felt that the phrase – 'an unfortunate choice of words' – was destined to widen existing divisions within the movement and to increase white hostility to it.[67] In an attempt to neutralise the chants, the SCLC's Hosea Williams encouraged marchers to shout 'Freedom Now' instead. Confirming King's fears, the rival chants quickly led to a contest to see which could be shouted the loudest. King was so concerned about the new development that he considered withdrawing the SCLC from the march altogether. The controversy over black power among marchers meant that the event was beginning to highlight internal movement divisions more than it was dramatising the need for civil rights.

King left the march for two more days, returning on Tuesday, 21 June, as marchers took a detour into Philadelphia, Mississippi, where SNCC workers James Chaney, Michael Schwerner and Andrew Goodman had been murdered two years previous. As King led 250 marchers into town, local whites taunted and harassed them in the absence of police protection. At the Neshoba County Courthouse, Chief Deputy Sheriff Cecil Ray Price prevented the marchers from holding a meeting on the courthouse lawn. King confronted Price. He asked, 'You're the one who had Schwerner and those fellows in jail?' Price proudly replied, 'Yes, sir.' King's further attempts to hold a memorial service out in the street were heckled by some three hundred whites. Shaken, King declared that 'I believe in my heart that the murderers are somewhere around me at this moment.' From behind him, Price muttered, 'You're damn right, they're right behind you right now.' At a prearranged signal from Price's men, whites began to hurl bottles and firecrackers at the marchers. Fights broke out between local whites and some of the marchers, finally prompting local lawmen to intervene. Back at Mount Nebo Baptist Church, King told reporters that Philadelphia was 'the worst city I have ever seen. There is a complete reign of terror here.'[68] He vowed to return with more marchers before the week was out.

The following day, march leaders talked over tactics. They agreed that they should return to Philadelphia on Friday. Arrangements were also made for the conclusion of the march in Jackson on Sunday. What took up the most time, however, was a discussion about the use of the black power slogan. King pleaded with Carmichael and McKissick to drop the slogan, arguing that it would 'confuse our allies, isolate the Negro community and give many prejudiced whites, who might otherwise be ashamed of their anti-Negro feeling, a ready excuse for self-justification'.[69] They refused to listen to King, pointing to the slogan's popularity with local blacks in Mississippi. Ultimately, the two sides agreed to allow the slogan to remain while putting a stop to the shouting matches between the rival 'Black Power' and 'Freedom Now' chants. As the meeting broke up, Carmichael admitted to King, 'I deliberately decided to raise this issue on the march in order to give it a national forum and to force you to take a stand for Black Power.' King wearily replied, 'I have been used before. One more time won't hurt.'[70]

On Thursday afternoon, the march wound up for the day in Canton where the Madison County sheriff arrested an advance party for trying to erect tents on the grounds of a local black school. When King and other march leaders arrived, they also attempted to make camp and to hold a rally on the school field. A stand-off between the marchers and state highway patrolmen soon developed. The patrolmen tried to disperse the marchers by firing tear gas at them. King initially stood his ground but the gas finally overwhelmed him and the other marchers, who were forced to retreat. The state highway patrolmen removed the few remaining stragglers with the use of billyclubs. These events infuriated the march leaders since they had received federal assurances that state highway patrolmen would protect them on Friday's planned return to Philadelphia. Their sworn protectors for the following day now tear-gassed them in Canton. Such duplicity totally undermined King's determined efforts to maintain a nonviolent movement and instead only strengthened the appeal of armed self-defence. 'The government has got to give me some victories if I'm gonna' keep people nonviolent,' King told white journalist Paul Good afterwards. 'I know I'm gonna' stay nonviolent no matter what happens. But a lot of people are getting hurt and bitter, and they can't see it that way anymore.'[71] Even SCLC staff members were near the end of their tether. 'I didn't say it, but I thought to myself, "If I had a machine gun, I'd *show* those motherfuckers!"' recalls Andrew Young.

On Friday, the march through Philadelphia proved uneventful as state highway patrolmen successfully guarded the demonstrators. It was back at Canton that afternoon, where the marchers again threatened to pitch tents at the local black school, that there was most tension. Eventually, city officials compromised by telling the march leaders that they could hold a rally at the school, but only if they agreed not to set up camp there. King left the decision to the local black leaders, who agreed to the compromise. However, when the compromise was announced at the rally, many march participants booed the decision as a needless climbdown.

Saturday brought more dissension. James Meredith, back for the final stages of the march, felt slighted when the march leaders completed the penultimate leg from Canton to Tougaloo College on the outskirts of Jackson without him. Meredith angrily set out walking on his own from Canton. When the SCLC's Andrew Young and Robert Green went to try to improve relations, Meredith pushed them aside. Meredith's temper only calmed when King went personally to apologise and to accompany him on the final mile into Tougaloo. That evening, there was more disagreement over who should be allowed to speak at Sunday's rally. NUL executive director Whitney Young was back and ready to endorse the march manifesto in return for a place on the podium. Though this was accepted, a similar courtesy to Mississippi NAACP state president Charles Evers was not. Evers, whose brother Medgar had been shot and killed in Jackson three years previously, had vacillated over his support for the march. Evers was now ready to lend his endorsement to the march but the national NAACP still refused to sign up to the march manifesto. Above the protests of King and the SCLC, leaders from SNCC, CORE and the MFDP vetoed the appearance of an NAACP speaker without the support of the national organisation.

On Sunday, the marchers took the eight-mile journey into Jackson. Somewhere between twelve thousand and sixteen thousand people reportedly attended the rally there, which turned out to be a prickly affair. Whites gathered to heckle the speakers, and bitter wrangling over the 'Freedom Now' and 'Black Power' chants continued to divide movement activists. The march ended in further acrimony when it appeared that the SCLC was being left to foot the bill for the march expenses. Moreover, there was no consensus between the participating civil rights organisations about how to successfully follow up on the march. Consequently, the SCLC, SNCC and the NAACP made their own separate arrangements for voter-registration drives in Mississippi. Unlike previous civil rights demonstrations, where latent tensions between various civil rights organisations had often been papered over to give at least a semblance of unity, the infighting on the Meredith March was laid bare for all to see.

'The phrase "civil rights movement" lay moribund, dead forever with the birth of Black Power,' declared SNCC's James Forman in his autobiography.[72] To be sure, black power seemed successfully to alienate core constituencies of civil rights movement support. Key federal supporters of the civil rights movement, including President Johnson, Vice President Hubert Humphrey and Senator Robert Kennedy, all condemned black power. *Time* magazine labelled it the 'new racism' that was 'almost indistinguishable from the wild-eyed doctrines of the Black Muslims'.[73] Even black supporters of the civil rights movement condemned black power. Roy Wilkins was among black power's most virulent critics, calling it 'a reverse Mississippi, a reverse Hitler, a reverse Ku Klux Klan'.[74] Although more muted in tone, A. Philip Randolph, Bayard Rustin and Whitney Young also rejected the slogan. Only CORE supported SNCC in its embrace of the black power slogan.

King attempted to ease these divisions by exploiting black power's main weakness, which was also in many ways its greatest strength: its lack of any coherent meaning or programme. This rendered the black power slogan a powerfully emotive term that was endlessly open to both creative and positive – as well as destructive and negative – definitions and connotations. In attempting to define black power, King recognised that the term had both 'assets and liabilities'. He acknowledged that black power was an understandable 'cry of disappointment' at how slow white America was to instigate change in response to black demands. He approved of black power's call 'to amass the political and economic strength' to achieve action on those demands. He understood black power's 'psychological call to manhood' after years of white domination and oppression. Yet King also dismissed what he considered to be black power's embrace of hate and despair over love and hope, of armed self-defence and violence over nonviolence, and of black nationalism and black separatism over integration and the forging of coalitions and allegiances with whites. These central tenets of the civil rights movement, King insisted, must remain to the fore as they had in the past if that movement was to continue to be successful.[75]

King's efforts to paper over movement divisions about black power, however, were constantly undermined by Carmichael and others who failed to refute the sensationalism and scaremongering of the white press over the slogan. This made sure that black power, Carmichael himself, whose penchant for self-publicity led some in the movement to label him 'Stokely Starmichael', and SNCC remained in the headlines. If black power did not mark the decisive end to the civil rights movement that James Forman claimed, it did mark the beginning of the end. Over the following years, King would play his own part in closing that chapter of the black freedom struggle. His direct condemnation of US foreign policy in Vietnam, his support for and involvement in the growing anti-war movement, and his pursuit of a more radical economic agenda in the final years of his life, would change for ever the civil rights movement as it had previously existed.

Chapter 6

New Directions, 1966–8

During the final years of King's life, he and the SCLC moved in a number of new directions. In July 1966, they launched their first concerted campaign of nonviolent, direct-action demonstrations in a northern city, holding open housing marches through Chicago's white neighbourhoods. The demonstrations were successful to the extent that they encountered white violence that prompted Mayor Daley and other white city leaders to come to the negotiating table. Yet when King got them there, he did not know exactly what to ask for. The problems faced by northern ghetto blacks were complex and multifaceted, and King evidently did not fully understand how to go about tackling them. Unlike the issues of segregation and disfranchisement in the South, racial discrimination in the north had no direct or simple solutions. In the face of mounting violence in the city King therefore accepted an agreement of vague paper promises to move towards better conditions. When King and the SCLC left Chicago, city leaders ignored their previous commitments and did nothing to implement them.

King's experience in Chicago forced him to reflect more deeply about the conditions that he had encountered there. Increasingly, he came to believe that the problems of urban black ghettoes could only be tackled through a fundamental reorientation of national social and economic values. As he told white journalist David Halberstam after the Chicago campaign, 'For years I labored with the idea of reforming the existing institutions of society, a little change here, a little change there. Now I feel quite differently. I think you've got to have a reconstruction of the entire society, a revolution of values.'[1] Talk of economic change and revolution did not mean that King had become a Marxist. He consistently dismissed what he believed were the excesses of both Marxism and unrestrained capitalism, but he did in his final years move towards a more democratic socialist political outlook.

In a sense, King found himself back where he had been after the Montgomery bus boycott ten years earlier, searching for a way to take his existing strategy for change and to develop it to address new issues, concerns and circumstances. As he pondered what this strategy would be, other events intruded. In 1967, the anti-war movement against US involvement in Vietnam replaced civil rights as the nation's main focus of domestic concern. King had remained largely silent over the Vietnam War, fearing a break with President Johnson, who displayed fervent support for it. When King did begin to speak up, relations between King and Johnson quickly soured. Alongside Johnson's increasing alienation from King and the rest of the civil rights movement came a so-called 'white backlash' as, challenged to consider more fundamental social and economic change, whites began to recoil from King's and the movement's new demands. Swimming against the political tide, King launched his most radical strategy for change yet. Evolving the Birmingham strategy to a new level, in late 1967 and early 1968 King formulated plans for a Poor People's Campaign (PPC) to unite blacks with other minorities and poor whites in a concerted campaign of civil disobedience in Washington, DC, to demand better economic opportunities and conditions. As King readied himself and the SCLC for the campaign, he was sidetracked into a black union dispute in Memphis. King agreed to assist in the dispute since he believed that it highlighted the intertwined nature of racism and economic injustice, and he thought that it might be used as a launch pad for the PPC. However, it was in the midst of the campaign in Memphis that King was assassinated. He would never get the chance to implement the next step beyond his Birmingham strategy for change.

The Chicago Open Housing Marches

The numbers at the 10 July Soldier Field rally fell disappointingly short of King and the SCLC's overambitious estimate of 100,000 people. In the event, the SCLC claimed 60,000 participants, with the press estimating the figure more at around 30,000. Aware of how events in the movement were unfolding elsewhere, and the growing popularity of black power, King told the audience that 'Our power does not reside in Molotov cocktails, rifles, knives and bricks. I am still convinced that nonviolence is a powerful and just weapon.'[2] Afterwards, King marched downtown to pin the movement's demands on the door of Chicago's City Hall, a move evoking the actions of his namesake, church reformer Martin Luther, who nailed his 95 Theses to the door of the castle church in Wittenberg in 1517. The next day, King and local movement representatives met with Mayor Daley. The meeting achieved little, with Daley insistent that the city was doing its best to tackle the problems of the slums, and movement representatives insistent that they were ready to engage in nonviolent direct action to compel the city to do more. That night, the SCLC announced that the nonviolent, direct-action phase of the Chicago campaign would begin by targeting housing discrimination in Gage Park, one of Chicago's exclusively white neighbourhoods.

Events on the ground in Chicago soon overtook the movement's plans. In the middle of a sweltering Midwest heatwave children in black neighbourhoods had turned on fire hydrants for a cooling spray, a not uncommon practice in the city. On 12 July, Chicago fire commissioner Robert Quinn ordered the fire hydrants to be turned off to stop the city's water pressure from falling. Attempts to enforce this policy led to conflict between police and local black residents that rapidly escalated into a full-pitched battle. King first learned of what was happening when he and Coretta witnessed gangs of black youths running in the streets. He immediately went down to the local police station to try to secure the release of six arrested black youths. Successful in this endeavour, he headed to the black Shiloah Baptist Church to show local residents that he had secured their release and to insist that they should put an end to the violence. Few were willing to listen. They angrily denounced the Chicago police for its actions and refused to listen to King's appeal for calm. Instead, they drifted outside to join a growing and hostile crowd of blacks. King was powerless to contain their anger.

Over the next few days a full-scale riot developed. Violence erupted in the very areas of the West Side ghetto where the SCLC had worked for almost a year. On 15 July, with two people dead, Illinois governor Otto Kerner called out the National Guard. King attempted to stop the violence by getting local movement leaders and local ministers to talk to the rioters, but this too met with little success. 'A lot of people have lost faith in the establishment,' King conceded. 'They have lost faith in the democratic process.'[3] Negotiations between the movement and Mayor Daley produced only token measures to address the short-term problems of the black community. Daley ordered the fire hydrants to be turned back on and for mobile swimming pools to be shipped into black neighbourhoods. Chicago news columnist Mike Royko sardonically noted Daley's determination to make 'Chicago's blacks the wettest in the country'. One local black activist mused, 'I think they're hoping we'll all grow gills and swim away.'[4]

To King and local movement leaders the rioting demonstrated the need to direct the anger and frustration felt by Chicago blacks into more peaceful and constructive channels. Over the following weeks, leading SCLC figures and local movement leaders launched nonviolent, direct-action demonstrations. They picketed selected Chicago real estate firms and held 'Open Housing' marches into white neighbourhoods, highlighting the problem of racial discrimination in the city's housing practices. The violence they encountered, with whites throwing rocks and bottles at them and wrecking their parked vehicles, evoked images of the SCLC's southern campaigns and effectively demonstrated that white prejudice and bigotry were present in the north as well as the South. As the campaign gathered momentum, King led his first open housing march, targeting four realty firms in the Gage Park and Chicago Lawn neighbourhoods. A caravan of 600 people in over 100 cars travelled to join him. Over 1,000 police officers were dispatched to offer the marchers protection. However, despite the considerable police presence, shortly after emerging from his car King was struck by a rock on the side of the head. After taking a few moments to recover, King continued the march through a volley of missiles. By the end of the march, police had made 41 arrests and 30 marchers had been injured. King told the press that he had 'been in many demonstrations all across the South, but I can say that I have never – even in Mississippi and Alabama – seen mobs as hostile and hate-filled as I've seen in Chicago.'[5]

As King left for Atlanta the following morning, the events of the previous day made national news headlines. To keep up pressure on the city to act, the following Monday James Bevel and Jesse Jackson, without first consulting King, announced plans to expand the marches to the white neighbourhoods of Bogan and Cicero, which were much tougher targets where even greater violence was expected. Cook County sheriff Richard B. Ogilvie warned that any attempt to march through Cicero would 'make Gage Park look like a tea-party'.[6] For Daley, historian of the Chicago movement James R. Ralph Jr suggests, the marches were 'a nightmare. They tarnished Chicago's image as a first-class city, threatened its civic order, and, most of all, imperiled his political dominance.'[7] Up to that point, Daley had tried to protect the marchers and to limit white violence. The new marches, however, threatened to bring violence on a scale beyond the control of the city. Daley pleaded, 'I am asking for calm. I will meet with anyone and do anything to prevent what is happening to our city. I will meet with Dr. Martin Luther King or anyone else at any time. We cannot get anywhere through violence.'[8]

Daley subsequently agreed to attend a 'Summit Conference' on Wednesday, 17 August, with movement leaders and leading white community figures, organised by the interracial Chicago Conference on Religion and Race. From the outset, Daley made clear his intention to stop the open housing marches whatever it took. Exploiting the vague agenda tabled by the movement, which was intended as a framework for discussion rather than a list of concrete demands, Daley said that he would agree to all movement proposals if the marches stopped forthwith. CCCO leader Albert Raby pressed Daley for more specific commitments. Attention then shifted to the pivotal role played by the Chicago Real Estate Board (CREB) in perpetuating housing discrimination. Under pressure from movement representatives, from Mayor Daley and from other members of the committee, CREB eventually came up with its own vague proposals for change. CREB promised to 'withdraw all opposition to the philosophy of open occupancy legislation at the state level', and to remind its members to obey the city's fair-housing ordinance.[9] When King asked for clarification of exactly what the statement meant, CREB chair Ross Beatty simply reread his statement. 'We've heard your statement,' Albert Raby told Beatty. 'We're just not sure what you are saying.'[10]

With talks still at a stalemate by the end of the meeting a subcommittee was formed to draw up further proposals. Daley later reported that he was 'disappointed and frustrated' with the fact that the Summit Conference had not brought a halt to the open housing marches.[11] The movement announced that more marches would take place on Sunday. As the subcommittee convened on Friday morning, news arrived that the city had obtained a state court injunction against the movement on the grounds that the open housing marches were a threat to the 'order, peace, and quiet, health, safety, morals, and welfare of the city'.[12] The injunction severely restricted further demonstrations. Marches could only take place in one part of the city each day, only during daylight hours (excluding the rush hour, when they were most likely to be disruptive), and only with a maximum of 500 participants. Furthermore, the movement would have to inform the police in writing of any marches at least 24 hours in advance, and to provide details of the route, the leaders and the size of the march. The injunction appeared to contradict the conciliatory tone taken by Daley at the Summit Conference. King called the injunction 'unjust, illegal, and unconstitutional'.[13] All the subcommittee members, black and white, were alarmed at Daley's action. Nevertheless, they decided to continue the meeting. The talks proved constructive, and members agreed to reconvene the following Monday.

James Bevel and local leaders were ready to step up demonstrations in Chicago to force concessions from the subcommittee. Bevel insisted that the movement would break Daley's injunction and fill the jails. 'Get ready,' Bevel told Chicago blacks. 'Get your grandmother up from the South so she can keep the kids while we're in jail.'[14] King, however, cautioned restraint. Sensing that the movement in Chicago had reached a critical juncture, King questioned whether it really had enough people ready and willing to fill the city's jails. Moreover, SCLC attorneys were telling King that the city was more likely to fine demonstrators who broke the injunction rather than send them to jail. King therefore decided not to break the injunction but instead to adjust the movement's existing plans to accommodate it. Three Sunday marches took place in neighbourhoods outside the city limits that were not covered by the injunction. At the same time, King warned that if discussions failed to progress when the planned second Summit Conference convened, the movement would indeed break the injunction and march through Cicero the following weekend. Emphasising their intent to march, movement leaders met with city officials to give advance notification and details of their plans as required by the injunction. Governor Kerner readied the Illinois National Guard for duty.

Despite further subcommittee meetings there was still no consensus over an agreement when the second Summit Conference began on Friday, 26 August. The situation was delicately balanced. On the one hand, the movement's stated plans to hold a march through Cicero the next day if an agreement was not reached put pressure on the city to negotiate. On the other, the plans also placed pressure on the movement. Local black activists in particular were afraid that if the march did go ahead and the expected violence occurred, the main issue in the Chicago campaign might shift from one of open housing to one of law and order. They feared that this would in turn be used by the city as an excuse to crack down even harder on movement activities. The conference began with the tabling of ten proposals put forward by the subcommittee that essentially codified the non-discriminatory pledges of the previous meeting. Daley, indicating again that his main goal was to stop the marches, called for an immediate vote to ratify the document.

There was still much concern within the local movement over how and when the proposals would be implemented. King, however, felt that the movement had reached a point where it had little choice but to accept a compromise. He decided that the risk of violence if the movement continued with demonstrations was far too great. Under these circumstances, King negotiated an agreement as favourable to the movement as possible. He insisted that in exchange for ending the marches the city should drop its court injunction against the movement and clarify details about how it intended to implement the terms of any agreement. Daley point-blank refused to drop the injunction. In a more conciliatory tone, the Chicago Conference on Religion and Race gave assurances that it would oversee the implementation of any agreement. Although local leaders and SCLC representatives still held deep misgivings about the sincerity of white commitments and promises, King indicated that the movement was willing to discuss the injunction as a separate and ongoing issue, and to accept the city's proposed settlement. The 'Summit Agreement' was adopted unanimously.

After the meeting, an upbeat King told the press that the Summit Agreement would mean 'The total eradication of housing discrimination' in Chicago, and that all further marches would be halted. Not everyone in the movement was so confident. James Bevel told the press that he would have to 'think about' if he was happy with the agreement or not. Others were less reserved. Local black leader Chester Robinson declared that 'we feel the poor Negro has been sold out by this agreement'.[15] There were many in Chicago who agreed with these sentiments. Subsequent events bore out the fears of local leaders that the city had no intention of carrying out the terms of its agreement. Over the ensuing months there was little apparent change in the city's housing practices. Attempts by the SCLC to sponsor a voter-registration campaign to pressure the city to live up to its commitments failed miserably. Hosea Williams, placed in charge of the campaign, claimed 32,000 new black registrations. The city put the figure nearer to 320. A distinct lack of federal pressure for change undermined King and the SCLC's efforts even further. In September 1966, attempts to pass the 1966 civil rights bill, which included provisions for fair housing, had finally failed. In April 1967, Mayor Daley was returned to office, winning over four-fifths of the black vote. With his political career intact, he ignored all the city's previous commitments. The local movement fell apart. The SCLC Chicago campaign had ended in defeat.

King's Defeat in Chicago

The failure of the Chicago campaign placed the spotlight on King's leadership once again. Some local black leaders complained that King had grasped defeat out of the jaws of victory by accepting a weak agreement just as the movement was applying its greatest pressure.

Local CORE leader Robert Lucas believed that 'had King broke[n the] injunction . . . he would have rallied thousands of black people in this city and perhaps around the country to Chicago'.[16] King later admitted that he might have made a tactical error in accepting the agreement and refusing to march. However, in King's defence, had he decided to proceed with the open housing marches, and had they led to a high number of casualties and/or fatalities, he faced the prospect of even greater criticism, both locally and nationally. Consistent with his leadership in the past, King considered putting lives recklessly at risk too big a price to pay for the gains that applying such pressure might provide in return. The risks King took were always measured and calculated. If they often erred on the side of caution, it was because King took his responsibilities as a leader seriously and because he held himself accountable for the welfare of those willing to follow him.

In truth, the failure of the Chicago campaign did not rest in King's negotiating and leadership skills but in much deeper-seated problems. Little about the Chicago campaign had turned out as King and the SCLC expected. Hopes of white receptivity to their demands proved to be unfounded. Mayor Daley was a shrewd, pragmatic and powerful politician, not the small-town southern official that King and the SCLC had dealt with in the past. When the movement criticised Daley he pointed, not entirely without justification, to the efforts the city was already making to try to alleviate the problems of the slums. Daley did not offer all-out opposition to King and the SCLC's demands as many southern opponents had in the past. Rather, Daley agreed with the aims of the movement, he agreed to meet most of its demands, and he even asked them what more he could do to help. In part, this was evidence of Daley's political strategy, King noted, of playing 'tricks with us – to say he's going to end the slums but not to do any concrete things . . . trying to stay ahead of us just enough to take the steam out of the movement'.[17] Yet King was equally forced to admit that he had no ready answers to offer for the complex problems blacks faced in Chicago. 'The truth is, if I were mayor of Chicago,' King reflected, 'it would take me ten years to make an impact on many of these problems.'[18]

Widespread support from white unions and the Catholic Church failed to materialise. Though many leaders of those institutions supported civil rights in the South, when the movement moved into their own backyards they were distinctly less comfortable with it. 'As long as the struggle was down in Alabama and Mississippi,' King wrote, 'they could look from afar and think about it and say how terrible people are.'[19] In Chicago, the unions and the Church were torn between supporting the movement and maintaining the support of their membership and congregations. Even if many union and Church leaders were genuinely sympathetic to the aims of the movement, personal pragmatism often dictated that they back their own vested interests. Many whites questioned the very legitimacy of the movement's goals in Chicago. Destroying overt legalised segregation and disfranchisement in the South was one thing. Invading neighbourhoods, infringing property rights, interfering with the right of citizens to live where they wanted (as many whites perceived the issues at stake in the campaign) was another. As biographers of Mayor Daley, Adam Cohen and Elizabeth Taylor, point out, 'What King viewed as [segregation], Daley saw as the natural instinct of free people to stick to their own kind.'[20] Unlike previous campaigns, where the issues had been relatively clear-cut, in Chicago there was far more ambiguity as to what exactly constituted civil rights.

The reaction of whites in Chicago formed part of what northern politicians identified as a nationwide 'white backlash' to the civil rights movement. The rise of black power and rioting in urban areas, they contended, had convinced whites that blacks wanted 'too much' and 'too fast'. 'To many whites,' writes movement historian James R. Ralph Jr, 'this New Negro seemed ungrateful, defiant, and dangerous, and with this perception white empathy for the black predicament shrank.'[21] The distinction in the minds of whites between riots and peaceful demonstrations became increasingly blurred. National opinion polls that had shown rising northern white support for civil rights in the early and mid 1960s now began to show that support rapidly subsiding. Nevertheless, the term 'white backlash' was not new and had been bandied around for a number of years. Moreover, as King noted, 'the white backlash has always existed underneath and sometimes on the surface of American life'.[22] The popularisation of the term in 1966 was in many ways linked to the discovery by northern whites that support for the civil rights movement might have direct implications for them too. The sentiment underlined Stanley Levison's contention before the Chicago campaign that whites would support specific and limited reforms, but not thoroughgoing social change.

If Chicago's white community had failed to live up to King and the SCLC's expectations, so too had Chicago's black community. At the outset of the Chicago campaign James Bevel had insisted that 'Chicago is not that different from the South. Black Chicago is Mississippi moved north a few hundred miles.'[23] The SCLC's actual experience in Chicago revealed that Bevel was quite clearly wrong. The black community in Chicago was very different from the black community in the South. Blacks made up an important component of Mayor Daley's political power, which partly explained his previously declared support for the civil rights movement. Chicago's black congressman, William L. Dawson, played a key role in running black politics in the city and enjoyed Daley's support and patronage, as did many other of the city's black political leaders. Dawson and other black politicians therefore sided with Daley and opposed King and the SCLC's presence in Chicago. The black church, the organisational foundation of King and the SCLC's campaigns in the South, was largely unreceptive to their presence in Chicago. Black ministers, claims historian James R. Ralph Jr, 'were afraid of inviting Dr. King to their churches because they were afraid they would alienate the feelings of Mayor Daley'.[24] President of the National Baptist Convention Joseph H. Jackson, a Chicago resident and a long-time conservative critic and rival of King's, led black church opposition to King and the SCLC's presence in the city. In later years, when the street on which Jackson's church was located was renamed after King, Jackson changed the church's entrance so that its address would not carry King's name. The SCLC'S Dorothy Tillman remembers that Chicago was the first city that she ever visited where the 'black leadership had a press conference and they told us to go back down south where we came from'.[25] The city's rank and file black population was in many cases even more hostile to King and the SCLC. The black population in Chicago was far more secular than the southern black population and therefore less inclined to bow to the authority of a black minister. They rejected King's appeals for nonviolence and for integration as irrelevant. King would remember Chicago as 'the only time I have been booed' by a black audience.[26] On the difference between working with southern blacks and northern blacks, the SCLC's Hosea Williams commented, 'The Negroes of Chicago have a greater feeling of powerlessness than I've ever seen ... they are beaten psychologically. We are used to working with people who want to be free.'[27]

The sheer physical scale of the problems that blacks faced in Chicago was beyond the comprehension of many SCLC staff. The city was ten times bigger than Birmingham and a hundred times bigger than Selma. 'As we drove through the South Side, where large segments of the black population lived,' Ralph Abernathy recalled of a car journey with Jesse Jackson, 'we kept waiting for the slum tenements to give way to warehouses, vacant lots, and country stores and open fields where cows were grazing ... Instead we saw more slum blocks. And more. And more.'[28] King was forced to conclude that 'the eradication of the slums housing millions is complex far beyond integrating buses and lunch counters'.[29] Or, as Andrew Young put it, 'We were realizing along with the rest of the country that the movement had passed the stage of easy solutions.'[30]

One revealing absence in the Chicago campaign was federal government support. In past campaigns in Birmingham and Selma, the SCLC had relied on federal intervention as an integral part of its success; where federal intervention had not been forthcoming, as in Albany and St. Augustine, campaigns had been much less successful. In Chicago, Mayor Daley's presence no doubt deterred any inclination that President Johnson might have had to intervene in events. Having alienated many white southern Democratic politicians and white southern voters with his civil rights stance, incurring the wrath of northern Democrats and risking white northern votes would have been political suicide. Like many whites in the nation, Johnson was also sceptical of the value of nonviolent, direct-action demonstrations, particularly since he felt that his civil rights legislation already tackled the very problems that King and the SCLC were demonstrating about. King and Johnson had no contact at all during the Chicago campaign, despite the fact that the campaign was focused on open housing at the same time that Johnson's civil rights bill containing fair housing provisions was being debated in Congress. More than anything else, Johnson's interest in the civil rights movement and the War on Poverty were in decline because of his preoccupation with the war in Vietnam. Increasingly, King too turned his attention to that issue, and particularly to the growing anti-war movement, which was threatening to displace civil rights as the nation's number one domestic concern.

King and the Vietnam War

United States involvement in Vietnam dated back to the 1950s, when it had supported the South Vietnam regime of President Ngo Dinh Diem as a Cold War imperative to prevent its takeover by communist North Vietnam under the leadership of Ho Chi Minh. Presidents Eisenhower, Kennedy and Johnson had all gradually committed more military personnel to bolster the South Vietnam regime. It was during President Johnson's second term in office from 1964 to 1968, however, that the first US combat soldiers were sent to Vietnam and a massive escalation of troops began. As the US became more heavily involved in and committed to the conflict, the Vietnam War, and growing public opposition to it, became one of the central issues of national concern.

Initially, King chose to stay silent about the war in Vietnam since he feared that linking civil rights and anti-war issues would dilute the national impact of the civil rights movement. Moreover, taking an overt anti-war stance risked alienating key constituencies of movement support, not least President Johnson. Yet, as an advocate of nonviolence and a man of conscience, it became increasingly difficult for King to remain silent. Early in 1965, at the encouragement of Bayard Rustin and Stanley Levison, King tentatively began to speak out against the war. His first public utterance came in a speech at Howard University in Washington, DC, on 2 March 1965, when he told the audience that 'The war in Vietnam is accomplishing nothing.'[31] By July 1965, King's statements on the war were becoming much bolder and were directly opposed to the Johnson administration's policy. As the SCLC conference approached in August 1965, King formulated a plan with his advisers to write to all of the principal countries involved in the Vietnam War to urge a negotiated settlement to the conflict. However, when King met with the SCLC board, he found its normally compliant members unsettled by the plan. Although the board recognised King's right to speak out against the war as an individual, the SCLC reaffirmed that its primary goal was the pursuit of 'full citizenship rights for Negro citizens', and maintained that 'resources are not sufficient to assume the burden of two major issues'.[32] Nevertheless, King remained determined to pursue his letter-writing initiative, regardless of the board's reservations.

Further pressure for King to curtail his comments about the Vietnam War came from President Johnson. Johnson rebuked King over his public anti war stance and initiated a meeting between King and Johnson's ambassador to the United Nations, Arthur Goldberg, with hopes of muting King's opposition. When King and Goldberg met, however, King continued to insist that the United States should work towards a negotiated settlement. In a further criticism of existing American foreign policy, King also suggested that the United States should drop its opposition to the People's Republic of China entering the United Nations. The following day, Connecticut senator Thomas Dodd, a close ally of the Johnson administration, lambasted King's comments on Vietnam and 'Red China'.[33] The pressure being exerted on him by the Johnson administration prompted King to call another meeting with his advisers. At the meeting, King indicated a willingness to heed Johnson's warnings to backtrack and to mute his statements about the war. King told his advisers that he felt isolated and vulnerable in speaking out on Vietnam, and feared that his position as a civil rights leader would be undermined as a result. His advisers agreed. A decision was made to drop the letter-writing proposal and to play down King's anti-war stance in the future.

Although Dodd's comments effectively silenced King in the short term, the growing momentum of the anti-war movement inevitably brought King back to the issue. In January 1966, the Bond affair indicated that civil rights and anti-war issues were becoming ever more intertwined. The Georgia state legislature refused to seat the recently elected Julian Bond, former SNCC communications director, because he endorsed SNCC's view that people should take up civil rights work rather than submit to military draft. King leapt to Bond's defence, telling the press that 'in my current role as a pacifist I would be a conscientious objector'.[34] King led a rally to the Georgia state capitol in support of Bond, but King's comments to the press revealed that he still remained cautious about being drawn too far on the Vietnam question. King said that he supported SNCC's stand against the draft in principle but pointed out that he personally was not prepared to encourage breaking the law by draft dodging. King's equivocation continued throughout 1966 as he studiously avoided participation in the burgeoning peace rallies and public discussions about the war. However, he did not keep totally silent on the subject. In an awkward compromise, he often referred to the war indirectly by assessing its damaging impact on civil rights and anti-poverty efforts. At its April 1966 convention, the SCLC adopted a resolution that 'The intense expectations and hopes of the neglected poor in the United States must be regarded as a priority more urgent than a conflict so rapidly degenerating into a sordid military adventure.'[35] At its August convention, the SCLC called for an immediate and unilateral de-escalation of the war, warning that it was 'corrupting American society from within and degrading it from without'.[36] Invited to speak before the US Senate's Government Operations Committee in December 1966, King identified the war in Vietnam as one of the principal reasons for resources being drained away from anti-poverty efforts.

King's decisive turning point over Vietnam came in January 1967. As he was preparing to fly to Jamaica to work on his latest book he came across an article by William Pepper in *Ramparts* magazine about 'The Children of Vietnam'. The article discussed and graphically illustrated the horrific injuries inflicted in Vietnam by the United States's use of chemical weapons such as napalm. While King was in Jamaica, James Bevel visited to ask for another leave of absence from the SCLC, this time to become national director of the anti-war Spring Mobilization Committee, which was planning a mass demonstration in New York. Bevel urged King to join the demonstration and to speak out more forthrightly against the war. Other SCLC staff members Harry Boyte, John Barber and Robert Green, along with former SCLC staff member

James Lawson, were also active in helping to organise anti-war rallies. When King returned from Jamaica, he indicated that he was finally ready to tie 'the peace movement to the civil rights movement or vice-versa', even if that meant an explicit break with the Johnson administration.[37] At a speech in Los Angeles on 25 February, King roundly condemned the 'triple evils of racism, extreme materialism and militarism', while criticising US foreign policy in Vietnam, which, he insisted, represented 'white colonialism', 'paranoid anti-communism', and 'deadly western arrogance'.[38]

Most of King's SCLC advisers remained adamantly against his participation in the Spring Mobilization, scheduled for 15 April 1967. Bayard Rustin warned that King's participation would mean a total and decisive breakdown in the civil rights movement's relationship with the Johnson administration. Stanley Levison had his own particular reservations about King marching alongside an eclectic group of demonstrators that would include pacifists, hippies and left-wing extremists, warning him that 'you will become identified as a leader of a fringe movement when you are so much more'.[39] Others worried about what impact King's participation in the march would have on SCLC funding. King carefully weighed the arguments put forward by his advisers before finally deciding to participate in the Spring Mobilization. On 25 March, King led his first anti-war march of five thousand people in Chicago, alongside noted paediatrician and anti-war spokesperson Dr Benjamin Spock.

Ultimately it was not King's eventual participation in the Spring Mobilization that grabbed the headlines, but rather his speech at New York's Riverside Church on 4 April, delivered to the group 'Clergy and Laymen Concerned about Vietnam'. The speech was actually designed to pre-empt and hopefully to 'neutralise' King's Spring Mobilization appearance.[40] Drafted with the help of black academic Vincent Harding, King's speech contained his harshest condemnation yet of the Vietnam War and the Johnson administration. Denouncing the United States as 'the greatest purveyor of violence in the world today', King demanded that the US halt its bombing of Vietnam, declare a unilateral ceasefire, curtail its forces in Thailand and Laos, accept Vietcong representation in peace negotiations and set a date for the withdrawal of US troops.[41]

Reaction to King's speech was far more negative than he had anticipated. 'Nationally, the reaction was like a torrent of hate and venom,' Andrew Young recalls.[42] On 6 April, the *Washington Post* summed up the prevailing sentiment when it announced that King 'has done a grave injury to those who are his natural allies . . . Many who have listened to him with respect will never again accord him the same confidence.' *Life* magazine called the speech 'a demagogic slander that sounded like a script for [North Vietnamese] Radio Hanoi'. John P. Roche, special assistant to the president, told Johnson in a memo that 'King . . . has thrown in with the communists' and 'is destroying his reputation as a Negro leader'.[43] Black columnist Carl T. Rowan bemoaned 'Martin Luther King's Tragic Decision' to speak out on Vietnam in America's most widely read magazine, *Reader's Digest*. Only a few newspapers and magazines backed King's statement, most notably the *Christian Century*, which called his speech 'a magnificent blend of eloquence and raw fact, of searing denunciation and tender wooing, of political sagacity and Christian insight, of tough realism and infinite compassion'.[44]

Within the civil rights movement, the NAACP's Roy Wilkins and NUL's Whitney Young both distanced themselves from King's anti-war stance. The NAACP board of directors warned that attempts to merge civil rights and anti-war movements would be a 'serious tactical mistake'.[45] A. Philip Randolph and Bayard Rustin both refused to comment on King's speech to the press. Later, however, Rustin wrote an article in the *New York Amsterdam News* on 'Dr. King's Painful Dilemma', in which he noted that 'the involvement of the civil rights organizations as such in peace activities' was 'unprofitable and perhaps even suicidal'.[46] Even Stanley Levison was critical of the incendiary way that the speech had dealt with the sensitive Vietnam question. King conceded that the speech may have been 'politically unwise', but at the same time insisted that it was 'morally wise'.[47] For FBI director J. Edgar Hoover, King's speech was grist to the mill for his allegations about subversive communist influence on the civil rights leader. President Johnson was now far more disposed to agree with Hoover's analysis. In private, Johnson called King 'a naïve black preacher [who] has been duped by a Communist', a reference to King's lasting friendship with Stanley Levison.[48]

Nevertheless, King remained unrepentant in the face of public criticism. On 15 April, he led the Spring Mobilization march as planned alongside James Bevel, Dr Spock and Harry Belafonte. 125,000 people marched from New York's Central Park to United Nations Plaza. Appearing on the Columbia Broadcasting System (CBS) 'Face the Nation' television programme on 16 April, King insisted that the civil rights and anti-war movements were indeed tied together 'from a content point of view, although the two are not joined together from an organizational point of view'.[49] King encouraged potential army draftees to apply for conscientious objector status, although he remained opposed to breaking federal law through draft evasion. At a meeting of civil rights leaders in Suffern, New York, on 27 April, King confronted Bayard Rustin, Roy

Wilkins and Whitney Young over their lack of support for his anti-war stance. King meanwhile told SCLC staff, 'I backed up a little when I came out [on Vietnam] in 1965. My name then wouldn't have been written in any book called Profiles in Courage. But now I have decided. I will not be intimidated. I will not be harassed. I will not be silent. And I will be heard.'[50]

On 23 April, King joined Dr Benjamin Spock to announce plans for a 'Vietnam Summer' in conjunction with Clergy and Laymen Concerned about Vietnam. With more than a passing resemblance to SNCC's 1964 'Freedom Summer' in Mississippi, 'Vietnam Summer' proposed to mobilise grassroots opposition to the war into a nationwide network. The next day, King joined a new peace group called 'Negotiation Now'. King's anti-war stance even began to filter through into his sermons at Ebenezer Baptist Church, where he praised black boxer Muhammad Ali's refusal to enlist in the US army to fight in Vietnam. King's name was even mooted as a potential third-party peace candidate for the 1968 presidential election. Meanwhile, polls suggested that, as many of King's advisers had feared, much of the black community did not share his anti-war stance. According to one Harris opinion poll, only a quarter of blacks backed King over the issue.

King nevertheless remained optimistic about tying together civil rights and anti-war sentiment, possibly by mobilising another March on Washington type of event. However, over the summer of 1967, the impetus of the Spring Mobilization began to fade. A short-lived Arab–Israeli war broke out in June that eclipsed the war in Vietnam in the national news headlines. The Middle East conflict muted much of the anti-war movement's liberal Jewish supporters, one of its key constituencies. 'Half of the peace movement is Jewish and the Jews have all become hawks,' noted Stanley Levison.[51] Israel's use of military might to resolve the conflict held out the promise that the United States's continuing use of force in Vietnam might bring about a similar victory. A new outbreak of urban riots during July and August in Newark, New Jersey, and Detroit, Michigan, also diverted attention away from the war. While these developments robbed the anti-war movement of momentum and publicity, the movement itself became increasingly fractious. By the end of the summer, the anti-war movement was left in disarray and appeared a spent force.

While King's attention was focused on the anti-war movement in 1967, the SCLC languished. Indicative of waning support for civil rights, a lack of financial contributions meant that the SCLC was forced to make a number of staff members redundant. Other disillusioned staff left of their own accord to take up new jobs elsewhere. Although SCLC finances met with an upturn later in the year, in part due to the success of its direct mail fund-raising and in part due to SNCC's alienation of white contributors who now gave to the SCLC instead, the organisation found it difficult to recruit able staff. The knock-on effect of diminishing finances and decreasing personnel was a downturn in the SCLC's civil rights activism. The one viable SCLC project in the South at Grenada, Mississippi, stuttered along with little direction. Efforts to launch open housing demonstrations in Louisville, Kentucky, met with scant success. In Cleveland, Ohio, the SCLC participated alongside the United Pastors Association and other local groups to help in Carl Stokes's election campaign to become the first black mayor of a major US city. Despite his success, Stokes played down the support he had received from King and the SCLC, and he even believed that it might have harmed rather than improved his chances of victory. Amid these strained campaigns, Jesse Jackson's successful Operation Breadbasket project in Chicago, one of the positive legacies of the SCLC's presence there, offered some hope of progress. King encouraged Jackson to expand the project nationwide. Nevertheless, he still held reservations over Operation Breadbasket's ability to exact the kind of far-reaching changes in the economy that King increasingly believed were necessary.

The Poor People's Campaign (PPC)

New initiatives in the autumn of 1967 were intended to move King and the SCLC out of the doldrums. In mid September, King arranged an SCLC retreat in Warrenton, Virginia, to discuss an idea put to him by Marian Wright, an NAACP attorney working in Mississippi. Wright's suggestion was to take the crippling poverty she had witnessed in Mississippi to the seat of power in Washington, DC, to dramatise the plight of the black poor. Her initial suggestion was to stage a sit-in at the national headquarters of the Office of Health, Education and Welfare. Expanding upon this idea, King suggested a more ambitious campaign. He proposed a march of several thousand volunteers to Washington, DC, to hold a concerted campaign of 'civil disobedience'. This would involve a significant escalation of nonviolent direct action to another level, expressly aimed at disrupting the normal day-to-day running of the nation's capital, with demands for 'jobs and income' for the poor. From the outset, the plan caused disagreement within the SCLC. SCLC board member Marian Logan thought the idea was 'too big and unwieldy for us to be able to handle'.[52] James Bevel also demurred, arguing that SCLC activities should continue to centre on participation in the anti-war movement. King insisted that federal support and public sympathy for helping the poor, black and white, would be much easier to mobilise than anti-war sentiment. King therefore insisted that all of SCLC's efforts should now be directed towards running a Poor People's Campaign (PPC) in Washington, DC, in spring 1968.

While preparations got under way for the PPC, on 9 October the US Supreme Court refused King and his co-defendants a rehearing of convictions for contempt charges dating back to the 1963 Birmingham campaign. King therefore served four days in jail in Alabama at the end of October and the beginning of November. Shortly before going to jail, King testified before the National Advisory Commission on Civil Disorders set up by the Johnson administration to look into the causes of the recent riots in US cities. After his release, King flew to the United Kingdom to receive an honorary degree from the University of Newcastle upon Tyne. Upon his return, he recorded a series of speeches to be broadcast by the Canadian Broadcasting Corporation. News of a $230,000 grant from the Ford Foundation for a Ministers Leadership Training Program provided a source of money to develop leadership in key cities for the PPC. In the midst of these commitments, King attended a series of movement fund-raising concerts featuring entertainers such as Joan Baez, Harry Belafonte, Sammy Davis Jr and Aretha Franklin.

Between 27 November and 1 December the SCLC held another retreat in Frogmore, South Carolina, to discuss progress on the PPC. There, King articulated an even more radical vision of how the PPC might unfold. He told SCLC staff that they had underestimated just how entrenched racism was in the United States. The gains made between 1955 and 1965 had barely scratched the surface, King said. The true challenge they now faced was 'bring[ing] the social change movements through from their early and now inadequate protest phase to a stage of massive, active, nonviolent resistance to the evils of the modern system'.[53] Doing so would mean moving beyond issues such as integration and voting rights towards a more fundamental reorientation of social and economic values. This could be achieved, King said, through building a coalition of the poor and oppressed, not just including blacks, but also 'Puerto Ricans, Mexicans, Indians from the reservations, and poor whites from Appalachia', too.[54] Initial goals would involve securing employment opportunities and a minimum income level, and include demands for an elimination of the slums. Andrew Young, promoted to SCLC executive vice president, further elucidated King's vision by suggesting that the movement might employ tactics such as 'lying on highways, blocking doors at government offices, and mass school boycotts'.[55] This campaign of disruption would culminate in another March on Washington. However, this time the demonstration would not last for just one day but would instead occupy the nation's capital indefinitely until the Johnson administration was forced to reassess its domestic and foreign policy. At the end of the retreat on 4 December, King informed the press that the campaign would begin in April.

The PPC represented the SCLC's most ambitious and most audacious campaign – critics would say its most desperate – to date. The campaign essentially combined a number of elements already tried or suggested in the past. In attempting to build a broader movement that went beyond civil rights to tackle economic injustice, the plans at first glance appeared to hark back to Bayard Rustin's earlier thoughts about the movement shifting from 'protest to politics'. Yet the PPC was considerably different from Rustin's suggestion in the sense that it proposed not a move into the area of coalition politics, but rather into coalition protest. The emphasis on mass activism remained the same; it was rather the movement's perceived constituency of support and the scale of demonstrations that had changed. The PPC also incorporated elements first suggested in the Bevel proposal for demonstrations in Alabama after the Sixteenth Street Church bombing, particularly in its advocacy of mass civil disobedience. However, the PPC was in many respects even more ambitious than the Bevel plan, since it suggested deploying such tactics at a national rather than a state level. In reprising the idea of a March on Washington, the PPC looked to borrow on past movement success as a benchmark for its contemporary aspirations. King was under no illusions about the enormity of the task the PPC faced. 'This is a mammoth job,' he noted. 'Before we have mobilized one city at a time, now we are mobilizing a nation.'[56] Moreover, this had to be achieved against the backdrop of an unsympathetic president, a more conservative Congress, continuing internal divisions in the movement, and the spectre of urban violence.

Although many of the factors that could affect the success of the PPC were beyond King's control, the reinvigoration of a flagging SCLC was something that King could directly influence. In December 1967, King hired William A. Rutherford as the SCLC's new executive director. Rutherford, a native of Chicago and a successful black businessman, had volunteered assistance to the SCLC in the past. King persuaded Rutherford to take a one-year contract to help get the SCLC back on track. King's first briefing of Rutherford indicated that he had a very clear idea about what the main problems within the SCLC were. He outlined two specific tasks. Firstly, he wanted Rutherford to look into the spending habits of two senior SCLC staff, Jim Harrison and Hosea Williams, whose lifestyles appeared to be far more lavish than their salaries seemed to allow. The situation was a reflection of persistent problems of economic laxity running throughout the SCLC although, unbeknown to King, in SCLC comptroller Jim Harrison's case, the extra funds came from his being on the FBI payroll for passing on inside information about the SCLC's activities. Second, King was concerned about the activities of Jesse Jackson, whose Operation Breadbasket threatened to become a rival to, rather than a subsidiary of, the SCLC. King wanted Jackson either reined back into the SCLC fold or pushed out of it altogether.

During November and December 1967, the Canadian Broadcasting Corporation aired King's earlier recorded speeches. They revealed more about King's thoughts on the PPC. King insisted that 'Nonviolent protest must now mature to a new level to correspond to heightened black impatience and stiffened white reaction. This higher level is mass civil disobedience.' This new departure would offer an antidote to recent black violence, King said, and 'transmute the deep rage of the ghetto into a constructive and creative force'.[57] The PPC would comprise 'A sustained, massive, direct action movement in Washington,' offering 'a new economic deal for the poor.'[58] King asserted that the United States needed 'not a new law, but a massive new national program'.[59] The goal of the PPC would be to 'prod and sensitize the legislators, the administrators, and all the wielders of power until they have faced the utterly imperative need' to address that agenda.[60]

The speeches revealed that alongside a nationalisation of demonstrations, King was also contemplating an agenda for the internationalisation of nonviolent direct action. 'Can a nonviolent, direct action movement find application on the international level, to confront economic and political problems?' King asked. 'I believe it can. It is clear to me that the next stage in the movement is to become international.' King hinted at just how wide-ranging this internationalisation might be, and how it was tied to the new economic focus of the civil rights movement. 'We in the West must bear in mind that poor countries are poor primarily because we have exploited them through political or economic colonialism,' King told listeners. 'Americans in particular must help their nation repent of her modern economic imperialism.'[61] King's comments encompassed global issues from South America – 'So many of Latin America's problem's have roots in the United States of America' – to South Africa – 'If just two countries, Britain and the United States, could be persuaded to end all economic interaction with the South African regime, they could bring that government to its knees in a relatively short space of time.'[62] Overall,

King's ambition appeared to be nothing short of an effort 'to planetize our movement for racial justice'.[63] King's linking of civil rights to human rights and to global issues was not a particularly new departure. Since his visits to Africa and India in the late 1950s, King had often located the civil rights movement within a wider context of international liberation struggles. As a recipient of the international Nobel Peace Prize in 1964, however, King's statements on the subject had an even greater relevance and urgency to them.

Despite King's apparent optimism, doubts about the viability of the PPC remained within the SCLC. SCLC staff members were finding the task of engaging and organising local support, as well as fund-raising for the PPC, very hard going. Jesse Jackson complained that even the SCLC staff did not fully understand what the aims and goals of the PPC were. James Bevel and Bayard Rustin disputed the very idea that civil disobedience could be used to pressure the federal government into action. 'We are not now in the period we were in 1963 at the time of Selma, Birmingham and the March on Washington, where there was absolute clarity in everyone's mind as to objectives,' Rustin told King. 'The confusion today around economic questions and the splintering of the movement, I am convinced, requires a clear statement as to objectives, strategy and tactics.'[64] King's old theology tutor L. Harold DeWolf meanwhile warned King that 'anything which looks like an attempt to coerce the action of Congress would be not only illegal, but would probably result in . . . the election of an even more reactionary Congress'.[65] In March 1968, one of the SCLC board's most respected members, Marian Logan, circulated a memo outlining her constant concerns about the PPC. Like DeWolf, Logan feared that the PPC would harden the conservative stance of Congress and win support for reactionary candidates in elections later that year, while contributing to the defeat of politicians sympathetic to the movement. Moreover, Logan voiced concerns about inadequate planning for the PPC, the risk of violence and the lack of clear objectives.

With grave doubts emanating from his supporters, King's opponents were predictably even more adamantly opposed to the PPC. President Johnson berated the campaign and urged the civil rights movement to use its energies more productively. Congress explored the possibility of banning all demonstrations in the nation's capital. The PPC caused the FBI to further intensify its campaign against the civil rights movement. In particular, the FBI was concerned about the 'rise of a "messiah" who could unify, and electrify, the militant black nationalist movement'. Though King consistently distanced himself from such movements, the FBI still felt that he 'could be a very real contender for that position'.[66]

George C. Moore, head of the new Racial Intelligence Section of the FBI, urged a 'rumor campaign' against the PPC. This might include, he indicated, stories about the SCLC's undisciplined organisation and finances, the likelihood of the PPC descending into violence, the withholding of welfare cheques from PPC participants, and the opposition in Washington, DC,'s black community to the demonstrations. FBI field officers came up with ideas such as circulating pictures of King with Nation of Islam leader Elijah Muhammad, advertising bogus meetings with King listed as the main speaker, and disrupting arrangements for the PPC by promising buses to help with transportation and then not delivering them.

King staunchly defended his plans to movement supporters and to political opponents. He insisted that the indistinct goals of the PPC was a strength rather than a weakness. King contended that the campaign needed a simple slogan of 'jobs and income' that people could rally around, not complicated and detailed policy programmes. He pointed out that previous campaigns in Montgomery, Birmingham and Selma had not had detailed blueprints. Rather, mobilisation had occurred first and the precise details had been worked out after the momentum of the demonstrations had been established. The same would be true of the PPC. When King explained the PPC to the press he played down the use of civil disobedience and portrayed it as a much more traditionally conceived nonviolent, direct-action demonstration. King said that the first phase of the PPC would involve a 'lobby-in' of Congress when it reconvened on 22 April. At the same time, three groups of recruits from Milwaukee, Boston and Mississippi would begin a pilgrimage to Washington, DC, by car, by foot and by mule cart, to arrive in early May. Although King did not release further details to the press, there were also plans for a march on Capitol Hill on 5 May, a Mother's Day demonstration on 12 May, and a school desegregation rally to mark the fourteenth anniversary of the 1954 *Brown* v. *Board of Education* decision on 17 May. By the end of May, a March on Washington type of event and an escalation of demonstrations to the level of civil disobedience was planned. Provisional plans to hold demonstrations at the Democratic Party and Republican Party conventions later in the year were also under consideration. A nationwide economic boycott might be instigated to accompany them. King also formulated a tentative list of demands for the PPC, the main goal being to win an annual $30 billion appropriation for anti-poverty efforts. As an 'absolute minimum' the PPC would press Congress to pass legislation to ensure a commitment to full employment, a guaranteed minimum annual income, and funds for the annual building of half a million units of low-cost housing.[67]

By March 1968, the indications were that the PPC was beginning to take shape. The recruitment quotas for each targeted area had not only been achieved but had been exceeded. Donations through the SCLC's direct mailing programme were beginning to pick up. Labour unions, religious organisations and other interracial groups were starting to lend their support to the PPC. Nevertheless, as Andrew Young admitted, 'we still hadn't worked out the details'.[68]

The Memphis Sanitation Workers' Strike and King's Assassination

Just as the PPC seemed to be gathering momentum, King was sidetracked by an escalating union dispute in Memphis, Tennessee. The 1,300-strong members of the predominantly black American Federation of State, County and Municipal Employees (AFSCME) had been on strike since 12 February, angered at unfair treatment of its members and at the refusal of city officials to negotiate over a union dues 'checkoff' system. The checkoff system meant that dues were deducted straight from pay packets, which ensured regular union contributions. Without it, already lowly paid workers were often reluctant to relinquish dues on payday.

Memphis mayor Henry Loeb refused to recognise the union at all, let alone the validity of its complaints. Attempts to broker a compromise by white union leaders, the Memphis Ministers Association and national AFSCME president Jerry Wurf all failed. On 23 February, the conflict escalated further when city police employed Mace (an irritant chemical in aerosol form), tear gas and billyclubs to break up a union march. In the melee, participating black ministers and federal observers were also gassed. The actions of the city police helped to galvanise support for the striking workers and the following day 150 blacks, half of them ministers, formed Community on the Move for Equality (COME) to coordinate black community support for the strike. To exert pressure on the city, COME launched a boycott of downtown stores and white newspapers, and organised daily movement marches and evening rallies. When the city still refused to budge, COME sought to attract national support for its cause. In March 1968, Roy Wilkins and Bayard Rustin travelled to Memphis to address AFSCME members. King's old friend James Lawson, a minister in Memphis and a member of COME, also requested King's support. Many in the SCLC warned King against getting involved in Memphis when both he and the SCLC were already over-burdened with preparations for the PPC. Dismissing these concerns,

King told Andrew Young, 'Well, Jim Lawson has been around for so long and here are garbage workers on strike, he just wants me to come in and make a speech and I'll be right back.'[69] King therefore agreed to make a detour to the city while on his People-to-People tour of Mississippi.

When King arrived in Memphis on 18 March, he addressed an enthusiastic crowd of fifteen thousand people at Mason Temple. King was encouraged by the enthusiastic reception he received. He later told black Memphis minister Billy Kyles that he had detected 'that old movement spirit' that night, and that the strike might be the beginning of a 'rejuvenation of the movement'.[70] So moved was King by the response that he told the crowd, 'In a few days you ought to get together and just have a general work stoppage in the city of Memphis,' to allow all blacks in the city to show solidarity with the striking workers and to put more pressure on city officials to negotiate.[71] After conferring with Lawson, King announced that he would return to Memphis on the day of the general strike, which was scheduled for 22 March. Recognising that the dispute highlighted the intertwined nature of racial justice and economic power, King specifically tied the situation in Memphis to the PPC by announcing that the one-day general strike would mark 'the beginning of the Washington movement [the PPC]'.[72]

King continued with his People-to-People tour of Mississippi, Alabama and Georgia before heading north to fulfil commitments in New York and New Jersey. The one-day strike in Memphis had to be rescheduled for 28 March after a heavy snowfall disrupted plans for 22 March. When King flew into Memphis on 28 March his flight was delayed, meaning that those who had assembled at Clayborn Temple AME Church were kept waiting for over an hour for the march in support of the strike to begin. The delay proved to be a fateful one. As they waited, the crowd grew restless and impatient. Usually, marches headed by King and the SCLC only took place after careful preparation and training in nonviolence, the SCLC's Marian Logan noted, 'To get people organized in nonviolence and make them understand how important it was. And these garbage workers were not trained like that. And it was really a polyglot group of men, a union movement.'[73] Organisation of the Memphis march was left in the hands of local black leaders who made only perfunctory preparations for it. Among the milling crowd were members of a local black power group, the Black Organizing Project, or the 'Invaders' as they called themselves, who had been left out of discussions about the march. Alongside the Invaders there were, one student on the march noted, 'fellows sitting around drinking wine and beer and waiting for the march to begin. They began talking about looting stores.'[74] When King,

Ralph Abernathy and other SCLC staff members finally arrived, they were unaware of the potentially volatile mix. There were warning signs of the unruliness of the crowd when King's arrival was greeted by a disorganised crush. Lawson suggested delaying the march further to address the problem, but SCLC staff dismissed his entreaties, mistaking the uneasy mood of the crowd for exuberance and enthusiasm. 'We've been in this kind of situation before,' they told Lawson. 'There's a lot of excitement in the beginning, but if we hold on and go on, the march will get itself straightened out and everything will be all right.'[75]

However, it did not take long for the march to descend into chaos. The crowd did not sort itself out but remained in a state of what minister Billy Kyles described as 'mass confusion'. Student Ronald Hooks, at the front of the column taking photographs, noted that 'People were trying to walk much too fast for a crowd of that size. Dr. King was being pushed and people were walking on each other's heels.'[76] As the marchers turned into Main Street, white attorney Walter Bailey 'saw a group of young punks with sticks hitting a pawn shop window, and I said to myself "Good heavens! What the hell are they trying to do? Get us all shot?" Cries of 'smash glass' and 'burn it down, baby' could be heard as looting broke out.[77] The march had lasted less than half an hour. At the outbreak of looting, Lawson took the decision to disband. 'This is Reverend Lawson speaking,' he said, using a borrowed police bullhorn. 'I want everyone who's in the march, in the Movement, to turn back around and go back to church.'[78] Before the retreat got under way, however, city police waded into the crowd and used Mace and tear gas to break up the demonstration. King, at Lawson's insistence, had already been whisked away down a side street, where the SCLC's Bernard Lee commandeered a private car with the permission of its owner to get King away from the scene. King fled, accompanied by a police escort. The day's events led to 282 arrests, 62 injuries and the death of 17-year-old Larry Payne, who was shot by a Memphis police officer. A 7.00 p.m. curfew was imposed, enforced by 3,800 members of the Tennessee National Guard. Back at King's hotel, infuriated aides demanded to know why COME leaders had allowed King to step into such a badly organised and badly planned march, and why they had brought them 'into a situation like this without really telling them that the possibility [of violence] was there'.[79] King told Lawson, 'I can see a lot of our critics now saying, "You can't have anymore nonviolent marches and you can't come to Washington."' King was extremely subdued. 'Never have I led a march where the demonstrators committed acts of violence,' he told Abernathy, adding somberly, 'Maybe we'll just have to let violence have its chance.'[80] Yet clearly another peaceful march was an absolute necessity. Since King had explicitly linked the situation in Memphis to the PPC, the whole Washington, DC, campaign now hinged upon King's ability to show that he could still hold a disciplined, nonviolent demonstration, without it descending into violence.

The next morning, three leaders of the Invaders, Charles Cabbage, Calvin Taylor and Charles Harrington, arrived at King's hotel room to defend their organisation over its alleged role in events. King agreed to see them. Cabbage, who like King was a Morehouse College graduate, explained that 'Lawson kept us out. If he had been listening to us, we could have warned him there was likely to be trouble.'[81] Even though King remained unconvinced at the Invaders' protestations of innocence, he was annoyed by the fact that Lawson had misled him over the presence of a black power faction in the city. Moreover, it was clear to King that, in order for a peaceful march to go ahead, the cooperation of the Invaders would be needed. 'What can I do ... to have a peaceful march,' King asked them, 'because you know that I have to lead one.'[82] The Invaders indicated that, in return for financial help for their community organising plans, they would cooperate with another march. However, they still insisted that they could not wholly guarantee a peaceful passage. King explained that the SCLC did not have the money to fund the Invaders' project but he agreed to make inquiries elsewhere on their behalf. At that uneasy truce, the Invaders left. Later, King told the press that the SCLC had not played a role in the organisation of the march the previous day but that it would take responsibility for running a second, peaceful march through the city.

As King expected, forces opposed to the civil rights movement used the violence in Memphis to discredit him personally and to insist that his inability to control the movement meant that plans for the PPC must be abandoned. The FBI concocted its own version of the events for release to 'cooperative media sources'. It depicted King as a 'judas goat leading lambs to slaughter ... and when the violence broke out he disappeared', and warned that 'Memphis may only be a prelude to civil strife in our Nation's Capitol [sic].' The *Memphis Commercial Appeal* printed a picture of King fleeing the march with the caption 'Chicken A La King'. The *St. Louis Globe-Democrat* warned that unless King was 'checked, he could wipe out most of the impressive civil rights gains made by Negroes in recent years'. Hostile forces in Congress lined up to condemn King. West Virginia senator Robert C. Byrd described King as a 'self-seeking rabble rouser'.[83] The black-owned, Memphis-based *Tri-State Defender* meanwhile placed the blame for the violence squarely on the city's shoulders.

'A disturbance was bound to occur sooner or later,' its editorial read. 'And Memphis authorities knew it. They made the fatal choice. Between settling the strike and clubbing the marchers into submission, they chose the latter.'[84]

In public, King confidently asserted that the situation in Memphis, which demonstrated the link between issues of race and class, underlined exactly why the PPC was necessary and insisted that it would still go ahead. In private, King was far more perturbed. He told Abernathy, 'Ralph, I want to get out of Memphis. Get me out of Memphis as soon as possible.'[85] In an afternoon phone call with Stanley Levison, King further lamented the current state of affairs. The Memphis march had been a disaster. It would make recruitment for the PPC more difficult than ever. Indeed, King believed that the PPC might now have to be cancelled altogether. His personal standing and his ability to successfully deliver on nonviolence had been brought into question. The only way to turn things around was to guarantee a second successful nonviolent march that could silence his critics. Levison disagreed with King's downbeat assessment and urged a sense of perspective. The failure of the march was not King's fault but down to the ineptitude of local organisers, Levison told him. Moreover, neither King nor the SCLC could ever absolutely guarantee that there would be no violence on a demonstration. It was simply unrealistic to claim that they could control everyone who turned up on the streets. Despite Levison's efforts to uplift him, King remained grim about the future prospects of the movement. A meeting with the SCLC's executive staff back in Atlanta was arranged to discuss developments the following day.

The Atlanta meeting highlighted just how deep King's disillusionment had become. When King outlined plans for a second Memphis march as a way of getting the PPC back on track, it inspired precious little enthusiasm. Some staff members thought that returning to Memphis was a bad idea and that concentrating efforts and resources there would undermine rather than help the PPC. Other staff members, particularly James Bevel and Jesse Jackson, voiced their lasting feeling that the PPC should be abandoned altogether. 'There was a general tone of lecturing Martin,' Andrew Young recalled.[86] After facing several hours of dissent, King stood up and announced that he was leaving the meeting and that they could probably sort out the organisation's problems better without him. As Jackson followed King to the door, King launched an uncharacteristically personal attack on him, saying 'Jesse it may be necessary for you to carve out your own individual niche in society. But you don't bother me.'[87] With that outburst King left.

Staff discussions continued without King. After a gruelling ten hours, some clarity over the PPC began to emerge. Rallying to find a consensus, the SCLC executive staff agreed that the twin objectives of returning to hold a peaceful second march in Memphis and continuing with the PPC were both achievable and mutually compatible. The SCLC would return to Memphis not to defend its ability to hold a nonviolent march, they said, but because the issues that were being raised there were relevant to the PPC. The violence in Memphis had not been the SCLC's doing, but it would exert its influence to assure a better level of preparedness for the second march. A successful second march would provide a fitting springboard for the PPC. With the feeling that the movement was now firmly back on track, the earlier gloom of the meeting was lifted. The following day, President Johnson made a dramatic national television appearance to tell the nation that he would not seek re-election to office in the forthcoming presidential election. The promise of political change heightened King and the SCLC's hopes for a renewal of the movement's fortunes.

SCLC staff James Orange, Jesse Jackson, James Bevel and Hosea Williams were sent to Memphis to pave the way for a second march scheduled for 5 April. Orange took on the nettlesome task of reconciling local Memphis factions the Invaders and COME. Though a great deal of personal antipathy remained on both sides, Orange got the two organisations to agree to work together on the forthcoming march, rescheduled for 8 April. King travelled to Washington, DC, to keep a prearranged engagement and returned to Atlanta for a couple of days before heading to Memphis on 3 April. As King participated in a meeting at James Lawson's church, news came through that federal district judge Bailey Brown had issued a restraining order against King, Abernathy, Williams, Bevel, Orange and Lee, as well as their 'servants, agents, employees and those in concert with them from organizing or engaging in a massive parade or march in the city of Memphis'.[88] Six Memphis attorneys agreed to help fight the order on the SCLC's behalf. King indicated that he intended to go ahead with the march whether the injunction was lifted or not. The attorneys meanwhile devised a strategy whereby they would ask for a modification of the injunction to allow a small, disciplined group to hold a limited downtown march. This would strike a note of compromise with the court while at the same time heightening the chances of the march passing off without violence. King agreed, and the attorneys prepared their arguments to present to the court the following morning. With the legal issue dealt with, King turned his attention to placating representatives from the Invaders. He promised to help with the planning and financing of their community organising plans in exchange for their support in keeping the 8 April march free from violence.

That evening, King was due to speak to a mass meeting at Mason Temple. However, exhausted, he sent Abernathy to deputise for him. Only two thousand people turned up owing to the stormy weather. Yet Abernathy sensed that those who had made the effort to get there were disappointed not to see King in person. Abernathy called King and told him, 'Martin, you know I would not ask you to come ordinarily, but these people want to hear you, and they want to see you.'[89] King agreed to go, although even as he took the stage, one of the people sharing the platform with him, the Revd Harold Middlebrook, thought 'that he looked harrowed and tired and wan and rushed'.[90] King's weariness added to the emotional intensity of his speech that night. Part of the address dwelt on the time that he had been stabbed and had stared death in the face. If he had merely sneezed, King told the crowd, the blade might have pierced his heart and killed him. But he had not sneezed and he had gone on to see the great achievements of the movement through the sit-ins, the Freedom Rides, the March on Washington, and SCLC campaigns in Albany, Birmingham and Selma. There were difficult days ahead, King told them, 'But it really doesn't matter to me now, because I've been to the mountaintop . . . and I've seen the promised land. I may not get there with you. But I want you to know tonight, that we as a people will get to the promised land. And so I'm happy tonight. I'm not worried about anything. I'm not fearing any man. Mine eyes have see the glory of the coming of the Lord.'[91] Afterwards, King and Abernathy dined with Memphis minister and SCLC board member Benjamin Hooks before heading back to their rooms at the Lorraine Hotel. There, they found that King's brother A. D. and other friends had arrived from Louisville. The group stayed up until the small hours in conversation.

On 4 April, King did not awake until noon, by which time Andrew Young and James Lawson had already headed off to the district court with movement attorneys in an attempt to get Judge Bailey to modify the injunction against the planned march. King waited anxiously for news in his hotel room throughout the afternoon while discussing the continuing problems posed by the unpredictable Invaders with SCLC staff. Later, Andrew Young and SCLC attorney Chauncey Eskridge returned from the court with the good news that the judge had agreed to their proposal for a scaled-down march the following Monday. King was in good humour at hearing the news and teased Young about his prolonged absence. Abernathy joined in the teasing and the three of them ended up in a pillow fight in a brief release from the tension-filled past few weeks.

Memphis minister Billy Kyles had invited King and his aides for a soul food supper that evening, so with the time approaching 6.00 p.m. they began to ready themselves. Shortly afterwards, Kyles called to collect them. King walked out on to his second-floor balcony beside Kyles, with driver Solomon Jones Jr, while Andrew Young, Chauncey Eskridge, James Bevel, Jesse Jackson and Hosea Williams waited for them in the courtyard below. Abernathy was still inside the hotel room fussing about and getting ready. Jones called up to King to put on a topcoat since it was getting cold. King sent Kyles on ahead while he went to get his coat from the room. Suddenly, a single rifle shot rang out, hitting King in the cheek. Abernathy rushed out of the room and Kyles and the others headed to the balcony. When Andrew Young reached King he was laid out on the balcony floor. Young looked over at Abernathy and said 'Oh, my God, my God, it's all over, it's all over.'[92] King was rushed to a Memphis hospital, but was pronounced dead not long after arrival.

Conclusion: Martin and the Movement

Although the civil rights movement had already been in decline for several years, no one single event signalled a decisive end to it more than King's assassination. Much of white America felt sympathy and remorse at King's death. President Johnson ordered flags to be flown at half mast and declared the following Sunday a national day of mourning. In Memphis, 300 black and white ministers marched on City Hall on 5 April. Eleven days later the city capitulated to the demands of the striking sanitation workers. Congress passed the 1968 Civil Rights Act on 10 April, although its provisions for fair housing and for the protection of civil rights workers had little practical impact. More white money poured into SCLC coffers than ever before. In black America, however, King's death was greeted with anger and violence. Racial disturbances rocked more than 130 cities in 29 states, resulting in 46 deaths, over 7,000 injuries and 20,000 arrests, with damage to property estimated at over $100 million.

Although the outbreak of such violence might seem paradoxical, given King's commitment to nonviolence, in fact it made every sense. King had maintained throughout his life that nonviolence was the most viable antidote to violence. Blacks viewed King's death as white America's final rejection of nonviolence and, just as King had predicted, turned decisively to violence instead. Black power advocate Stokely Carmichael asserted that 'when white America killed Dr. King, she declared war on us . . . Black people have to survive, and the only way they will survive is by getting a gun.'[1] As King had also predicted, the use of black violence only brought greater white counter-violence. The federal government ruthlessly suppressed and quickly crushed a black militant insurgency within a few short years. Without King, the SCLC's influence quickly melted away. Ralph Abernathy took over as president of the organisation and presided over an ill-fated Poor People's Campaign that failed to win any significant concessions. Shortly afterwards, many of the influential members of the SCLC during King's lifetime left the organisation, which had become riddled with factionalism and disagreements in his absence.

As events unfolded after King's death, they underscored just what his presence had meant to the civil rights movement. 'Ultimately,' King once reflected, 'a genuine leader is not a searcher for consensus but a molder of consensus.'[2] As president of the SCLC, King had acted as a lightning conductor to attract a cadre of talented local black southern leaders. King had kept conflicting egos within the SCLC largely at bay during his lifetime. Never resorting to autocratic leadership, King allowed SCLC staff members a great deal of leeway to develop new ideas and tactics, while reining in their over-ambition and cautioning against excess.

King's leadership of the SCLC was in many ways a microcosm of his leadership role in the civil rights movement. As part of what was an often fractious and factious movement, King commanded more respect and trust in more sections of the black community than any other black leader of the time. Central to King's ability to achieve this respect and trust was his grounding in the black southern Baptist Church tradition. King used the black church as a spiritual and organisational base for the movement. He tapped the latent religious sentiment and fervour of the black church while using his position at the head of a key black community institution to appeal to more secular sections of the black community as well. King made the idea of nonviolence and the tactic of nonviolent direct action appear like a seamless extension of the black church and black religion. Yet in fact, in employing nonviolent, direct-action tactics, King managed to combine what was often a very conservative black community institution with a far more radical tradition of nonviolence developed by pacifists and socialists on the American political left. In this way, he was able to appeal to both conservative and to militant wings of the movement. As historian and activist August Meier noted at the time, King could very well be described as a 'conservative militant'.[3]

King effectively acted as a bridge between different sections of the black community. In a decade when American youth would implore their generation not to trust anyone over 30, King turned 31 in January 1960. This placed him on the cusp of being young enough to relate to influential student demonstrators, but mature and respected enough to mediate between them and older and more conservative black leaders such as the NAACP's Roy Wilkins and the NUL's Whitney Young. King also used his status and authority as a black minister to successfully appeal to both the 'classes' and the 'masses', or, as King put it, 'the PhDs and the no "Ds"' in the southern black community.[4] Of course, King could not appeal to everyone all of the time. Many black northerners did not identify with King's distinctly southern and religious sensibilities.

As the civil rights movement became more fragmented after 1965, King often found himself stranded in the middle ground, too old, too conservative and too bourgeois for a new generation of younger, more working-class-oriented black militants, yet too young and too radical for older, more conservative middle-class black leaders.

Just as important as King's ability to unite the black community was his ability to reach out to large and significant sections of America's white community, and to engage them in the civil rights movement. Nonviolent direct action highlighted the inconsistency of brutal southern enforcement of segregation and disfranchisement with white America's claims to be a fundamentally democratic and moral society. The tactic therefore appealed to whites on the very grounds on which they were most likely to listen and to make concessions. King also had the ability to verbally articulate the demands of the black community in a way that both blacks and whites could identify with and understand. Combining his experience as an orator in the black folk pulpit tradition with ideas, rhetoric and values imbibed in his northern white liberal seminary and university education, King skilfully fused texts such as the Bible with the Constitution and the Declaration of Independence to provide a vision of social and racial justice that merged, as one historian notes, 'prophetic Christianity and the American civic creed'.[5] Black writer James Baldwin was not the only one to note that 'King's secret lay in the intimate knowledge of his audience, black or white, and in the forthrightness with which he spoke of the things that hurt or baffled them.'[6]

A number of scholars have traced King's ideas, influences and abilities.[7] The main aim of this book has been to demonstrate how King translated those ideas, influences and abilities into action, by formulating a strategy to pursue social, political and economic change for blacks. The most readily apparent markers of King's success are the 1964 Civil Rights Act and the 1965 Voting Rights Act. The 1964 Civil Rights Act was passed in a climate for racial reform created by King and the SCLC's 1963 Birmingham campaign and the 1963 March on Washington, and was speeded by the grief over the assassination of President Kennedy and by the political skill and commitment to civil rights of his successor President Johnson. The 1964 Civil Rights Act ended the practice of legalised segregation in the South that had provided a highly visible, day-to-day enforcement of black social inferiority. The 1965 Voting Rights Act, passed as a direct consequence of King and the SCLC's 1965 Selma campaign, opened up a path for blacks to join the southern body politic and to begin in earnest the process of building black political power. The 1965 Voting Rights Act meant that far larger numbers of southern blacks were able to vote without impediment. It also meant that blacks could actually run for election to positions such as president, US Congress, state congress, governor and mayor, as well as for election to positions such as local judge, local sheriff and local school board member, with a far more realistic chance of success.

An integral part of civil rights struggles was also a transformation in black self-awareness, self-confidence and self-respect. Participation in the movement enabled many blacks to stand shoulder to shoulder in opposition to white oppression and in the process to overcome their fear of white violence and intimidation. However, not all of King's and the movement's endeavours were successful: King's efforts to focus on economic issues during his final years were only at an embryonic stage at the time of his death, and he never achieved the kind of far-reaching redistribution of wealth and resources that he sought.

Ultimately, King and the civil rights movement helped blacks to gain access to and build a platform for social and political power. In doing so, they fostered a sense of black empowerment and psychological liberation that provided the foundations for implementing and furthering those gains. Yet King and the civil rights movement barely had a chance to begin the much larger and far more complex task of translating notional rights under the law into actual social, political and economic power. That new phase of the struggle for black freedom and equality succeeded King and the movement and continues today.

Notes

Introduction

1. David J. Garrow, *Bearing the Cross: Martin Luther King, Jr. and the Southern Christian Leadership Conference* (New York, 1986), p. 625.
2. Richard Lischer, *The Preacher King: Martin Luther King, Jr. and the Word That Moved America* (New York, 1995), p. 192.
3. Martin Luther King Jr, *Where Do We Go From Here?: Chaos or Community* (New York, 1967), p. 37.
4. Charles M. Payne, *I've Got the Light of Freedom: The Organizing Tradition and the Mississippi Freedom Struggle* (Berkeley, California, 1995), p. 418.
5. Martin Luther King Jr, *Stride Toward Freedom: The Montgomery Story* (New York, 1958), p. 85.
6. David J. Garrow, *Protest at Selma: Martin Luther King, Jr., and the Voting Rights Act of 1965* (New Haven, Connecticut, 1978), p. 221.

Chapter 1

1. J. Harvie Wilkinson III, *From Brown to Bakke: The Supreme Court and School Integration, 1954–1978* (New York, 1979), p. 69.
2. David R. Goldfield, *Black, White, and Southern: Race Relations and Southern Culture, 1940 to the Present* (Baton Rouge, Louisiana, 1990), pp. 75–6.
3. James T. Patterson, *Brown v. Board of Education: A Civil Rights Milestone and Its Troubled Legacy* (New York, 2001), p. 60.
4. Rosa Parks interview in Henry Hampton and Steven Fayer (eds), *Voices of Freedom: An Oral History of the Civil Rights Movement from the 1950s through the 1980s* (New York, 1995), pp. 19–20; Rosa Parks, with Jim Haskins, *Rosa Parks: My Story* (New York, 1992), p. 1.
5. E.D. Nixon interview in Howell Raines (ed.), *My Soul is Rested: Movement Days in the Deep South Remembered* (New York, 1977), p. 39.
6. Fred D. Gray, *Bus Ride to Justice: Changing the System by the System: The Life and Works of Fred D. Gray, Preacher, Attorney, Politician: Lawyer for Rosa Parks* (Montgomery, Alabama, 1999), pp. 48–9.

7. E.D. Nixon interview in Hampton and Fayer (eds), *Voices of Freedom*, p. 21; Douglas Brinkley, *Mine Eyes Have Seen the Glory: The Life of Rosa Parks* (London, 2000), p. 114.

8. Jo Ann Robinson interview in Hampton and Fayer (eds), *Voices of Freedom*, p. 22.

9. Fred D. Gray, *Bus Ride to Justice*, pp. 40–1.

10. 'Don't Ride the Bus', leaflet, 2 December 1955, in Clayborne Carson, Susan A. Carson, Peter Holloran, Dana L. Powell and Stewart Burns (eds), *The Papers of Martin Luther King, Jr. Vol. III.: Birth of a New Age, December 1955–December 1956* (Berkeley, California, 1997), p. 67.

11. Rosa Parks, *Rosa Parks: My Story*, p. 125.

12. Adam Fairclough, *To Redeem the Soul of America: The Southern Christian Leadership Conference and Martin Luther King, Jr.* (Athens, Georgia, 1987), p. 16.

13. Martin Luther King Jr, 'An Autobiography of Religious Development', 22 November 1950, in Clayborne Carson, Ralph E. Luker and Penny A. Russell (eds), *The Papers of Martin Luther King, Jr Vol. I: Called To Serve, January 1929–June 1951* (Berkeley, California, 1992), p. 363.

14. Ibid., p. 360.

15. Ibid., p. 362.

16. Clayborne Carson (ed.), *The Autobiography of Martin Luther King, Jr.* (New York, 1998), p. 10.

17. Martin Luther King Jr, 'An Autobiography of Religious Development', p. 363.

18. Benjamin E. Mays, *Born to Rebel: An Autobiography* (Athens, Georgia, 1987), p. 265.

19. Martin Luther King Jr, 'An Autobiography of Religious Development', p. 361.

20. Ibid.

21. Carson (ed.), *The Autobiography of Martin Luther King, Jr.*, p. 16.

22. Ibid., p. 12.

23. Martin Luther King Sr, with Clayton Riley, *Daddy King: An Autobiography* (Boston, Massachusetts, 1980), pp. 150–1.

24. David J. Garrow, *Bearing the Cross: Martin Luther King, Jr. and the Southern Christian Leadership Conference* (New York, 1986), p. 50.

25. Martin Luther King Jr, *Stride Toward Freedom: The Montgomery Story* (New York, 1958), p. 150.

26. Ibid., p. 43.

27. Roy Wilkins, *Standing Fast: The Autobiography of Roy Wilkins* (New York, 1982), p. 227.

28. Coretta Scott King interview in Hampton and Fayer (eds), *Voices of Freedom*, pp. 23–4.

29. 'MIA Mass Meeting at Holt Street Baptist Church', 5 December 1955, in Carson et al., *The Papers of Martin Luther King, Jr. Vol. III*, pp. 71–9.

30. Martin Luther King Jr, *Stride Toward Freedom*, p. 119.

31. MIA Press Release, 'The Bus Protest is Still On', 22 January 1956, in Carson et al., *The Papers of Martin Luther King, Jr. Vol. III*, pp. 100–1.

32. Garrow, *Bearing the Cross*, p. 55.

33. Martin Luther King Jr, *Stride Toward Freedom*, p. 121.

34. Ibid., p. 128.

35. Garrow, *Bearing the Cross*, pp. 57–8.

36. Martin Luther King Jr, *Stride Toward Freedom*, pp. 128–9.

37. Ibid., p. 134.

38. Coretta Scott King, *My Life With Martin Luther King, Jr.* (New York, 1969), p. 144.

39. Ibid., p. 146.

40. Martin Luther King Jr, *Stride Toward Freedom*, p. 139.

41. Daniel Levine, *Bayard Rustin and the Civil Rights Movement* (New Brunswick, New Jersey, 2000), p. 83.

42. Bayard Rustin interview in Howell Raines (ed.), *My Soul is Rested*, p. 53.

43. Fairclough, *To Redeem the Soul of America*, p. 24.

44. Jervis Anderson, *Bayard Rustin: Troubles I've Seen: A Biography* (Berkeley, California, 1997), p. 189.

45. Garrow, *Bearing the Cross*, p. 68.

46. Martin Luther King Jr, *Stride Toward Freedom*, p. 154.

47. Garrow, *Bearing the Cross*, p. 81.

48. Martin Luther King Jr, *Stride Toward Freedom*, pp. 160–4.

49. Ibid., p. 164.

50. Harris Wofford, *Of Kennedys and Kings: Making Sense of the Sixties* (New York, 1980), p. 119.

51. Martin Luther King Jr, *Stride Toward Freedom*, p. 156.

52. Ibid., p. 177.

53. James Forman, *The Making of Black Revolutionaries* (Washington, DC, 1985), pp. 84–5.

Chapter 2

1. Carolyn Calloway-Thomas and John Louis Lucaites (eds), *Martin Luther King, Jr. and the Sermonic Power of Public Discourse* (Tuscaloosa, Alabama, 1993), p. 46.

2. Martin Luther King Jr, *Why We Can't Wait* (New York, 1964), p. 132.

3. Lerone Bennett Jr, *What Manner of Man: A Biography of Martin Luther King, Jr.* (Chicago, 1964), pp. 80–1.

4. Martin Luther King Jr, 'Give Us the Ballot – We Will Transform the South', in James M. Washington (ed.), *A Testament of Hope: The Essential Writings and Speeches of Martin Luther King, Jr.* (San Francisco, California, 1986), pp. 197–200.

5. Clayborne Carson (ed.), *The Autobiography of Martin Luther King, Jr.* (New York, 1998), p. 109.

6. Jervis Anderson, *Bayard Rustin: Troubles I've Seen: A Biography* (Berkeley, California, 1997), p. 207.

7. Carson (ed.), *The Autobiography of Martin Luther King, Jr.*, p. 114. King also visited Nigeria, Rome, Geneva, Paris and London on the trip.

8. Ibid., pp. 132, 134.

9. J. Mills Thornton, *Dividing Lines: Municipal Politics and the Struggle for Civil Rights in Montgomery, Birmingham, and Selma* (Tuscaloosa, Alabama, 2002), p. 100.

10. David L. Lewis, *King: A Critical Biography* (Urbana, Illinois, 1970), p. 96.

11. David J. Garrow, *Bearing the Cross: Martin Luther King, Jr. and the Southern Christian Leadership Conference* (New York, 1986), p. 109.

12. Carson (ed.), *The Autobiography of Martin Luther King, Jr.*, p. 117.

13. Ibid., p. 118.

14. Ibid., p. 120.

15. Adam Fairclough, *To Redeem the Soul of America: The Southern Christian Leadership Conference and Martin Luther King, Jr.* (Athens, Georgia, 1987), p. 32.

16. Aldon D. Morris, *The Origins of the Civil Rights Movement: Black Communities Organizing for Change* (New York, 1984), p. 45.

17. The SCLC eventually introduced individual membership in 1963.

18. Fairclough, *To Redeem the Soul of America*, p. 43.

19. Garrow, *Bearing the Cross*, p. 115.

20. Carson (ed.), *The Autobiography of Martin Luther King, Jr.*, p. 136.

21. Garrow, *Bearing the Cross*, p. 125.

22. Howard Zinn, *SNCC: The New Abolitionists* (Boston, Massachusetts, 1965), p. 16.

23. Garrow, *Bearing the Cross*, p. 129.

24. Clayborne Carson, *In Struggle: SNCC and the Black Awakening of the 1960s* (Cambridge, Massachusetts, 1981), p. 20.

25. Ella J. Baker, 'Bigger than a Hamburger', in Clayborne Carson, David J. Garrow, Gerald Gill, Vincent Harding and Darlene Clark Hine (eds), *The Eyes on the Prize Civil Rights Reader: Documents, Speeches, and Firsthand Accounts from the Black Freedom Struggle* (New York, 1991), pp. 120–2.

26. Carson, *In Struggle*, pp. 22–3.

27. Zinn, *SNCC*, p. 35.

28. Garrow, *Bearing the Cross*, p. 144.

29. Harris Wofford, *Of Kennedys and Kings: Making Sense of the Sixties* (New York, 1980), p. 14.

30. Ibid., p. 11.

31. Carson (ed.), *The Autobiography of Martin Luther King, Jr.*, p. 147.

32. Coretta Scott King interview in Henry Hampton and Steven Fayer (eds), *Voices of Freedom: An Oral History of the Civil Rights Movement from the 1950s through the 1980s* (New York, 1995), pp. 69–70.

33. Harris Wofford interview in Hampton and Fayer (eds), *Voices of Freedom*, p. 70.

34. Wofford, *Of Kennedys and Kings*, p. 21.

35. Clifford M. Khun, '"There's a Footnote to History!" Memory and the History of Martin Luther King's October 1960 Arrest and Its Aftermath', *Journal of American History* 84 (Sept. 1997), p. 590.

36. Ibid.

37. Ibid., p. 587.

38. Harris Wofford interview in Hampton and Fayer (eds), *Voices of Freedom*, p. 71.

39. Wofford, *Of Kennedys and Kings*, p. 22.

40. Carson (ed.), *The Autobiography of Martin Luther King, Jr.*, pp. 143–4.

41. Garrow, *Bearing the Cross*, p. 140.

42. Daniel Levine, *Bayard Rustin and the Civil Rights Movement* (New Brunswick, New Jersey, 2000), p. 121.

43. Wofford, *Of Kennedys and Kings*, p. 151.

44. James Farmer interview in Hampton and Fayer (eds), *Voices of Freedom*, p. 79.

45. Catherine Barnes, *Journey from Jim Crow: The Desegregation of Southern Transit* (New York, 1983), pp. 159–60.

46. James Peck interview in Hampton and Fayer (eds), *Voices of Freedom*, p. 78.

47. Hank Thomas interview in Howell Raines (ed.), *My Soul is Rested: Movement Days in the Deep South Remembered* (New York, 1977), p. 115.

48. Diane Nash interview in Hampton and Fayer (eds), *Voices of Freedom*, p. 82.

49. Pat Watters, *Down to Now: Reflections on the Southern Civil Rights Movement* (New York, 1971), p. 103.

50. Andrew M. Manis, *A Fire You Can't Put Out: The Civil Rights Life of Birmingham's Fred Shuttlesworth* (Tuscaloosa, Alabama, 1999), p. 273.

51. Wofford, *Of Kennedys and Kings*, p. 153.

52. Manis, *A Fire You Can't Put Out*, p. 274.

53. Wofford, *Of Kennedys and Kings*, p. 154.

54. John Lewis interview in Hampton and Fayer (eds), *Voices of Freedom*, p. 86.

55. Manis, *A Fire You Can't Put Out*, p. 229. According to the New Testament, Golgotha was the place of Christ's crucifixion.

56. Lewis, *King*, p. 134.

57. James Farmer interview in Hampton and Fayer (eds), *Voices of Freedom*, p. 92.

58. Zinn, *SNCC*, p. 50.

59. Ibid., p. 51.

60. Barnes, *Journey from Jim Crow*, p. 166.

61. Ibid.

62. Wofford, *Of Kennedys and Kings*, p. 378.

63. August Meier and Elliott Rudwick, *CORE: A Study in the Civil Rights Movement, 1942–1968* (New York, 1973), p. 133.

64. Wofford, *Of Kennedys and Kings*, p. 155.

65. Barnes, *Journey from Jim Crow*, p. 184.

66. Stephen B. Oates, *Let the Trumpet Sound: The Life of Martin Luther King, Jr.* (New York, 1982), p. 308.

Chapter 3

1. Laurie Pritchett interview in Howell Raines (ed.), *My Soul is Rested: Movement Days in the Deep South Remembered* (New York, 1977), p. 361.
2. Laurie Pritchett interview in Henry Hampton and Steven Fayer (eds), *Voices of Freedom: An Oral History of the Civil Rights Movement from the 1950s through the 1980s* (New York, 1995), p. 106.
3. Martin Luther King Jr, *Stride Toward Freedom: The Montgomery Story* (New York, 1958), p. 69.
4. David L. Lewis, *King: A Critical Biography* (Urbana, Illinois, 1970), p. 145.
5. Clayborne Carson, *In Struggle: SNCC and the Black Awakening of the 1960s* (Cambridge, Massachusetts, 1981), p. 59.
6. Howard Zinn, *SNCC: The New Abolitionists* (Boston, Massachusetts, 1965), p. 130.
7. Ibid.
8. Ibid., p. 123.
9. Aldon D. Morris, *The Origins of the Civil Rights Movement: Black Communities Organizing for Change* (New York, 1984), p. 243.
10. James Forman, *The Making of Black Revolutionaries* (Washington, DC, 1985), p. 255.
11. Morris, *The Origins of the Civil Rights Movement*, p. 242.
12. Coretta Scott King, *My Life With Martin Luther King, Jr.* (New York, 1969), p. 203.
13. David J. Garrow, *Bearing the Cross: Martin Luther King, Jr. and the Southern Christian Leadership Conference* (New York, 1986), p. 181.
14. Zinn, *SNCC*, p. 131.
15. Martin Luther King Jr, *Why We Can't Wait* (New York, 1964), p. 61.
16. Garrow, *Bearing the Cross*, p. 100.
17. Lewis, *King*, p. 149.
18. Clayborne Carson (ed.), *The Autobiography of Martin Luther King, Jr.* (New York, 1998), p. 156.
19. Taylor Branch, *Parting the Waters: Martin Luther King and the Civil Rights Movement, 1954–1963* (New York, 1988), p. 556.
20. Ibid., p. 557.
21. Adam Fairclough, *To Redeem the Soul of America: The Southern Christian Leadership Conference and Martin Luther King, Jr.* (Athens, Georgia, 1987), p. 85.
22. John A. Ricks, 'De Lawd Descends and is Crucified: Martin Luther King, Jr. in Albany, Georgia', *Journal of Southwest Georgia History* 2 (Fall 1984), p. 7.
23. Pat Watters, *Down to Now: Reflections on the Southern Civil Rights Movement* (New York, 1971), p. 149.

24. Zinn, *SNCC*, p. 134.

25. Carson (ed.), *The Autobiography of Martin Luther King, Jr.*, p. 159.

26. Zinn, *SNCC*, p. 134.

27. Fairclough, *To Redeem the Soul of America*, pp. 102–3.

28. Forman, *The Making of Black Revolutionaries*, pp. 274–5.

29. Charles Sherrod interview in Hampton and Fayer (eds), *Voices of Freedom*, p. 112.

30. Morris, *The Origins of the Civil Rights Movement*, p. 248.

31. Ricks, 'De Lawd', p. 9.

32. Carson (ed.), *The Autobiography of Martin Luther King, Jr.*, p. 160.

33. Watters, *Down to Now*, p. 214.

34. Carson, *In Struggle*, p. 61.

35. Telegram to President Kennedy, 2 August 1962, in Carson (ed.), *The Autobiography of Martin Luther King, Jr.*, p. 164.

36. Garrow, *Bearing the Cross*, pp. 211–13.

37. Carson (ed.), *The Autobiography of Martin Luther King, Jr.*, p. 165.

38. Ricks, 'De Lawd', p. 11.

39. Garrow, *Bearing the Cross*, p. 215.

40. Ibid., p. 216.

41. Fairclough, *To Redeem the Soul of America*, p. 106.

42. Stephen G.N. Tuck, *Beyond Atlanta: The Struggle for Racial Equality in Georgia, 1940–1980* (Athens, Georgia, 2001), p. 147.

43. Roy Wilkins, *Standing Fast: The Autobiography of Roy Wilkins* (New York, 1982), p. 286.

44. Glenn T. Eskew, *But for Birmingham: The Local and National Movements in the Civil Rights Struggle* (Chapel Hill, North Carolina, 1997), p. 53.

45. Walker interview in Hampton and Fayer (eds), *Voices of Freedom*, p. 126.

46. Martin Luther King Jr, *Why We Can't Wait*, p. 54.

47. Fred Shuttlesworth interview in Hampton and Fayer (eds), *Voices of Freedom*, p. 125.

48. Martin Luther King Jr, *Why We Can't Wait*, p. 115.

49. Forman, *The Making of Black Revolutionaries*, p. 312.

50. Martin Luther King Jr, *Why We Can't Wait*, p. 56.

51. Andrew M. Manis, *A Fire You Can't Put Out: The Civil Rights Life of Birmingham's Fred Shuttlesworth* (Tuscaloosa, Alabama, 1999), p. 361.

52. Martin Luther King Jr, *Why We Can't Wait*, p. 54.

53. Garrow, *Bearing the Cross*, p. 235.

54. Eskew, *But for Birmingham*, p. 222.

55. Martin Luther King Jr, *Why We Can't Wait*, p. 69.

56. Manis, *A Fire You Can't Put Out*, p. 348.

57. Ibid., pp. 350–1.

58. Forman, *The Making of Black Revolutionaries*, p. 312.

59. Martin Luther King Jr, *Why We Can't Wait*, p. 72.

60. Ibid., p. 73.

61. Andrew Young interview in Hampton and Fayer (eds), *Voices of Freedom*, p. 136.

62. Eskew, *But for Birmingham*, p. 241.

63. Garrow, *Bearing the Cross*, p. 243.

64. Martin Luther King Jr, 'Letter from Birmingham City Jail', in James M. Washington (ed.), *A Testament of Hope: The Essential Writings and Speeches of Martin Luther King, Jr.* (San Francisco, California, 1986), pp. 289–302.

65. Eskew, *But for Birmingham*, p. 261.

66. Bevel interview in Hampton and Fayer (eds), *Voices of Freedom*, p. 131.

67. Lawrence D. Reddick, *Crusader Without Violence: A Biography of Martin Luther King, Jr.* (New York, 1959), p. 153.

68. Manis, *A Fire You Can't Put Out*, p. 370.

69. Eskew, *But for Birmingham*, p. 259.

70. Martin Luther King Jr, *Why We Can't Wait*, p. 97.

71. David Vann interview in Hampton and Fayer (eds), *Voices of Freedom*, p. 133.

72. Garrow, *Bearing the Cross*, p. 250.

73. James Bevel in Hampton and Fayer (eds), *Voices of Freedom*, p. 134.

74. Eskew, *But for Birmingham*, p. 280.

75. Martin Luther King Jr, *Why We Can't Wait*, p. 104.

76. Carson (ed.), *The Autobiography of Martin Luther King, Jr.*, p. 219.

Chapter 4

1. Roy Wilkins, *Standing Fast: The Autobiography of Roy Wilkins* (New York, 1982), p. 292.

2. It took 31 years to secure De La Beckwith's conviction for the crime.

3. Taylor Branch, *Pillar of Fire: America in the King Years, 1963–65* (New York, 1998), p. 108.

4. Jervis Anderson, *Bayard Rustin: Troubles I've Seen: A Biography* (Berkeley, California, 1997), pp. 244–5.

5. Martin Luther King Jr, *Why We Can't Wait* (New York, 1964), p. 122.

6. Paula F. Pfeffer, *A. Philip Randolph: Pioneer of the Civil Rights Movement* (Baton Rouge, Louisiana, 1990), p. 244.

7. The best starting point on Malcolm X's life and career is: Malcolm X, with Alex Haley, *The Autobiography of Malcolm X* (New York, 1965).

8. Kenneth O'Reilly, *Racial Matters: The FBI's Secret File on Black America, 1960–1972* (New York, 1989), p. 134.

9. The Profumo scandal involved revelations that the British Conservative Government's Secretary of State for War John Profumo had had an affair with showgirl Christine Keeler, a woman who had also been in a relationship with Soviet Embassy attaché Yevgeny Ivanov. The Cold War scandal came to a head in 1963, when Profumo insisted in Parliament that there was 'no impropriety whatsoever' about his relationship with Keeler, a statement he later retracted, leading to his resignation from office. A month later, British Prime Minister Harold Macmillan also resigned.

10. John Lewis, *Walking With the Wind: A Memoir of the Movement* (New York, 1998), pp. 216–18.

11. Anderson, *Bayard Rustin*, p. 261.

12. Martin Luther King Jr, 'I Have A Dream', in James M. Washington (ed.), *A Testament of Hope: The Essential Writings and Speeches of Martin Luther King, Jr.* (San Francisco, California, 1986), pp. 217–20.

13. Andrew M. Manis, *A Fire You Can't Put Out: The Civil Rights Life of Birmingham's Fred Shuttlesworth* (Tuscaloosa, Alabama, 1999), p. 401.

14. Ralph David Abernathy, *And the Walls Came Tumbling Down* (New York, 1989), p. 281.

15. Anderson, *Bayard Rustin*, p. 263.

16. Anne Moody, *Coming of Age in Mississippi* (New York, 1968), p. 275.

17. O'Reilly, *Racial Matters*, p. 126.

18. Anderson, *Bayard Rustin*, p. 263.

19. Pfeffer, *A. Philip Randolph*, p. 267.

20. Taylor Branch, *Parting the Waters: Martin Luther King and the Civil Rights Movement, 1954–1963* (New York, 1988), p. 874.

21. Martin Luther King Jr, *Why We Can't Wait*, p. 122.

22. O'Reilly, *Racial Matters*, p. 131.

23. Abernathy, *And The Walls Came Tumbling Down*, p. 281.

24. Anderson, *Bayard Rustin*, p. 264.

25. A 1965 FBI investigation pointed the finger of suspicion at four local Ku Klux Klan members for the bombing and recommended their prosecution. FBI director J. Edgar Hoover rejected the recommendation. The case has been reopened several times since. In 1977, Robert E. Chambliss was sentenced to life imprisonment for murder. He died eight years later. In 2001, Thomas E. Blanton Jr was sentenced to life imprisonment for murder. In 2002, Bobby Frank Cherry was sentenced to life imprisonment for murder. A fourth suspect, Herman Frank Cash, died in 1994 without ever being charged.

26. Martin Luther King Jr, 'Eulogy for Martyred Children', in Washington (ed.), *A Testament of Hope*, p. 221.

27. David J. Garrow, *Bearing the Cross: Martin Luther King, Jr. and the Southern Christian Leadership Conference* (New York, 1986), p. 293.

28. Coretta Scott King, *My Life With Martin Luther King, Jr.* (New York, 1969), p. 243.

29. A filibuster is an attempt to prolong a debate to prevent a vote being taken on proposed legislation.

30. Adam Fairclough, *To Redeem the Soul of America: The Southern Christian Leadership Conference and Martin Luther King, Jr.* (Athens, Georgia, 1987), p. 179.

31. R.O. Mitchell et al., 'Racial and Civil Disorders in St. Augustine: Report of the Legislative Investigation Committee, February 1965', in David J. Garrow (ed.), *St. Augustine, Florida, 1963–1964: Mass Protest and Racial Violence* (Brooklyn, New York, 1989), p. 180.

32. David R. Colburn, *Racial Change and Community Crisis: St. Augustine, Florida, 1877–1980* (New York, 1985), p. 67.

33. Mitchell et al., 'Racial and Civic Disorders in St. Augustine', p. 187.

34. Robert W. Hartley, 'A Long, Hot Summer: The St. Augustine Racial Disorders of 1964', in Garrow (ed.), *St. Augustine, Florida, 1963–1964*, p. 38.

35. Colburn, *Racial Change and Community Crisis*, p. 79.

36. Hartley, 'A Long, Hot Summer,' p. 41.

37. Colburn, *Racial Change and Community Crisis*, p. 84.

38. Ibid., p. 87.

39. Hartley, 'A Long, Hot Summer,' p. 48.

40. Colburn, *Racial Change and Community Crisis*, p. 89.

41. Ibid., p. 99.

42. Ibid., p. 102.

43. Ibid., p. 101.

44. Hartley, 'A Long, Hot Summer,' p. 67.

45. Mitchell et al., 'Racial and Civic Disorders in St. Augustine', pp. 198–9.

46. Colburn, *Racial Change and Community Crisis*, p. 110.

47. Ibid., p. 112.

48. Ibid.

49. Ibid., p. 190.

50. Clayborne Carson (ed.), *The Autobiography of Martin Luther King, Jr.* (New York, 1998), p. 242.

51. Ibid., p. 249.

52. Charles Sherrod, 'Mississippi at Atlantic City', in Clayborne Carson, David J. Garrow, Gerald Gill, Vincent Harding, and Darlene Clark Hine (eds), *The Eyes on the Prize Civil Rights Reader: Documents, Speeches, and Firsthand Accounts from the Black Freedom Struggle* (New York, 1991), p. 186.

53. John Dittmer, *Local People: The Struggle for Civil Rights in Mississippi* (Urbana, Illinois, 1994), p. 288.

54. Ibid., p. 289.

55. Fairclough, *To Redeem the Soul of America*, p. 204.

56. Chana Kai Lee, *For Freedom's Sake: The Life of Fannie Lou Hamer* (Urbana, Illinois, 1999), p. 100.

57. Dittmer, *Local People*, p. 302.

58. James Forman, *The Making of Black Revolutionaries* (Washington, DC, 1985), p. 405.

59. Andrew Young, *An Easy Burden: The Civil Rights Movement and the Transformation of America* (New York, 1996), p. 308.

60. Lee, *For Freedom's Sake*, p. 95.

61. Eric Burner, *And Gently Shall He Lead Them: Robert Paris Moses and Civil Rights in Mississippi* (New York, 1984), p. 183.

62. Barbara Ransby, *Ella Baker and the Black Freedom Movement: A Radical Democratic Vision* (Chapel Hill, North Carolina, 2002), p. 342.

63. O'Reilly, *Racial Matters*, p. 142.

64. David J. Garrow, *The FBI and Martin Luther King, Jr.: From "Solo" to Memphis* (New York, 1981), p. 122.

65. O'Reilly, *Racial Matters*, p. 141.

66. Garrow, *The FBI and Martin Luther King, Jr.*, pp. 122–4.

67. O'Reilly, *Racial Matters*, p. 144.

68. Ibid., p. 146.

69. Ibid.

70. Ibid., p. 144.

71. Garrow, *Bearing the Cross*, p. 374.

72. Garrow, *The FBI and Martin Luther King, Jr.*, p. 134.

73. Martin Luther King Jr, *Strength to Love* (New York, 1963), p. 68.

74. Frederick L. Downing, *To See the Promised Land: The Faith Pilgrimage of Martin Luther King, Jr.* (Macon, Georgia, 1986), p. 236.

75. Garrow, *The FBI and Martin Luther King, Jr.*, p. 219.

Chapter 5

1. Clayborne Carson (ed.), *The Autobiography of Martin Luther King, Jr.* (New York, 1998), p. 271.

2. Nicolas Katzenbach interview in Henry Hampton and Steven Fayer (eds), *Voices of Freedom: An Oral History of the Civil Rights Movement from the 1950s through the 1980s* (New York, 1995), p. 212.

3. Andrew Young interview in Hampton and Fayer (eds), *Voices of Freedom*, p. 214; John Lewis interview in Howell Raines (ed.), *My Soul is Rested: Movement Days in the Deep South Remembered* (New York, 1977), p. 206.

4. Joseph Smitherman interview in Hampton and Fayer (eds), *Voices of Freedom*, p. 216.

5. James Forman, *The Making of Black Revolutionaries* (Washington, DC, 1985), p. 347.

6. Julian Bond interview in Raines (ed.), *My Soul is Rested*, p. 214.

7. Andrew Young, *An Easy Burden: The Civil Rights Movement and the Transformation of America* (New York, 1996), p. 342.

8. J.L. Chestnut, with Julia Cass, *Black in Selma: The Uncommon Life of J.L. Chestnut, Jr.* (New York, 1991), p. 199.

9. Wilson Baker interview in Raines (ed.), *My Soul is Rested*, p. 198.

10. Amelia Boynton Robinson interview in Hampton and Fayer (eds), *Voices of Freedom*, p. 217.

11. Jim Clark interview in Hampton and Fayer (eds), *Voices of Freedom*, p. 218.

12. David J. Garrow, *Protest at Selma: Martin Luther King, Jr. and the Voting Rights Act of 1965* (New Haven, Connecticut, 1978), p. 43.

13. Wilson Baker interview in Raines (ed.), *My Soul is Rested*, p. 196.

14. Adam Fairclough, *To Redeem the Soul of America: The Southern Christian Leadership Conference and Martin Luther King, Jr.* (Athens, Georgia, 1987), p. 234.

15. Martin Luther King Jr, 'A Letter from a Selma, Alabama, Jail', in Clayborne Carson, David J. Garrow, Gerald Gill, Vincent Harding and Darlene Clark Hine (eds), *The Eyes on the Prize Civil Rights Reader: Documents, Speeches, and Firsthand Accounts from the Black Freedom Struggle* (New York, 1991), p. 210.

16. Stephen L. Longenecker, *Selma's Peacemaker: Ralph Smeltzer and Civil Rights Mediation* (Philadelphia, Pennsylvania, 1987), p. 159.

17. Ibid., p. 163.

18. John Lewis interview in Raines (ed.), *My Soul is Rested*, p. 207.

19. Ibid.

20. Garrow, *Protest at Selma*, p. 74.

21. John Lewis interview in Hampton and Fayer (eds), *Voices of Freedom*, p. 228.

22. Sheyann Webb interview in Raines (ed.), *My Soul is Rested*, p. 204.

23. Sheyann Webb and Rachel West Nelson, *Selma, Lord, Selma: Girlhood Memories of the Civil Rights Days* (Tuscaloosa, Alabama, 1980), p. 96.

24. Chestnut, *Black in Selma*, p. 208.

25. Wilson Baker interview in Raines (ed.), *My Soul is Rested*, p. 202.

26. Ibid., p. 203.

27. Garrow, *Protest at Selma*, p. 76.

28. John Lewis interview in Raines (ed.), *My Soul is Rested*, p. 212.

29. Young, *An Easy Burden*, p. 358.

30. Carson, *The Autobiography of Martin Luther King, Jr.*, p. 279.

31. Garrow, *Protest at Selma*, p. 82.

32. Wilson Baker interview in Raines (ed.), *My Soul is Rested*, p. 215.

33. Carson, *The Autobiography of Martin Luther King, Jr.*, p. 280.

34. Ibid., p. 282.

35. David J. Garrow, *Bearing the Cross: Martin Luther King, Jr. and the Southern Christian Leadership Conference* (New York, 1986), p. 407.

36. Roy Wilkins, *Standing Fast: The Autobiography of Roy Wilkins* (New York, 1982), p. 307.

37. Joseph T. Smitherman interviewed by Charles Wheeler on BBC Television's *Wheeler on America*, 'Part Three, America's Long March', first broadcast on BBC 2, March 1996.

38. Martin Luther King Jr, 'Our God is Marching On!', in James M. Washington (ed.), *A Testament of Hope: The Essential Writings and Speeches of Martin Luther King, Jr.* (San Francisco, California, 1986), p. 229.

39. Martin Luther King Jr, *Where Do We Go From Here?: Chaos or Community* (New York, 1967), p. 9.

40. Ibid., p. 3.

41. Young, *An Easy Burden*, p. 376.

42. James R. Ralph Jr, *Northern Protest: Martin Luther King, Jr., Chicago, and the Civil Rights Movement* (Cambridge, Massachusetts, 1993), p. 29.

43. Bayard Rustin, 'From Protest to Politics: The Future of the Civil Rights Movement', *Commentary* 42 (February 1964), pp. 25–31.

44. Daniel Levine, *Bayard Rustin and the Civil Rights Movement* (New Brunswick, New Jersey, 2000), pp. 184–5.

45. Jervis Anderson, *Bayard Rustin: Troubles I've Seen: A Biography* (Berkeley, California, 1997), p. 301.

46. Levine, *Bayard Rustin*, p. 187.

47. Adam S. Cohen and Elizabeth J. Taylor, *American Pharaoh: Mayor Richard J. Daley, His Battle for Chicago and the Nation* (Boston, Massachusetts, 2000), p. 348.

48. Peter J. Ling, *Martin Luther King, Jr.* (London, 2002).

49. Coretta Scott King, *My Life With Martin Luther King, Jr.* (New York, 1969), p. 4.

50. Ralph, *Northern Protest*, p. 33.

51. Cohen and Taylor, *American Pharaoh*, p. 347.

52. Coretta Scott King, *My Life With Martin Luther King, Jr.*, p. 279.

53. Ralph David Abernathy, *And the Walls Came Tumbling Down* (New York, 1989), pp. 370–1.

54. Fairclough, *To Redeem the Soul of America*, p. 290.

55. Garrow, *Bearing the Cross*, p. 465.

56. Fairclough, *To Redeem the Soul of America*, p. 290.

57. Cohen and Taylor, *American Pharaoh*, p. 366.

58. Young, *An Easy Burden*, p. 395.

59. Martin Luther King Jr, *Where Do We Go From Here?*, p. 23.

60. Ibid., p. 24.

61. Clayborne Carson, *In Struggle: SNCC and the Black Awakening of the 1960s* (Cambridge, Massachusetts, 1981), p. 207.

62. Martin Luther King Jr, *Where Do We Go From Here?*, pp. 25–6.

63. Carson, *In Struggle*, p. 208.

64. Carmichael interview in Hampton and Fayer (eds), *Voices of Freedom*, p. 340.

65. Fairclough, *To Redeem the Soul of America*, p. 316.

66. Ibid., p. 316.

67. Carson, *In Struggle*, p. 210.

68. Garrow, *Bearing the Cross*, p. 483.

69. Martin Luther King Jr, *Where Do We Go From Here?*, p. 31.

70. Ibid.

71. Carson, *In Struggle*, p. 210.

72. Forman, *The Making of Black Revolutionaries*, p. 458.

73. Adam Fairclough, *Better Day Coming: Blacks and Equality, 1890–2000* (New York, 2001), p. 313.

74. Fairclough, *To Redeem the Soul of America*, p. 320.

75. For King's discussion of black power, see Chapter 2 in Martin Luther King Jr, *Where Do We Go From Here?*

Chapter 6

1. Michael Eric Dyson, *I May Not Get There With You: The True Martin Luther King, Jr.* (New York, 2000), p. 39.

2. James R. Ralph Jr, *Northern Protest: Martin Luther King, Jr., Chicago, and the Civil Rights Movement* (Cambridge, Massachusetts, 1993), p. 107.

3. Ibid., p. 112.

4. Mike Royko, *Boss: Richard J. Daley of Chicago* (London, 1971), p. 154.

5. Adam S. Cohen and Elizabeth J. Taylor, *American Pharaoh: Mayor Richard J. Daley, His Battle for Chicago and the Nation* (Boston, Massachusetts, 2000), p. 396.

6. Alan B. Anderson and George W. Pickering, *Confronting the Color Line: The Broken Promise of the Civil Rights Movement in Chicago* (Athens, Georgia, 1986), p. 230.

7. Ralph, *Northern Protest*, p. 141.

8. Ibid., p. 130.

9. Gerald D. McKnight, *The Last Crusade: Martin Luther King Jr., the FBI, and the Poor People's Campaign* (Denver, Colorado, 1998), p. 123.

10. John McKnight, 'The Summit Negotiations: Chicago, August 17, 1966–August 26, 1966', in David J. Garrow (ed.), *Chicago 1966: Open Housing Marches, Summit Negotiations, and Operation Breadbasket* (Brooklyn, New York, 1989), p. 124.

11. David J. Garrow, *Bearing the Cross: Martin Luther King, Jr. and the Southern Christian Leadership Conference* (New York, 1986), p. 514.

12. Cohen and Taylor, *American Pharaoh*, p. 414.

13. Ibid.

14. Ralph, *Northern Protest*, p. 162.

15. Garrow, *Bearing the Cross*, p. 524.

16. Stephen Grant Meyer, *As Long As They Don't Move Next Door: Segregation and Racial Conflict in American Neighborhoods* (Lanham, Maryland, 2000), p. 178.

17. Cohen and Taylor, *American Pharaoh*, p. 392.

18. Andrew Young, *An Easy Burden: The Civil Rights Movement and the Transformation of America* (New York, 1996), p. 406.

19. Clayborne Carson (ed.), *The Autobiography of Martin Luther King, Jr.* (New York, 1998), p. 306.

20. Cohen and Taylor, *American Pharaoh*, p. 338.

21. Ralph, *Northern Protest*, p. 184.

22. Martin Luther King Jr, *Where Do We Go From Here?: Chaos or Community* (New York, 1967), p. 3.

23. Ibid., p. 330.

24. Ibid., p. 137.

25. Dorothy Tillman interview in Henry Hampton and Steven Fayer (eds), *Voices of Freedom: An Oral History of the Civil Rights Movement from the 1950s through the 1980s* (New York, 1995), p. 300.

26. Martin Luther King Jr, *Where Do We Go From Here?*, p. 45.
27. Cohen and Taylor, *American Pharaoh*, p. 358.
28. Ibid.
29. Martin Luther King Jr, *Where Do We Go From Here?*, p. 6.
30. Young, *An Easy Burden*, p. 413.
31. Garrow, *Bearing the Cross*, p. 394.
32. Ibid., p. 438.
33. Ibid., p. 445.
34. Ibid., p. 458.
35. Ibid., p. 470.
36. Ibid., p. 502.
37. Ibid., p. 545.
38. Ibid., pp. 545–6.
39. Adam Fairclough, *To Redeem the Soul of America: The Southern Christian Leadership Conference and Martin Luther King, Jr.* (Athens, Georgia, 1987), p. 340.
40. Ibid., p. 337.
41. Martin Luther King Jr, 'A Time to Break Silence', in James M. Washington (ed.), *A Testament of Hope: The Essential Writings and Speeches of Martin Luther King, Jr.* (San Francisco, California, 1986), pp. 231–44.
42. Andrew Young interview in Hampton and Fayer (eds), *Voices of Freedom*, p. 344.
43. Jervis Anderson, *Bayard Rustin: Troubles I've Seen: A Biography* (Berkeley, California, 1997), p. 300.
44. Garrow, *Bearing the Cross*, p. 554.
45. Ibid., p. 555.
46. Daniel Levine, *Bayard Rustin and the Civil Rights Movement* (New Brunswick, New Jersey, 2000), pp. 198–9.
47. Garrow, *Bearing the Cross*, p. 554.
48. Fairclough, *To Redeem the Soul of America*, p. 340.
49. Garrow, *Bearing the Cross*, p. 557.
50. Fairclough, *To Redeem the Soul of America*, p. 342.
51. Ibid., p. 343.
52. Marian Logan interview in Hampton and Fayer (eds), *Voices of Freedom*, p. 455.
53. Garrow, *Bearing the Cross*, p. 581.
54. Coretta Scott King, *My Life With Martin Luther King, Jr.* (New York, 1969), p. 299.
55. Garrow, *Bearing the Cross*, p. 582.
56. Coretta Scott King, *My Life With Martin Luther King, Jr.*, p. 299.
57. Martin Luther King Jr, *The Trumpet of Conscience* (New York, 1968), p. 15.
58. Ibid., pp. 60–1.
59. Ibid, p. 61.
60. Ibid, p. 62.
61. Ibid.

62. Ibid., p. 63.

63. Ibid., p. 64.

64. Levine, *Bayard Rustin*, p. 203.

65. Fairclough, *To Redeem the Soul of America*, p. 364.

66. Ibid., p. 368.

67. Garrow, *Bearing the Cross*, pp. 595–6, 600.

68. Young, *An Easy Burden*, p. 451.

69. Andrew Young interview in Hampton and Fayer (eds), *Voices of Freedom*, p. 459.

70. McKnight, *The Last Crusade*, pp. 51, 60.

71. Joan Turner Biefuss, *At the River I Stand: Memphis, the 1968 Strike, and Martin Luther King* (Memphis, Tennessee, 1985), p. 194.

72. Ibid., p. 195.

73. Marian Logan interview in Hampton and Fayer (eds), *Voices of Freedom*, p. 462.

74. Biefuss, *At the River I Stand*, p. 220.

75. Ibid., p. 221.

76. Ibid., pp. 221, 223.

77. Ibid., pp. 224–5.

78. Ibid., p. 225.

79. Ibid., p. 252.

80. Abernathy, *And the Walls Came Tumbling Down*, p. 419.

81. Young, *An Easy Burden*, p. 456.

82. Biefuss, *At the River I Stand*, p. 254.

83. McKnight, *The Last Crusade*, pp. 60–3.

84. Biefuss, *At the River I Stand*, p. 248.

85. Ralph Abernathy interview in Howell Raines (ed.), *My Soul is Rested: Movement Days in the Deep South Remembered* (New York, 1977), p. 465.

86. Young, *An Easy Burden*, p. 458.

87. Abernathy, *And the Walls Came Tumbling Down*, p. 425.

88. Biefuss, *At the River I Stand*, p. 267.

89. Ralph Abernathy interview in Hampton and Fayer (eds), *Voices of Freedom*, p. 464.

90. Biefuss, *At the River I Stand*, p. 277.

91. Martin Luther King Jr, 'I See The Promised Land', in Washington (ed.), *A Testament of Hope*, p. 286.

92. Ralph Abernathy interview in Raines (ed.), *My Soul is Rested*, p. 470.

Conclusion

1. John Lewis, *Walking With the Wind: A Memoir of the Movement* (New York, 1998), p. 389.

2. James H. Cone, 'The Theology of Martin Luther King, Jr.', in David J. Garrow (ed.), *Martin Luther King, Jr.: Civil Rights Leader, Theologian, Orator, Volume One* (Brooklyn, New York, 1989), p. 228.

3. August Meier, 'On the Role of Martin Luther King, Jr.', in David J. Garrow (ed.), *Martin Luther King, Jr.: Civil Rights Leader, Theologian, Orator, Volume Three* (Brooklyn, New York, 1989), pp. 635–42.

4. Martin Luther King Jr, *Stride Toward Freedom: The Montgomery Story* (New York, 1958), p. 86.

5. Rosemary R. Ruether, 'The Relevance of Martin Luther King for Today', in David J. Garrow (ed.), *Martin Luther King, Jr.: Civil Rights Leader, Theologian, Orator, Volume Three* (Brooklyn, New York, 1989), pp. 781–2.

6. Carolyn Calloway-Thomas and John Louis Lucaites (eds), *Martin Luther King, Jr., and the Sermonic Power of Public Discourse* (Tuscaloosa, Alabama, 1993), p. 106.

7. See the Bibliographical Essay at the back of this book.

Bibliographical Essay

Primary Sources

The civil rights movement was a period of high drama, visual spectacle and emotional intensity, to which the written word cannot always do justice. For that reason, executive producer Henry Hampton's superlative documentary *Eyes on the Prize: America's Civil Rights Years, 1954–1965* (Boston, 1987) makes an excellent starting point for King and the civil rights movement. The documentary uses archival footage and oral history interviews to tell the story of the civil rights struggle from the point of view of those people who participated in it. A second series, *Eyes on the Prize II: America at the Racial Crossroads, 1969–1985* (Boston, 1990) updates the story to the 1980s. The oral history collection inspired by the series, Henry Hampton and Steve Fayer (eds), *Voices of Freedom: An Oral History of the Civil Rights Movement from the 1950s through the 1980s* (New York, 1994), alongside an earlier collection of oral histories, Howell Raines (ed.), *My Soul is Rested: Movement Days in the Deep South Remembered* (New York, 1983), also make a fine introduction to King and the movement based upon an important primary source for civil rights historians. The series also produced the best edited collection of other movement primary sources in Clayborne Carson, David J. Garrow, Gerald Gill, Vincent Harding and Darlene Clark Hine (eds), *The Eyes on the Prize Civil Rights Reader: Documents, Speeches, and Firsthand Accounts from the Black Freedom Struggle* (New York, 1991).

The Martin Luther King Jr Papers Project under the directorship of Clayborne Carson at Stanford University, California, is currently in the process of assembling a 14–volume edited collection of King's personal papers, which should, when finished, provide the definitive published written primary source for King scholars. To date there are four volumes covering the period up to December 1958: Clayborne Carson, Ralph E. Luker and Penny A. Russell (eds), *The Papers of Martin Luther King, Jr. Vol. I.: Called to Serve, January 1929–June 1951* (Berkeley, California, 1992); Clayborne Carson, Ralph E. Luker, Penny A. Russell and Peter Holloran (eds), *The Papers of Martin Luther King, Jr. Vol. II.: Rediscovering Precious*

Values, July 1951–November 1955 (Berkeley, California, 1994); Clayborne Carson, Susan A. Carson, Peter Holloran, Dana L. Powell and Stewart Burns (eds), *The Papers of Martin Luther King, Jr. Vol. III.: Birth of a New Age, December 1955–December 1956* (Berkeley, California, 1997); Clayborne Carson, Susan A. Carson, Adrienne Clay, Virginia Shadron and Kieran Taylor (eds), *The Papers of Martin Luther King, Jr. Vol. IV.: Symbol of the Movement, January 1957–December 1958* (Berkeley, California, 2000). Clayborne Carson (ed.), *The Autobiography of Martin Luther King, Jr.* (New York, 1998), provides an edited collection of King's reflections about his life and career. The King Papers Project website at http://www.stanford.edu/group/King is the best starting point for accessing King on the Internet and contains a treasury of primary sources. The most comprehensive single volume of King's writings, speeches and sermons is James M. Washington (ed.), *A Testament of Hope: The Essential Writings and Speeches of Martin Luther King, Jr.* (San Francisco, California, 1986).

The King Papers Project has already had an impact on King scholarship, not least in breaking the news in 1990 that King had 'used the words of others without credit' in his college essays and, more seriously, in large chunks of his Boston University PhD thesis. King's plagiarism, as others quickly labelled it, raised a storm of controversy. The implications of these revelations are examined by contemporaries of King, academic scholars and experts in plagiarism in 'Becoming Martin Luther King, Jr.: Plagiarism and Originality: A Round Table', *Journal of American History* 78 (Summer 1991), pp. 11–123. After allegations about King's sexual promiscuity, the 'plagiarism' debate has been the biggest scandal to impact upon King's reputation. Theodore Pappas, *Plagiarism and the Culture War: The Writings of Martin Luther King, Jr. and Other Prominent Americans* (Tampa, Florida, 1998), looks at King's 'plagiarism' from the perspective of the American right, although his somewhat self-righteous glee at exposing King's shortcomings quickly proves wearing. Eugene D. Genovese, *The Southern Front: History and Politics in the Cultural Cold War* (Columbia, Missouri, 1995), is also highly critical of King's plagiarism. A far more measured, thoughtful and insightful response to the plagiarism controversy, to revelations about King's sexual promiscuity, and to other King controversies, is Michael Eric Dyson, *I May Not Get There With You: The True Martin Luther King, Jr.* (New York, 2000).

The plagiarism debate is part of a wider debate over what constitutes a primary source in the study of King. Three books were published under King's name during his lifetime: *Stride Toward Freedom: The Montgomery Story* (New York, 1958); *Why We Can't Wait* (New York, 1964); and

Where Do We Go From Here: Chaos or Community? (New York, 1967). Two collections of King's sermons were also published as *The Measure of a Man* (Philadelphia, 1959), and *Strength to Love* (New York, 1963). *The Trumpet of Conscience* (New York, 1968) is a transcript of the recordings King made for the Canadian Broadcasting Corporation in 1967, which was published posthumously. Alongside these works, King published numerous essays, articles and speeches. However, King scholars David J. Garrow and James H. Cone have both disputed the validity of King's writings as a primary source. Garrow in particular has pointed out that since King was kept constantly busy by the demands of movement leadership he had little time to write such work, which was therefore heavily ghostwritten by others. Professional ghostwriter Al Duckett, Garrow claims, wrote most of *Why We Can't Wait*, and Stanley Levison, Bayard Rustin, Harris Wofford and other King advisers played a large role in writing King's other two books. King scholar Lewis V. Baldwin contends that, although admittedly largely ghostwritten, King personally approved the publication of work that appeared under his name and that such work therefore accurately reflects King's views. Moreover, Baldwin points out that the practice of ghostwriting is common to many public figures, and that if we begin to question the authenticity of King's writings, those of others must equally be subject to scrutiny. Problematically, it is still not precisely clear which of King's writings were ghostwritten and, if so, how heavily. Hopefully, the King Papers Project team will shed more light on this in the future.

King's sermons have also come under scrutiny. Keith D. Miller, *Voice of Deliverance. The Language of Martin Luther King, Jr., and Its Sources* (New York, 1992), points out that King's sermons 'borrowed' heavily from white liberal preachers. Miller terms this practice 'voice-merging' and argues that it is part of a distinct black oral tradition of melding the words of others into new forms without always fully attributing their origin. Richard Lischer, *The Preacher King: Martin Luther King, Jr. and the Word that Moved America* (New York, 1995), claims that Miller may have exaggerated the extent of King's 'borrowing' in his sermons and that in any case it was the actual performance of and the technique used in King's speeches that is more important. For other perspectives on King's use of rhetoric see the essay collection Carolyn Calloway-Thomas and John Louis Lucaites (eds), *Martin Luther King, Jr., and the Sermonic Power of Public Discourse* (Tuscaloosa, Alabama, 1993), and Frank Sunnemark, *An Inescapable Network of Mutability: Discursivity and Ideology in the Rhetoric of Martin Luther King, Jr.* (Gothenburg, 2001). Readers are certainly advised to seek out and to listen to King's speeches and sermons in recorded form as well as the written word. A number of King's recorded speeches and sermons are available, although unfortunately there is no one well-chosen, well-edited, easily available and definitive compilation. The King Papers Project website is a good starting point for samples of such recordings.

One important primary source comes from FBI surveillance of King. David Garrow (ed.), *The Martin Luther King, Jr. File* (Frederick, Maryland, 1984), is an edited microfilm collection of the material gathered from FBI wiretaps, which consist of 17,000 pages on sixteen reels. Part One contains wiretaps of King and Part Two contains wiretaps of Stanley Levison. David J. Garrow, *The FBI and Martin Luther King, Jr.: From 'Solo' to Memphis* (New York, 1981), is based in part on this material and looks at the FBI's wider campaign of harassment against King. Kenneth O'Reilly, *Racial Matters: The FBI's Secret File on Black America, 1960–1972* (New York, 1989), offers a chapter on King in a book about the FBI's wider campaign against the civil rights and black power movements. The FBI's illicit bugging of King's hotel rooms might well offer further insights into King's most intimate, unguarded, private thoughts. However, at the request of several former SCLC board members, those tapes are sealed by federal court order until 2027. Recent questions raised about the conditions in which the tapes are kept have reflected concerns that they might not survive long enough to be used at all.

A number of autobiographies provide a primary source for understanding King. Accounts by family members include King's father, Martin Luther King Sr, with Clayton Riley, *Daddy King: An Autobiography* (Boston, Massachusetts, 1980); King's sister Christine Farris King, *My Brother Martin: A Sister Remembers Growing Up with Rev. Dr. Martin Luther King, Jr.* (New York, 2003); King's wife Coretta Scott King, *My Life With Martin Luther King, Jr.* (New York, 1969); and King's son Dexter Scott King, *Growing Up King: An Intimate Memoir* (New York, 2003). There is even a memoir by an alleged former lover, Georgia David Powers, *I Shared the Dream: The Pride, Passion and Politics of the First Black Woman Senator from Kentucky* (Far Hills, New Jersey, 1995). Benjamin E. Mays, *Born to Rebel: An Autobiography* (Athens, Georgia, 1987), provides some recollections about King's Morehouse College days by its then president. Ralph David Abernathy, *And the Walls Came Tumbling Down* (New York, 1989), is the autobiography of one of King's most trusted SCLC confidants. Abernathy's autobiography is, however, disappointing in its lack of insight and most notable as a source of revelations about King's sexual promiscuity. A far better SCLC insider account is Andrew Young, *An Easy Burden: The Civil Rights Movement and the Transformation of America*

(New York, 1996). A number of leaders of other civil rights organisations offer their observations on King and the SCLC in their autobiographies: for the NAACP, Roy Wilkins, *Standing Fast: The Autobiography of Roy Wilkins* (New York, 1982); for CORE, James Farmer, *Lay Bare the Heart: An Autobiography of the Civil Rights Movement* (New York, 1985); and for SNCC, John Lewis, *Walking With the Wind: A Memoir of the Movement* (New York, 1998). James Forman, *The Making of Black Revolutionaries* (Washington, DC, 1985), articulates the continuing concerns about King's leadership within the civil rights movement from the militant SNCC point of view, as does Clyde Sellers, with Robert Terrell, *The River of No Return: The Autobiography of a Black Militant and the Life and Death of SNCC* (New York, 1973). For those leaders who do not have autobiographies, there are biographies in their place: for the National Urban League, Nancy J. Weiss, *Whitney M. Young, Jr. and the Struggle For Civil Rights* (Princeton, New Jersey, 1989), and Dennis C. Dickerson, *Militant Mediator: Whitney M. Young, Jr.* (Lexington, Kentucky, 1998); and for the Brotherhood of Sleeping Car Porters, Jervis Anderson, *A. Philip Randolph: A Biographical Portrait* (New York, 1973), and Paula F. Pfeffer, *A. Philip Randolph: Pioneer of the Civil Rights Movement* (Baton Rouge, Louisiana, 1990).

In writing this book, I have drawn upon a number of the sources listed above, using them advisedly and fully conscious of their problems and limitations – as anyone approaching any type of historical material is surely obliged to do.

Secondary Sources

A triumvirate of works published in the 1980s still sets the standard for King scholarship. Adam Fairclough, *To Redeem the Soul of America: The Southern Christian Leadership Conference and Martin Luther King, Jr.* (Athens, Georgia, 1987), brings superb analytical verve to King's public leadership career with the SCLC. David J. Garrow, *Bearing the Cross: Martin Luther King, Jr. and the Southern Christian Leadership Conference* (New York, 1986), offers exhaustive research and a mastery of the sources as its particular strength. Taylor Branch, *Parting the Waters: Martin Luther King and the Civil Rights Movement, 1954–63* (New York, 1988), weighs in at 1,000 pages plus and represents just the first of three projected volumes that will place King's life within the context of the broader civil rights movement and the history of the times on a truly epic scale. The second volume, again 1,000 pages plus, is *Pillar of Fire: America in the King Years, 1963–65* (New York, 1998). The third and final volume is currently in progress.

These books apart, one of the best, and one of the earliest and frankest, assessments of King following his assassination is David L. Lewis, *King: A Critical Biography* (Urbana, Illinois, 1970). Works by Stephen B. Oates, *Let the Trumpet Sound: The Life of Martin Luther King, Jr.* (New York, 1982), and Frederick L. Downing, *To See the Promised Land: the Faith Pilgrimage of Martin Luther King, Jr.* (Macon, Georgia, 1986), fill the gap between Lewis's and later studies. The most recent updates of King biography are Peter J. Ling, *Martin Luther King, Jr.* (New York, 2002), and Stewart Burns, *To the Mountaintop: Martin Luther King, Jr.'s Sacred Mission to Save America, 1955–1968* (San Francisco, California, 2003). Notable early biographies of King include Lawrence D. Reddick, *Crusader Without Violence: A Biography of Martin Luther King, Jr.* (New York, 1959); Lerone Bennett Jr, *What Manner of Man: A Biography of Martin Luther King, Jr.* (Chicago, Illinois, 1964); William Robert Miller, *Martin Luther King, Jr.: His Life, Martyrdom and Meaning for the World* (New York, 1968); Lionel Lokos, *House Divided: The Life and Legacy of Martin Luther King* (New Rochelle, New York, 1968); and Jim Bishop, *The Days of Martin Luther King* (New York, 1971). Lokos's book is a rarity in that it is a published attack on King and his use of nonviolent direct action.

For the larger context of the black struggle for freedom and equality, see the useful short overviews by Robert Cook, *Sweet Land of Liberty: The African American Struggle for Civil Rights in the Twentieth Century* (New York, 1998), and Adam Fairclough, *Better Day Coming: Blacks and Equality, 1890–2000* (New York, 2001). On the NAACP's legal struggle against segregation, see Mark V. Tushnet, *Making Civil Rights Law: Thurgood Marshall and the Supreme Court, 1936–1961* (New York, 1994), and Jack Greenberg, *Crusaders in the Courts: How a Dedicated Band of Lawyers Fought for the Civil Rights Revolution* (New York, 1994). In the field of higher education, see Mark V. Tushnet, *The NAACP's Legal Strategy Against Segregated Education, 1925–1950* (Chapel Hill, North Carolina, 1987); on the successful battle against the all-white Democratic Party primaries, see Darlene Clark Hine, *Black Victory: The Rise and Fall of the White Primary in Texas* (Millwood, New York, 1979); and on the desegregation of interstate transport, see Catherine Barnes, *Journey From Jim Crow: The Desegregation of Southern Transit* (New York, 1983).

Richard Kluger, *Simple Justice: The History of Brown v. Board of Education and Black America's Struggle for Equality* (New York, 1976), provides an exhaustive account of that 1954 landmark court case, and James T. Patterson, *Brown v. Board of Education: A Civil Rights Milestone and its*

Troubled Legacy (New York, 2001), assess *Brown*'s long-term impact – or, in some respects, the lack of it. Michael J. Klarman, *From Jim Crow to Civil Rights: The Supreme Court and the Struggle for Racial Equality* (New York, 2004), locates these black legal struggles within their wider twentieth-century constitutional, political and social context. On white resistance to *Brown*, see Numan V. Bartley, *The Rise of Massive Resistance: Race and Politics in the South during the 1950s* (Baton Rouge, Louisiana, 1969); Neil R. McMillen, *The Citizens' Council: Organized Resistance to the Second Reconstruction, 1955–1964* (Urbana, Illinois, 1971); Michael J. Klarman, 'How Brown Changed Race Relations: The Backlash Thesis', *Journal of American History* 81 (June 1994), pp. 81–118; George Lewis, *'With Bated Breath': Segregationists, Anti-Communism and Massive Resistance in the South of the United States, 1945–1965* (Gainesville, Florida, 2004); and the most recent collection of essays on the subject, Clive Webb (ed.), *Massive Resistance: Southern Opposition to the Second Reconstruction* (New York, 2005). John A. Kirk, *Redefining the Color Line: Black Activism in Little Rock, Arkansas, 1940–1970* (Gainesville, Florida, 2002), places the 1957 Little Rock school crisis in its local, state and national context. The impact of the Cold War on black civil rights is covered in Mary L. Dudziak, *Cold War Civil Rights: Race and the Image of American Democracy* (Princeton, New Jersey, 2000), and Thomas Borstelmann, *The Cold War and the Color Line: American Race Relations in the Global Arena* (Cambridge, Massachusetts, 2001).

On King's early life, Branch, *Parting the Waters*, offers the most thorough account of the King biographies. Clayborne Carson's introductory essay to Volume I of the King Papers is a particularly useful addition. On the 1955–6 Montgomery bus boycott, Stewart Burns (ed.), *Daybreak of Freedom: The Montgomery Bus Boycott* (Chapel Hill, North Carolina, 1997), weaves together a collection of primary sources to tell the story. Burns is one of the joint editors of Volume III of the King Papers, which gives an even more comprehensive documentary history of the bus boycott. The bus boycott does not have a dedicated monograph, in part because it is covered in depth by many of the existing King studies. The nearest equivalent is J. Mills Thornton, *Dividing Lines: Municipal Politics and the Struggle for Civil Rights in Montgomery, Birmingham, and Selma* (Tuscaloosa, Alabama, 2002), which offers an important analysis of the bus boycott from a local perspective and is, as the title suggests, particularly good on the role played by municipal politics. Catherine Barnes, *Journey From Jim Crow*, places the bus boycott within the larger context of the desegregation of public transportation facilities in the decades before and after the events in Montgomery.

There are a number of useful first-hand accounts of the bus boycott. King's *Stride Toward Freedom* is one of them but must be approached carefully, bearing in mind the reasons cited above and because the book was written with the intention of providing a popular representation of the bus boycott rather than a searching or even accurate historical analysis. Jo Ann Robinson, with David Garrow, *The Montgomery Bus Boycott and the Women Who Started It* (Knoxville, Tennessee, 1989), is the best of the memoirs, highlighting the role played by the Women's Political Council. Robinson's book indicates the pivotal role played by women and women's organisations in the civil rights movement, a point expanded upon in Belinda Robnett, *How Long? How Long? African American Women in the Struggle for Civil Rights* (New York, 1997), and three collections of essays: Vicki Crawford, Jacqueline Rouse and Barbara Woods (eds), *Women in the Civil Rights Movement: Trailblazers and Torchbearers, 1941–1965* (Brooklyn, New York, 1990); Peter J. Ling and Sharon Monteith (eds), *Gender in the Civil Rights Movement* (New York, 1999, reprinted New Jersey, 2004); and Bettye Collier-Thomas and V.P. Franklin (eds), *Sisters in the Struggle: African American Women in the Civil Rights–Black Power Movement* (New York, 2001). Rosa Parks's account of her role in the bus boycott and the part that it played in her life is told in Rosa Parks, with Jim Haskins, *Rosa Parks: My Story* (New York, 1992), and in Douglas Brinkley, *Mine Eyes Have Seen the Glory: The Life of Rosa Parks* (New York, 2000). Fred D. Gray, *Bus Ride to Justice: Changing the System by the System: The Life and Works of Fred D. Gray, Preacher, Attorney, Politician: Lawyer for Rosa Parks* (Montgomery, Alabama, 1999), gives the MIA attorney's version of the events; Robert Graetz, *A White Preacher's Memoir: The Montgomery Bus Boycott* (Montgomery, Alabama, 1999), views the boycott from the perspective of a sympathetic liberal white minister; Solomon S. Seay, *I Was There By The Grace Of God* (Montgomery, Alabama, 1990), is an account by a black MIA minister; and U.J. Fields, *The Montgomery Story: The Unhappy Effects of the Montgomery Bus Boycott* (New York, 1959), is noteworthy since it provides a critical contemporary account of events in Montgomery by a disgruntled member of the MIA. Virginia Durr, *Outside the Magic Circle* (Tuscaloosa, Alabama, 1986), has disappointingly little insight into the bus boycott itself, but does provide a useful account of the life of a white woman liberal activist in the South, who lived through the Montgomery bus boycott.

On the origins and the early years of the SCLC see Fairclough, *To Redeem the Soul of America*, Garrow, *Bearing the Cross*, Branch, *Parting the Waters*, and Aldon D. Morris, *The Origins of the Civil Rights Movement: Black Communities Organizing for Change* (New York, 1984). Three biographies of Bayard Rustin: Jervis Anderson, *Bayard Rustin: Troubles I've Seen: A Biography* (Berkeley, California, 1997); Daniel Levine, *Bayard Rustin and the Civil Rights Movement* (New Brunswick, New Jersey, 2000); and John D'Emillio, *Lost Prophet: The Life and Times of Bayard Rustin* (New York, 2003); and two of Ella Baker: Joanne Grant, *Ella Baker: Freedom Bound* (New York, 1998), and Barbara Ransby, *Ella Baker and the Black Freedom Movement: A Radical Democratic Vision* (Chapel Hill, North Carolina, 2002), throw light on the role played by those influential figures in the formation of the SCLC. There is no autobiography or biography of the third person instrumental in founding the SCLC, and one of King's key advisers, Stanley Levison.

On the 1960 sit-ins and SNCC, see Clayborne Carson, *In Struggle: SNCC and the Black Awakening of the 1960s* (Cambridge, Massachusetts, 1981), and Emily Stoper, *The Student Nonviolent Coordinating Committee: The Growth of Radicalism in a Civil Rights Organization* (Brooklyn, New York, 1989). Howard Zinn, *SNCC: The New Abolitionists* (Boston, Massachusetts, 1965), offers a near-contemporary evaluation of events that is still useful. Aldon D. Morris, *The Origins of the Civil Rights Movement*, offers an instructive sociological analysis of events. William Chafe, *Civilities and Civil Rights: Greensboro, North Carolina, and the Black Struggle for Freedom* (New York, 1980), is one of the earliest of the civil rights community studies. It situates the first Greensboro sit-ins within the context of the unfolding struggle for black freedom and equality in the city and the state. Journalist David Halberstam, *The Children* (New York, 1998), writes what is essentially a collective biography of the influential group of Nashville SNCC students. Reflections on the movement by a number of SNCC activists can be found in Cheryl Greenberg (ed.), *A Circle of Trust: Remembering SNCC* (New Brunswick, New Jersey, 1998). On King's role in the sit-ins and the involvement of the Kennedys, see Harris Wofford, *Of Kennedys and Kings: Making Sense of the Sixties* (New York, 1980), and the important revisionist article, Clifford M. Kuhn, '"There's a Footnote to History!" Memory and the History of Martin Luther King's October 1960 Arrest and Its Aftermath', *Journal of American History* 84 (Sept. 1997), pp. 583–95.

There is no comprehensive account of the 1961 Freedom Rides at the time of writing, although historian Raymond Arsenault is currently in the process of completing one. Catherine Barnes's study *Journey from Jim Crow* is the best place to look meanwhile, along with Clayborne Carson's *In Struggle*, and see also the autobiographies of James Farmer, John Lewis and James Forman. On the history of the Congress of Racial Equality, which organised the Freedom Rides, see August Meier and Elliott Rudwick,

CORE: A Study in the Civil Rights Movement, 1942–1968 (New York, 1973).

The 1961–2 Albany Movement does not have its own study. The *Journal of Southwest Georgia History* 2 (Fall 1984) contains a collection of articles on the Albany Movement, including the useful overview by John A. Ricks, 'De Lawd Descends and is Crucified: Martin Luther King, Jr. in Albany, Georgia', pp. 3–14. Journalist Pat Watters, who covered the Albany Movement, offers his observations on events in Pat Watters and Reese Cleghorn, *Climbing Jacob's Ladder* (New York, 1967), and Pat Watters, *Down to Now: Reflections on the Southern Civil Rights Movement* (New York, 1971). Stephen G.N. Tuck, *Beyond Atlanta: The Struggle for Racial Equality in Georgia, 1940–1980* (Athens, Georgia, 2001), locates the Albany Movement within the context of SNCC organising in south-west Georgia, and within the broader context of the black struggle for freedom and equality within the state.

On King and the SCLC's 1963 Birmingham campaign, see Glenn T. Eskew, *But For Birmingham: The Local and National Movements in the Civil Rights Struggle* (Chapel Hill, North Carolina, 1997). J. Mills Thornton, *Dividing Lines*, locates unfolding events within the context of municipal politics. Andrew M. Mannis, *A Fire You Can't Put Out: The Civil Rights Life of Birmingham's Fred Shuttlesworth* (Tuscaloosa, Alabama, 1999), provides an account of the life and career of that important local civil rights leader. Dianne McWhorter, *Carry Me Home: Birmingham, Alabama – The Climactic Battle of the Civil Rights Revolution* (New York, 2001), looks at the role played by the Ku Klux Klan in Birmingham, and Jonathan S. Bass, *Blessed Are The Peacemakers: Martin Luther King, Jr., Eight White Religious Leaders, and the 'Letter from Birmingham City Jail'* (Baton Rouge, Louisiana, 2001), looks at the role played by Birmingham's white clergymen, whose criticism of King's nonviolent, direct-action tactics prompted King's response in 'Letter from Birmingham City Jail'.

The 1963 March on Washington does not have its own monograph. Branch, *Parting the Waters*, has a chapter on the subject, and Drew D. Hansen, *The Dream: Martin Luther King, Jr. and the Speech that Inspired a Nation* (New York, 2003), has a short chapter on the march but his book focuses mostly on King's 'I Have A Dream' speech. The best approach is through the biographies and autobiographies of march participants such as Bayard Rustin (see the Anderson, Levine and D'Emillio biographies); Whitney Young (see the Weiss and Dickerson biographies); Fred Shuttlesworth (see the Mannis biography); Ralph Abernathy; James Farmer; James Forman; Coretta Scott King; John Lewis; Roy Wilkins; and Andrew Young.

David R. Colburn, *Racial Change and Community Crisis: St. Augustine, Florida, 1877–1980* (New York, 1985), covers the 1964 St. Augustine campaign and makes no bones about King and the SCLC's shortcomings. On the political machinations of and difficulties in passing the 1964 Civil Rights Act, see Charles W. Whalen and Barbara Whalen, *The Longest Debate: A Legislative History of the 1964 Civil Rights Act* (Cabin John, Maryland, 1985), and Robert D. Loevy, *To End All Segregation: The Politics of the Passage of the Civil Rights Act of 1964* (Lanham, Maryland, 1990). Hugh D. Graham, *The Civil Rights Era: Origins and Development of National Policy, 1960–1972* (New York, 1990), places the act within the broader context of federal civil rights policy.

Civil rights struggles in Mississippi have received the most attention outside the King-inspired campaigns. The two best studies are John Dittmer, *Local People: The Struggle for Civil Rights in Mississippi* (Urbana, Illinois, 1994), and Charles Payne, *I've Got the Light of Freedom: The Organizing Tradition and the Mississippi Freedom Struggle* (Berkeley, California, 1995). Doug McAdam, *Freedom Summer* (New York, 1988), offers a sociological analysis of the 1964 Freedom Summer. William Bradford Huie, *Three Lives For Mississippi* (London, 1965), and Seth Cagin and Philip Dray, *We Are Not Afraid: The Story of Goodman, Schwerner and Chaney and the Civil Rights Campaign for Mississippi* (New York, 1988), both focus on the murders of the three young civil rights workers. Two autobiographies offer insights about Freedom Summer from the perspective of young, white, northern, women participants in events: Sally Belfrage, *Freedom Summer* (London, 1965), and Mary King, *Freedom Song: A Personal Story of the 1960s Civil Rights Movement* (New York, 1987). Anne Moody, *Coming of Age in Mississippi* (New York, 1968), provides an autobiographical insight into growing up as a black woman in segregated Mississippi, as does Fannie Lou Hamer, *To Praise Our Bridges: An Autobiography* (Jackson, Mississippi, 1967). Biographies of Mississippi movement participants include Eric R. Burner, *And Gently Shall He Lead Them: Robert Parris Moses and Civil Rights in Mississippi* (New York, 1994); Kay Mills, *This Little Light of Mine: The Life of Fannie Lou Hamer* (New York, 1994); and Chana Kai Lee, *For Freedom's Sake: The Life of Fannie Lou Hamer* (Urbana, Illinois, 1999). Frank Parker, *Black Votes Count: Political Empowerment in Mississippi after 1965* (Chapel Hill, North Carolina, 1990), examines the long-term impact of Freedom Summer on Mississippi politics.

On King and the SCLC's 1965 Selma campaign and the 1965 Voting Rights Act, David J. Garrow, *Protest at Selma: Martin Luther King, Jr., and the Voting Rights Act of 1965* (New Haven, Connecticut, 1978), provides the most comprehensive analysis. J. Mills Thornton, *Dividing Lines*, again offers the local municipal politics perspective. Stephen L. Longencker, *Selma's Peacemaker: Ralph Smeltzer and Civil Rights Mediation* (Philadelphia, Pennsylvania, 1987), bases his account on the journal of a white clergyman involved in events. Mary Stanton, *From Selma to Sorrow: The Life and Death of Viola Liuzzo* (Athens, Georgia, 1998), investigates the life and murder of the white woman killed by members of the Ku Klux Klan at the end of the Selma to Montgomery march. J.L. Chestnut Jr, with Julia Cass, *Black in Selma: The Uncommon Life of J.L. Chestnut, Jr.* (New York, 1991), views events from the perspective of a local black attorney, and Sheyann Webb and Rachel West Nelson, *Selma, Lord, Selma: Girlhood Memories of the Civil Rights Days* (Tuscaloosa, Alabama, 1980), remember their roles from the perspective of two young, black schoolgirls who participated in the campaign. Charles Fager, *Selma, 1965: The March that Changed the South* (New York, 1974), recalls his involvement in Selma as a white SCLC staff member, and Richard D. Leonard, *Call to Selma: Eighteen Days of Witness* (Boston, Massachusetts, 2002), provides a memoir of his role as a New York Unitarian Universalist minister who answered King's call for the support of white clergy on the Selma to Montgomery march.

James R. Ralph Jr, *Northern Protest: Martin Luther King, Jr., Chicago, and the Civil Rights Movement* (Cambridge, Massachusetts, 1993), is the best starting point for King and the SCLC's 1965–6 Chicago campaign. Alan B. Anderson and George W. Pickering, *Confronting the Color Line: The Broken Promise of the Civil Rights Movement in Chicago* (Athens, Georgia, 1986), is also useful, but is somewhat heavy going in its social scientific approach. Mike Royko, *Boss: Richard J. Daley of Chicago* (New York, 1971), offers a city insider's view on Daley and the Chicago campaign from the perspective of a white *Chicago Daily News* columnist, and Alan S. Cohen and Elizabeth J. Taylor, *American Pharaoh: Mayor Richard J. Daley, His Battle for Chicago and the Nation* (Boston, Massachusetts, 2000), provide a more substantial academic treatment. On the politics of race and housing, see Stephen Grant Meyer, *As Long As They Don't Move Next Door: Segregation and Racial Conflict in American Neighborhoods* (Lanham, Maryland, 2000). Two important articles on white northern grassroots opposition to civil rights, particularly in relation to housing, are Thomas Sugrue, 'Crabgrass-Roots Politics: Race, Rights and the Reaction against Liberalism in the Urban North, 1940–1964', *Journal of American History* 82 (Sept. 1995), pp. 551–78, and Arnold R. Hirsch, 'Massive Resistance in the Urban North: Trumbull Park, Chicago, 1953–1966, *Journal of American History* 82 (Sept. 1995), pp. 522–50.

Dan T. Carter, *The Politics of Rage: George Wallace, the Origins of the New Conservatism, and the Transformation of American Politics* (New York, 1995), looks at the long-term impact of the 'white backlash' on American politics.

King's thoughts on the 1966 Meredith March Against Fear and the emergence of black power can be found in Chapter 2 of *Where Do We Go From Here?*. Stokely Carmichael and Charles V. Hamilton, *Black Power: The Politics of Liberation in Black America* (New York, Random House, 1967), gives a contemporary introduction to black power, part-written by the man who popularised the slogan. Timothy B. Tyson, *Radio Free Dixie: Robert F. Williams and the Roots of Black Power* (Chapel Hill, North Carolina, 1999), makes the important point that people like the NAACP's Robert F. Williams in North Carolina predated the emergence of black power in many ways, not least in staunchly advocating black armed self-defence. William L. Van DeBurg, *New Day in Babylon: The Black Power Movement and American Culture, 1965–1975* (Chicago, Illinois, 1992), provides the most comprehensive analysis of black power in its broadest dimensions.

Far fewer studies exist on King's final years, an indication of the relative neglect of King's more radical later bent, a fact noted in Vincent Harding, *Martin Luther King: The Inconvenient Hero* (New York, 1996). Fairclough, *To Redeem the Soul of America*, and Garrow, *Bearing the Cross*, provide the most extensive discussion of King's stand against the Vietnam War. The 1968 Poor People's campaign is covered in Gerald D. McKnight, *The Last Crusade: Martin Luther King Jr., the FBI, and the Poor People's Campaign* (Denver, Colorado, 1998). Joan Turner Biefuss, *At the River I Stand: Memphis, the 1968 Strike, and Martin Luther King* (Memphis, Tennessee, 1985), documents the issues and events in the last community campaign that King was involved in before his assassination. Michael Honey (ed.), *Black Workers Remember: An Oral History of Segregation, Unionism and the Freedom Struggle* (Berkeley, California, 1999), has a chapter of oral histories by black Memphis workers involved in the strike and places that event within the wider context of the intersection of black unionism and civil rights.

King's assassination has been the subject of much controversy. The official line is that career criminal and known racist James Earl Ray shot and killed King. In 1977–8 the House Select Committee on Assassinations concluded that 'there is a likelihood' that Ray did not plan the assassination alone. In 1997, King's son, Dexter Scott King, met with Ray in prison and declared that he believed Ray was innocent of the crime. The following year, US Attorney General Janet Reno opened a limited investigation into events without finding evidence of a conspiracy. In December 1999, a Memphis jury awarded the King family token damages of $100 in a wrongful death suit. The jury concluded that King's death had been the result of a conspiracy. The first book to raise questions about the King assassination was William Bradford Huie, *He Slew the Dreamer: My Search with James Earl Ray for the Truth about the Murder of Martin Luther King* (Montgomery, Alabama, 1970), followed by Gerold Frank, *An American Death: The True Story of the Assassination of Dr. Martin Luther King, Jr. and the Greatest Manhunt of Our Time* (London, 1972), and Mark Lane and Dick Gregory, *Code Name 'Zorro': The Murder of Martin Luther King, Jr.* (New York, 1977), updated in *Murder in Memphis: The FBI and the Assassination of Martin Luther King* (New York, 1993). James Earl Ray's attorney William F. Pepper, *Orders to Kill: The Truth Behind the Murder of Martin Luther King, Jr.* (New York, 1995), also puts forward the case for a conspiracy, updated in *An Act of State: The Execution of Martin Luther King* (London, 2003). James Earl Ray, *Who Killed Martin Luther King, Jr.?: The True Story by the Alleged Assassin* (New York, 1992), issued a plea of innocence before his death in prison in 1998. Gerald Posner, *Killing the Dream: James Earl Ray and the Assassination of Martin Luther King, Jr.* (New York, 1998), offers a comprehensive review of available materials from a journalist who has also investigated the Kennedy assassination. Posner concludes that the evidence that Ray killed King is compelling.

David J. Garrow (ed.), *Martin Luther King, Jr.: Civil Rights Leader, Theologian, Orator*, three volumes (Brooklyn, New York, 1989), is particularly helpful in gathering together the most important disparate articles on King up to the late 1980s. Useful companions and updates to these volumes are 'A Round Table: Martin Luther King, Jr.', *Journal of American History* 74 (Sept. 1987), pp. 436–81; Charles W. Eagles (ed.), *The Civil Rights Movement in America* (Jackson, Mississippi, 1986); Peter J. Albert and Ronald Hoffman (eds), *We Shall Overcome: Martin Luther King, Jr., and the Black Freedom Struggle* (New York, 1990); Brian Ward and Tony Badger (eds), *The Making of Martin Luther King and the Civil Rights Movement* (London, 1996); and Lewis V. Baldwin with Rufus Burrow Jr, Barbara A. Holmes and Susan Holmes Winfield (eds), *The Legacy of Martin Luther King, Jr.: The Boundaries of Law, Politics, and Religion* (Notre Dame, Indiana, 2002).

A number of studies have been written on what might be broadly termed as King's thought and culture. Kenneth L. Smith and Ira G. Zepp, *Search for the Beloved Community: The Thinking of Martin Luther King, Jr.* (Lanham, Maryland, 1986); Noel Leo Erskine and Bernice A. King,

King Among Theologians (Cleveland, Ohio, 1995); Luther D. Ivory, *Toward a Theology of Radical Involvement: The Theological Legacy of Martin Luther King, Jr.* (Nashville, Tennessee, 1997); and Russell Moldovan, *Martin Luther King, Jr.: An Oral History of his Religious Witness and his Life* (Lanham, Maryland, 1999), all examine King's theological ideas. An important corollary to this work is David L. Chappell, *A Stone of Hope: Prophetic Religion and the Death of Jim Crow* (Chapel Hill, North Carolina, 2004), which looks at the role played by prophetic religion in the civil rights movement. John J. Ansbro, *Martin Luther King, Jr.: The Making of a Mind* (New York, 1983, reprinted as *Martin Luther King, Jr.: Nonviolent Strategies and Tactics for Social Change* (Lanham, Maryland, 2000)); James P. Hanigan, *Martin Luther King, Jr. and the Foundations of Nonviolence* (Lanham, Maryland, 1984); William D. Watley, *Roots of Resistance: The Nonviolent Ethic of Martin Luther King, Jr.* (Valley Forge, Pennsylvania, 1985); and Greg Moses, *Revolution of Conscience: Martin Luther King, Jr., and the Philosophy of Nonviolence* (New York, 1997), examine King's ideas in relation to nonviolence. Sudarshan Kapur, *Raising Up a Prophet: The African American Encounter with Gandhi* (Boston, Massachusetts, 1992), locates King's nonviolence within the context of a larger tradition of black American encounters with Gandhism. Hanes Walton, *The Political Philosophy of Martin Luther King, Jr.* (Newport, Connecticut, 1972), and Richard H. King, *Civil Rights and the Idea of Freedom* (New York, 1992; Martin Luther King Jr is covered in Chapters 4 and 5) both examine King's political ideas. Ervin Smith, *The Ethics of Martin Luther King, Jr.* (New York, 1981), examines King's ethics. Michael G. Long, *Against Us, But For Us: Martin Luther King, Jr. and the State* (Macon, Georgia, 2002), looks at King's ideas in relation to the concept of the state. Lewis V. Baldwin, *There is a Balm in Gilead: The Cultural Roots of Martin Luther King, Jr.* (Minneapolis, Minnesota, 1991), and *To Make the Wounded Whole: The Cultural Legacy of Martin Luther King, Jr.* (Minneapolis, Minnesota, 1992), examine, as they suggest, King's cultural roots and his cultural legacy.

King has inspired a number of comparisons. Two of the most useful are James H. Cone, *Martin, Malcolm and America: A Dream or Nightmare?* (Maryknoll, New York, 1991), and Mary King, *Mahatma Gandhi and Martin Luther King, Jr.: The Power of Nonviolent Direct Action* (Paris, 1999), though Mary King tends to simply parallel the lives of Gandhi and Martin Luther King Jr rather than providing the more searching analysis of King and Malcolm X provided by Cone. Surprisingly little has been written about King, the movement and the media. Richard Lentz, *Symbols, the News Magazines and Martin Luther King* (Baton Rouge, Louisiana,

1990), offers a start, and Brian Ward (ed.), *Media, Culture and the Modern African American Freedom Struggle* (Gainesville, Florida, 2001), provides a collection of suggestive essays that point to where such studies might go in the future.

For presidential perspectives on King and the movement, see James C. Durham, *A Moderate Amongst Extremists: Dwight D. Eisenhower and the School Desegregation Crisis* (Chicago, Illinois, 1981); Robert F. Burk, *The Eisenhower Administration and Black Civil Rights* (Knoxville, Tennessee, 1984); Carl M. Brauer, *John F. Kennedy and the Second Reconstruction* (New York, 1977); Mark Stern, *Calculating Visions: Kennedy, Johnson and Civil Rights* (New Brunswick, New Jersey, 1987); Jonathan Rosenberg and Zachary Karabell, *Kennedy, Johnson, and the Quest For Justice: The Civil Rights Tapes* (New York, 2003); Robert Mann, *The Walls of Jericho: Lyndon Johnson, Hubert Humphrey and the Struggle For Civil Rights* (New York, 1996); Dean J. Kotlowski, *Nixon's Civil Rights: Politics, Principle and Policy* (Cambridge, Massachusetts, 2002); and Kenneth O' Reilly, *Nixon's Piano: Presidents and Racial Politics from Washington to Clinton* (New York, 1995).

Index